The Immaculate Conception of Data

The Immaculate Conception of Data

Agribusiness, Activists, and Their Shared Politics of the Future

Kelly Bronson

McGill-Queen's University Press
Montreal & Kingston | London | Chicago

ISBN 978-0-2280-1121-7 (cloth)
ISBN 978-0-2280-1122-4 (paper)
ISBN 978-0-2280-1253-5 (ePDF)
ISBN 978-0-2280-1254-2 (ePUB)

Legal deposit third quarter 2022
Bibliothèque nationale du Québec

This book has been published with the help of a grant from the Federation for the Humanities and Social Sciences, through the Awards to Scholarly Publications Program, using funds provided by the Social Sciences and Humanities Research Council of Canada.

Funded by the Government of Canada | Financé par le gouvernement du Canada | Canada

Canada Council for the Arts | Conseil des arts du Canada

We acknowledge the support of the Canada Council for the Arts.
Nous remercions le Conseil des arts du Canada de son soutien.

Library and Archives Canada Cataloguing in Publication

Title: Immaculate conception of data : agribusiness, activists, and their shared politics of the future / Kelly Bronson.
Names: Bronson, Kelly, author.
Description: Includes bibliographical references and index.
Identifiers: Canadiana (print) 2022020649X | Canadiana (ebook) 20220206651 | ISBN 9780228011217 (cloth) | ISBN 9780228011224 (paper) | ISBN 9780228012535 (ePDF) | ISBN 9780228012542 (ePUB)
Subjects: LCSH: Agriculture—Data processing. | LCSH: Big data. | LCSH: Artificial intelligence—Agricultural applications. | LCSH: Agriculture—Economic aspects. | LCSH: Food industry and trade.
Classification: LCC S494.5.D3 B76 2022 | DDC 630.28/557—dc23

For Oscar and Iza

In urgent times, many of us are tempted to address trouble in terms of making an imagined future safe, of stopping something from happening that looms in the future, of clearing away the present and the past in order to make futures for coming generations. Staying with the trouble does not require such a relationship to times called the future.

Donna Haraway, *Staying with the Trouble*

Contents

Figures ix

Acknowledgments xi

1 Facebook, Google, and ... Monsanto? 3

2 Revolutions, Disruptions, and the Future of Farming 24

3 Appropriate, Open, and Alternative 62

4 The Immaculate Conception of Data 82

5 The Politics of Digital Farm Technologies 113

Notes 155

Bibliography 161

Index 195

Figures

2.1 Photograph of the author standing next to an expensive precision agriculture tractor, which she got to ride on a hot day in June 2019 in southern Ontario. Photo taken by author. 30

2.2 Article from farmforum.ca from January 2017. 41

4.1 Final slide on a deck shared with the author at an agricultural technology convention in 2018. 101

Acknowledgments

As I sit down to write these acknowledgements, things feel dire: I submitted the book manuscript four months into what is a continuing, global human bid to manage the spread and impact of a so-called COVID-19 virus. I find myself wondering whether we will ever push this boulder back up the hill? But perhaps more urgently, I wonder whether enough of us have learned lessons about the environmental and social vulnerabilities we have created in order to motivate lasting change?

For me, the pandemic has brought to the surface those ethical and political commitments that motivated me to write this book in the first place, and I wish to acknowledge those commitments because they played such an important role: First, a commitment to cultivating justice and equity, specifically in a global food system that has for so long been characterized by unbelievable power imbalance; and second, a commitment to environmental sustainability – to seeking redress for the harms of colonial land practices and intensive agriculture that have eroded biodiversity and ecological redundancy and ultimately our ability to live well together into the twenty-first century.

I hold (embody) the commitments I do in large part because of my parents. Neither of my parents has a university degree; both grew up in working-class families though their stories are slightly different. My mother's immigrant family took for granted that women managed domestic affairs in the home, while my father was forced to leave his science degree after the first year, broke and with no options but to head north to work in a nickel mine. Because I carry their history forward, my parents have gifted me a desire to engender justice as well as an intense gratitude for being able to make a living doing what I do. Thank-you is not an adequate word, mom and dad.

That I ended up writing a book about how big data might be furthering historic patterns of inequity and unsustainability in food would not have happened, *ever*, if it weren't for Irena Knezevic who planted a seed of interest over a glass of wine in my living room back in 2015. I credit this book to this fated conversation and to our friendship and collaboration. Thank you Irena for turning my attention toward big data but also for always being honest. Everyone needs a friend whom they trust will tell the truth. You are that person for me.

My partner Nathan Harron was also there for that early living room conversation, and he has gifted me many, many conversations since – idea-shaping moments and intellectual contributions. Like how wind forms a rock over geological time, the influence has been subtle (due to our over-full lives, I think you never read full chapters), but the book would not have its final shape without your Socratic questioning and your incredible knowledge and care. Your care often took (takes) the form of cups of coffee and delicious meals and dish washing. I hate washing dishes! I owe much of my happiness to you and Oscar and Iza.

Several colleagues who are also friends helped me along this book journey. First, there is an incredible group of international collaborators who were with me, first out of the gate, on this topic: Steven Wolf (Cornell University), Michael Carolan (Colorado State University), Laurens Klerkx (Wageningen Research University), Simon Fielke (CSIRO), Emma Jakku (CSIRO), David Rose (University of Reading), Vaughan Higgins (University of Tasmania). You have all been so pivotal in how this subject and my book have taken shape. There are others closer to home who allowed me to ramble and puzzle through problems with wit and good nature and seemingly endless patience. These colleagues are Kristi Allain (St Thomas University), Michael Orsini (I am indebted a mountain of scones) (University of Ottawa) and Amanda Clark (Carleton University). Indeed, Amanda gave me the bravery to broadcast the "immaculate conception" framework, bringing the provocation into the title. Thanks also to Phoebe Sengers for being so smart and funny and supportive. Thanks also to my colleagues at the School of Sociological and Anthropological Studies at University of Ottawa who supported me emotionally: Loes Knappen, David Jaclin, and Vincent Mirza (and his espresso machine). And three non-academic friends need to be thanked: Jasmine Cady for counsel through episodic crises unrelated to the book, Jess Malkin for her artistry, and kind, kind Christine Thiessen.

A huge thank you to all of my students in the Science and Society Collective from whom I continuously learn so much more than I give. Thanks in particular to Alana Lajoie-O'Malley; I feel so lucky that you were the first PhD student to choose me as I cannot imagine a better relationship for developing my mentor muscles, but also I cannot imagine a more competent person to help me pursue so many testy and challenging but fulfilling projects that ran contemporaneous to this book. To Matthew Zucca who is now doing great world-altering things (or at least anti-colonial things) for helping me connect with so many of the participants I engaged in this book, some of whom you may have found on the backchannels of the web (I remember urging you: "Just don't do anything illegal!"). Thanks to Ursula Bero for calling farmers across Canada. Thanks also to Salwa Khan for her keen eye and close attention to my citations and bibliography. A sincere thank you to all my classes – undergraduate and graduate. I love teaching and learning from teaching, and this book is richer because of my students.

To several groups of people whom I was able to think in-depth with during the development of the book. First and foremost, the working group STS-FAN led by Drs Julie Guthman, Mascha Gugganig and Karly Burch. When this group interested in food and agriculture first meet up at 4S in 2019 I remember thinking, "Where have you been all of my life?" to members Charlotte Biltekoff, Mark Bomford, Garrett Broad, Samara Brock, Matt Comi, Ritwick Ghosh, Ke Hu, Zenia Kish, Charlie Mather, and Summer Sullivan. Thanks in particular to Saul Halfon and Madeleine Fairbairn who through their comments pushed me to clarify that immaculate conception of data is not so much an heuristic but a productive device that actors wield in their attempt to gain support for their version of the (data-driven) future of food.

There were other early audiences too, some of whom allowed me to test out emerging ideas in exchange for trips to interesting places such as Lawrence, Kansas (the Sociology Department at Kansas State University), Durham, North Carolina (the Center for Genetic Engineering in Society at North Carolina State University), Wageningen, Netherlands (Wageningen Research University), and Toronto, Ontario (York, STS). I am positive I got more than you received from these encounters.

A sincere thank-you to the two generous reviewers of the book who took enormous care with the text during an unprecedented time of pandemic, when all of us were juggling work and other commitments (and fears and anxieties). The process of peer review for the text, while taking longer than I impatiently wanted, reinforced for me just what peer review can do: strengthen, sharpen and add to the conversation, rather than knock down. I'd like to acknowledge that some of the funding to support this book's publication came from the Canada Research Chair in Science and Society. Thanks also to the internal editing, production, and marketing teams at McGill-Queen's University Press. Thanks also to my copy editor Stephanie Dotto for your help with signposting and making my claims more transparent and thus my writing more inclusive.

And finally, an acknowledgement of gratitude for the place from where I work and live. I make my life on the borrowed, unceded ancestral home of the Anishinaabe Algonquin Nation, who have nurtured the land, water, and air of this place for millennia and continue to do so today. Beyond this general acknowledgement of indebtedness to Ottawa I would like to also specifically thank the trees of Nakkertok Nordique in Gatineau, Quebec, especially the towering pines and cedars which literally inspired my ideas.

The Immaculate Conception of Data

1

Facebook, Google and ... Monsanto?

"Lots of people in suits over there. I think this is where you're going," says the cab driver as we pull up to the building housing the Impact AI convention. He has placed me as part of this congregation as I too am wearing a suit. The event space is unremarkable: a windowless basement with grey carpeting and poor lighting. All 680 of us in attendance are jammed awkwardly around square tables, and only half of us have a view of the stage. Clearly, the venue itself is not the draw for big data and artificial intelligence enthusiasts, who, as one attendee live tweets, "are at Impact AI to learn about the future." What the experience offers is a particular narrative of the future – one that positions digital technologies as all-powerful and driving inevitable positive change. Impact AI's organizer Eli Fathi takes to the podium to begin today's inculcation of this story, saying, "AI can help us grapple with fundamental problems ... but technology without humans is hollow and full of hubris. A technology with a human element is a world of limitless promise and it's a world I hope you are able to explore and imagine today."

This book challenges narratives like Fathi's, which suggest that big data and AI stand outside of the human and somehow need to be brought into relationship with it. Drawing on hours spent at technology conventions, in laboratories, in farm fields, and among activist groups, I present evidence to suggest that human effort, values, and interests are necessarily present all along; they structure which data get collected, how they come to be made useful for particular purposes, and how they serve particular interests. I add to critical data scholarship on big data in sectors like social media and health (e.g. Couldry and Turow 2014; Crawford, Miltner, and Gray 2014; Langlois, Redden, and Elmer 2015; Hall and Schulman 2009) by exploring big data and computing in the domain of food production, which is an important new site for investigating the reproduction of power via digitization. There is no good reason why we should not be looking at large agricultural corporations the same way we look at Facebook (Bronson and Sengers 2022). As Alvin, a high-level information scientist for the agricultural corporation Bayer/Monsanto, told me proudly, given the volume of environmental data collected from farms, "The notions of big data are really just the data of agriculture, today." I also add to a history of food studies scholarship that has detailed the role of historic agricultural technologies (e.g., genetically modified organisms or GMOs) in furthering corporate power with particularly negative impacts on the food system (see Clapp 2012; Friedmann 2005; Koç, Sumner, and Winson 2012; McMichael 2009). Last, and centrally, I add to science and technology studies scholarship by focusing on big data and AI in their wider social and notably imaginative context. Just as GMOs are made powerful because they are surrounded by a restrictive intellectual property regime that limits who can use them (Bronson 2015; Magnan 2004; Parthasarathy 2017), access to many agricultural big datasets – even those farmers help to generate – is concentrated in the hands of corporations. Moreover, farmer clients readily accept this restriction in part because they assume that "raw" data are useless without the corporate capacity and expertise to manipulate them into meaning. The book traces this view of big data as raw – or immaculately conceived and as powerful – as it gets used by a variety of ideologically distinct social groups and actors competing to control the future of food. The ultimate argument of the book is that the immaculate conception of data (ICD) is useful for actors intent on generating support for their data science projects, but it is a dangerous framework for imagining what big data are and what they can do for society; ICD obfuscates the political economies and moral orders that have come to define food systems and the everyday lives of many, many people.

Critical Data Awakening

Since 2018, there has been a public backlash against "big tech" – notably, against Facebook and Google, who have been labelled "ethical miscreants" abusing personal data collected from internet[1] use for corporate profit (Birch and Bronson, 2022; Solon 2017; Zuboff 2019).[2] Less visible both in terms of popular outcry and critical scholarship are some of the largest and longest-standing oligopoly corporations in North America – big agribusinesses – who increasingly centre their business models on the collection and processing of data. Every John Deere tractor manufactured today, for example, contains built-in sensors that passively and continuously collect and stream data (about soil and crop conditions, for example) to cloud-based data collection infrastructures. Deere & Company has signed more than one dozen agreements with corporations such as Monsanto, establishing channels for data transfer between their tractors and seed/chemicals corporations, just as Facebook transfers user data to non-social media corporations.

Critical data studies scholars and members of the public alike have detailed the implications of the misuses of big data on individual privacy, civil liberties, and even the whole of democratic society (Kitchin 2014; Lyon 2014). In March of 2018, the aptly named Christopher Wylie blew the whistle on Cambridge Analytica (CA), the British political consulting firm for whom he had worked as a data analyst. Wylie described to newspaper journalists how the company wilfully misused social media data in order to influence both American electoral politics as well as Brexit, the referendum on the United Kingdom's exit from the European Union. The data scientist, originally from Canada, confessed to having built "psychological warfare tools" for CA. He and others at the company had accessed Facebook data without users' consent and had used these data to build personal profiles for thousands of fictitious social media participants. These profiles were the same as those used in everyday targeted marketing for the sale of jeans or juicers. Corporations capture the online movements of others as data points, which they then use to generate predictions about a user's interests, triggers, and behaviour. In this case, CA had used internet participation data to harness weaknesses, or "demons" in Wylie's words, and to prey upon these demons in order to nudge voters in Britain toward an exit from the European Union and voters in the US toward electing Donald Trump as president. The "disinformation" tactics used by Cambridge Analytica to sway votes allegedly included the production of fake news and even fake or fully automated social media accounts (see Woolley and Howard 2016).[3]

A further surprising detail about Wylie's confession was his claim that senior executives at Facebook were aware of the nonconsensual uses of the big datasets built from their platform. Only months before, on 31 October 2017, general counsel for Facebook, Colin Stretch, had testified under oath to the United States Senate Judiciary Subcommittee on Crime and Terrorism about the firm's commitment to transparency and ethical data management. The committee called Stretch to testify because evidence had surfaced that "malevolent" foreign actors (both humans and computer programs) had used big data to influence the incredibly divisive 2016 American presidential election. Unlike Wylie in his confessional video, Stretch appeared broad-shouldered and confident during this testimonial. He commended the senators on their attention to "threats to our national security" but reassured them that Facebook was using its technical prowess to do everything possible to combat data misuses. This effort, in Stretch's words, was underpinned by the firm's commitment to "building community and bringing the world closer together" (US Senate 2017).

In the wake of the Cambridge Analytica revelations, an active public discourse emerged on the commercial, political, and legal/regulatory architecture lurking behind the collection and uses of big data on internet participation. Mark Zuckerberg attempted to shore up support for a view of the internet as a neutral tool for good or bad use, declaring on his Facebook profile that the company was making efforts to build computer programs that would be able to spot bad actors intent on gaming the system. Yet Zuckerberg and others toeing this techno-fix line were unable to prevent the surfacing of details that revealed that the system itself was flawed or always already gamed – structured in ways that directly facilitated misuse. Corporate data scientists and engineers have structured the internet's digital ecosystem so that those collecting big data online can use it in the social engineering of human subjects or what is known as "social physics" (Pentland 2015). Think tank researchers Dipayan Ghosh and Ben Scott wrote in early 2018 about the sophisticated tools for collecting and using personal data, which were leveraged by marketers, advertisers, and political muckrakers alike to command user attention. These tools include web browser cookies, which collect data on our behaviour as we move about "in" online spaces, aggregating those data into powerful resources for prediction and manipulation, which makes big datasets valuable as an economic and political resource. "There is an alignment of interests between advertisers and the platforms," Ghosh and Scott wrote, "and disinformation operators are typically indistinguishable from any other advertiser" (2018, para. 3). In a public talk in late 2017 at Stanford University's Graduate School of Business, former vice-president of user growth at Facebook Chamath Palihapitiya admitted to feeling "tremendous guilt," stating, "I think we have created tools that are ripping apart the social fabric of how society works" (Stanford Graduate School of Business 2017). Society has always recognized the internet as a powerful tool, but this confession confirmed that it was humans who had shaped its development and given it power. Now, Palihapitiya said, "We have a chance to control it and rein it in" (Stanford Graduate School of Business 2017).

Starting in early 2018, I noticed an explosion of interest in the powerful forces that shape data use and collection and the negative implications of their use. A staggering number of books released between 2017 and early 2018 focused on this topic, with titles such as *Move Fast and Break Things: How Facebook, Google and Amazon Cornered Culture and Undermined Democracy* (Taplin 2017), *Automating Inequality* (Eubanks 2018), *How to Fix the Future* (Keen 2018), and *The Know-It-Alls: The Rise of Silicon Valley as a Political Powerhouse and Social Wrecking Ball* (Cohen 2017). A number of books have focused in particular on the harmful effects of systemic racism as it influences the collection of personal data from vulnerable populations, reproducing marginalization (please see Umoja Noble 2018). By late 2017, surveys of public sentiment toward Facebook, Google, and Amazon showed a serious wane in trust in big tech companies, even among those populations benefiting from them most, like people living and working in Silicon Valley (see Edelman 2018). The uses and misuses of big data collected via sophisticated computer algorithms for corporations like Facebook and Google (among others) were the subject of numerous newspaper and magazine articles in late 2017 and early 2018 (see Clifford Chance 2018; Streitfeld, Singer, and Erlanger 2018). Indeed, *The Guardian* newspaper declared that 2017 was "the year the world turned on Silicon Valley" (Solon 2017). In 2018, my undergraduate sociology students were animated into a critical discussion of the uses of social media data to target them with advertising, and some of them even "quit" their Facebook accounts following Elon Musk's call to action (see Limer 2018). Other students asked me for obfuscation techniques they might deploy to prevent engineers and marketers from capitalizing on data they were creating through participation online.

Then in May of 2018, only a few months after the Cambridge Analytica scandal broke and amidst mounting awareness that big data were a tool for wielding power and economic gain, the US courts gave Bayer AG permission to purchase Monsanto Company – for US$63 billion – and divest much of its seeds and chemicals portfolio to the German corporation BASF (Philpott 2018). Many people, including federal regulators, were wary of this merger as a potential "marriage made in hell" in terms of corporate concentration and anti-trust or anti-competitive practices (see Neate 2016). This economic relationship would allow for continued vertical integration and market domination of these seed and chemical supplies in the agricultural supply chain, which would reduce certain financial risks for these businesses. Those of us with an interest in big data were aware that this merger would also secure data as a significant future revenue stream for Bayer/Monsanto. At the time of the merger, Bayer CropScience had already (since 2014) joined John Deere to develop digital machinery for collecting farm-level data, and Monsanto was in possession of The Climate Corporation, a valuable software developer they had purchased in 2013 for US$930 million (Kanaracus 2013). The Climate Corporation itself had acquired a number of start-up companies (e.g., 640 Labs) focused on producing tools for collecting and using farm data. While food producers have used computers, satellite monitoring (say, of weather), and global positioning system technologies for decades, The Climate Corporation's digital practices are different. Namely, they involve sensors embedded right into farm machinery, called "precision" farm equipment, as well as sophisticated digital tools for aggregating and mining big datasets for information, which can be sold alongside the datasets themselves. Due to its sheer market share, Bayer/Monsanto together have the capability to access data from and sell digitally derived advice to a majority of farmers. The merging of Bayer and Monsanto not only grew their conjoined market power by bringing together two of the largest agribusinesses in the world, it also increased the reach of this power. While Monsanto marketed largely to the US farmer/customer, Bayer had and retains access to markets not only in the US but also Europe (Belgium, Germany, France, Netherlands, Switzerland), Latin America (Argentina, Brazil), and Asia/Pacific (India).

While privacy agreements keep us from knowing the corporate uses of agricultural data, we can infer, from what we now know is done with data collection via social media (Zuboff 2019), that agribusinesses will use farm-level data to develop profiles of farmers in particular geographic areas and target them with advertisements for specific seed and chemical products, as one example. Social scientist Isabelle Carbonell (2016) says that whatever the specific uses, possessing agricultural big data "gives Monsanto a privileged position with unique insights into what farmers are doing around the clock, on a field-by-field, crop-by-crop basis into what is currently a third or more of the US farmland" (2). ETC Group – a watchdog organization tuned into technological justice issues who paid close attention to the Bayer/Monsanto merger – wrote in a 2016 report that "all agribusinesses meet in the Cloud ... It's all about who can profit most from the control of data."

A (Very Short) History of Agricultural Data Critiques

Widespread critical attention to the powerful forces behind the collection and use (or misuse) of big data – what Foroohar (2019) dubs "techlash" – has not bled over into visible critical attention toward *agricultural* big data. In October 2016 roughly one thousand people landed in Saint John, New Brunswick (population 70,000), to attend what is described as "North America's largest customer-focused data technology conference," Big Data Congress (IEEE 2016). Geoff Flood, the organizer of the 2016 Big Data Congress, commented to a conference room of 200 people (the vast majority of whom were white men in suits), "For years, people have wondered what it would be like to play god. Well, now we know. This is because of big data and data science." Situating himself and the conference in a larger epistemic community, he continued: "The heroes today all share a vision for data to build a better world. We have terrible problems, such as how to produce enough food and global warming." The messaging was clear: a society ordered under big data is the right kind of society – progressive and just. To the extent that I witnessed critical conversations at Big Data Congress or the other conventions I attended, they centred around helping everyone transition toward this utopic "data-driven" future, and quickly. Attendees repeatedly mentioned the UN's Global Open Data for Agriculture and Nutrition (GODAN), not just at this conference but also at others I attended from 2016 to 2018. GODAN is arguably leading efforts toward big data access, especially for the world's poorest. But even this conversation, which was on one level about big agricultural data's societal dimensions, seemed always to focus on technical challenges, like developing a nomenclature for the sharing of disparate datasets brought together by open data initiatives. Callum, a Canadian public sector data scientist and GODAN representative, told me in an interview that "open data is useless unless you publish it in an interoperable standard. This is the biggest challenge we face." At these conventions I met many smart people devoting enormous amounts of time and money to problems of interoperability or encryption in an attempt to open agricultural datasets for environmental and social good.[4] None of the panels at these conventions discussed the potential limits of what data might be able to deliver or the potential unintended consequences of leaving governance and other decisions putatively in the hands of machines. Even outside of these conventions where blind enthusiasm might be expected, I had difficulty finding critical news about agricultural big data amidst the noise over Facebook.

The research for this book started in 2016 as my attempt to fill a gap in critical academic as well as public discourse surrounding agricultural big data, but by 2018 the project had become an inquiry into the existence of this gap itself. In 2017 I joined a then-small group of international critical social scientists interested in the topic of big data in agriculture (see Bronson and Knezevic 2016; Carbonell 2016; Carolan 2017; Driessen and Heutinck 2015; Eastwood, Klerkx, and Nettle 2017; Higgins et al. 2017; building on Wolf and Buttel 1996; Wolf and Wood 1997). In 2017, the social science scholarship to date on big data and computing in agriculture had been largely survey-based (e.g., Silva, Moraes, and Molin 2011) and focused on the economic potential of big data applications (Campbell et al. 2014; Tesfom and Birch 2010). The sociologist Michael Carolan wrote in *Sociologia Ruralis* in early 2017 that the "relative silence among critical agro food scholars is made even more pronounced when one considers how much research colleagues in the information and crop sciences do on the subject, whom all evaluate practices through a distinctly productivist lens" (4). Michael Carolan and I, in fact, experienced this relative silence first-hand. In June of 2017, Carolan and I presented on a panel at a critical data studies academic conference, Data Power, which was otherwise lively with debate over big data but where only four people, including conference support staff, attended our session on agricultural data.

I began this book project wondering whether big agricultural data might perpetuate some of the issues flagged by food studies scholars who have studied other agricultural technologies like GMOs. For instance, I wondered: Is full access to commercial agricultural big datasets restricted, even for those farmers who are helping to generate the data in the first place, as happens with social media data (Crossley et al. 2015, 67)? I was also curious about the effects of restricted data access on the food system, following from research that has revealed that the licensing structure around genetically modified (GM) seeds is limiting for farmers (notably, restricting their ability to save seed) and fostering market concentration among agribusiness (Bronson 2014, 2015; see also: Clapp 2016; de Beer 2005; Howard 2016; Kinchy 2012). Moreover, after having studied critical public engagements with GM seeds, I wondered about Bayer's decision to buy Monsanto, a company whose name is a synecdoche for evil among environmentalists, anti-corporate globalization activists, and many unconventional farmers. In my earlier research, GMO activists had described to me the "terrible things agribusinesses do," such as use their market concentration to put an economic "squeeze" on farmers, and they told me that GM seeds were an embodiment of this immoral "corporate value system." Monsanto's already poor public image became even worse in July 2018 when law firms (see Baum Hedlund Law 2021) released incriminating documents that revealed Monsanto employees were "bullying" scientists and regulatory agents and suppressing evidence regarding the negative health effects of its best-selling glyphosate herbicide Roundup. Evidence of flagrantly unethical behaviour, such as influencing the peer review process, surfaced in the context of a lawsuit between Dewayne Johnson and the Monsanto Company (Krimsky and Gillam 2018). Johnson won his lawsuit and a jury awarded him US$289 million in damages; glyphosate, the jury determined, had caused Johnson's cancer. As of November 2017, there were still 3,500 plaintiffs with ongoing cases against Monsanto and thousands of civil suits have been settled. If society was judging big agriculture's products as hazardous to human and animal health, and their corporate behaviour as reckless and harmful, how would it view big agricultural data collected and controlled by these same companies? I assumed that the Bayer/Monsanto merger would signal to activists the appearance of a new site – big agricultural data – for food system corporatization, would it not? By 2017, some activists had turned attention to machinery manufacturers' copyright licensing on digital farm equipment for the ways it was preventing tinkering (see IFIXIT n.d.; Phillips et al. 2019),[5] but there was no highly visible organizing around the collection and use of big data. By July 2018, I wondered about the force field that seemed to have been erected around big agricultural data that protected agribusinesses from the "techlash."

The Power of "Raw" Data

The ultimate argument I make in this book is that a relative gap in popular and academic concern over agricultural big data relates to conceptual forces quietly aiding the stabilization of historic relationships of power and authority in the food system and beyond. The significant force I explore in this book is an uninterrogated "imaginary" of big data (Jasanoff and Kim 2015; Taylor 2003): one where data are viewed as capable of driving positive social change unmediated by human intervention. I call this the immaculate conception of data (ICD). It is a vision that data are "raw" and thereby provide truths about the world as it really is; consequently, the advice putatively "driven" by data and automated decision systems is conceived of as all-powerful. I trace the ICD across various arenas, from contained laboratory and convention spaces to messy farm fields.

A conversation I had with Chris,[6] a corporate ambassador for analytics at a big agricultural firm, is emblematic of the workings of ICD. Chris was describing a proprietary algorithm for detecting insects when he said, "It has one thousand examples to draw from, but once it has fifty thousand examples to draw from, it ... in many different lighting scenarios and different stages of life ... gets smarter and smarter." Rather than talking about confidence intervals and statistical improvements in predictability, he spoke to me about a digital technology anthropomorphically getting *smarter*. Yet in the very same conversation, Chris boasted about his company's suite of "mathematicians and computer scientists who are coding these algorithms that look at an image and tell you what's in it based on training sets that we've generated." Through the course of this project, I met many people who were a necessary part of the process of data collection, storage, and use. In one field visit to an experimental station, a data scientist walked me through a field and pointed to exact locations where an agronomist – a person with expertise in plant science – had "ground truthed," or verified and corrected for, a prediction made algorithmically using a big dataset. As one data scientist told me, "We fly the image and we have this multi-spectral picture of the fields and we are noticing like big vast differences in the reflectants in the field and the computer can't tell you what that means if it has never seen it before."

As Chris's story makes clear, despite the obvious role of people in creating and mediating data and the production of insights or information, these same people use ICD to frame their work and, significantly, their aspirations. One common expression of the ICD that I heard repeatedly is the phrase "data-driven," which connotes that data have agency quite apart from the humans who select and organize them. Michael Stenta, an activist scientist and farmer involved in the production of an open-source farm management platform called farmOS, told me that he believes that data have the capability of "driving" radical food system "transformation." He is therefore attempting to "collect as much data from as many farms as possible." Those farmOS volunteers I spoke with embrace GODAN's call for open data, having collaborated with the UN agency in the past. They are also motivated by a "development methodology" that farmOS leader Dorn Cox told me is "all about agriculture as a shared human endeavor and public participation in science ... and production through environmental improvement ... and ... expressions of that through open source, open science hardware and data systems." The belief is that local and sustainable farming systems will come about via open data innovation.

As can be seen, futurity is central to the ICD framework. Indeed, currently digital innovations applied to food are both academically and colloquially referred to as "food frontiers" and the fully realized digital farm that is predicted to arrive in the future is commonly – even by critical academics – called "agriculture 4.0" (Glaros et al. 2022). Almost every one of the big data and AI conventions I attended had "future" in its title – from IoTForum's "Future of Agrifood Industry" (online, October 2021) to Microsoft Research Summit 2021 (online), which included sessions with titles such as "New Future of Work," "The Future of Cloud Networking," and "The Future of Search and Recommendation" among many other "futures." Academic work on digital agriculture is also often casting toward the future; at the ic-ETITE international conference 2020, Bhojwani et al. claimed that "Internet of Things (IoT) is the future. IoT is the change that is required in every field."

In practice, those people whose stories animate this book do not just receive "data-driven" advice as if it fell from the sky, but rather they participate in the challenging work of bringing data into being and making them useful. In other words, ICD as a framework for imagining big data and the future it supposedly delivers contradicts the daily grind of digitally mediated scientific and farming practices. Recognizing this tension or contradiction, I came to see ICD not as a faulty belief system but instead as a tool that actors tactically leverage. I witnessed the ICD imaginary put to work: by public sector scientists attempting to gather grant money for a technological research program, by commercial big data platforms advertising to farmers, and by leaders of a volunteer network of food and technology activists intent on catalyzing a social movement to rebuild or "regenerate" food systems.

In outlining how the ICD framework gets used, this book extends work in critical data studies that has *described* how people view big data as objective and truthful; I put forward ICD as an *analytical* device which helps *explain* why people appear to hold this view, at least publicly – because it has social force. In the most recent *Handbook of Science and Technology Studies*, Konrad et al. (2017) give an overview of "the performative force" of claims that science and technology will lead to a better future or what science studies scholars call "sociotechnical imaginaries" (Jasanoff and Kim 2015). Such imaginaries help to mobilize and legitimate the activities of technologists and policymakers along with activists (465). Instead of treating ICD as false consciousness, I elaborate on ICD as a useful imaginary for particular people in particular networks of power. This book is thus distinct from critical data studies or psychology, which since the early days of AI has troubled over the "deeply powerful and delusional thinking" that humans seem to display in their assessment of the efficacy of automated systems (Weizenbaum 1975). A key example of such scholarship is the work in cognitive psychology on "automation bias" or the propensity for humans to put undue trust in machines over humans. Psychologists or others working on this subject stage experiments to test the human propensity to choose machine-derived insights or outcomes over those derived by humans, where the latter is referred to as a "heuristic replacement for vigilant information seeking and processing" (e.g., Mosier 2009, 162).

Rather than treating ICD as epistemic distortion like a cognitive psychologist might, I draw on science studies scholarship and treat ICD as a logical framework for actors to animate because ICD draws on long-standing assumptions about scientific and technological neutrality (immaculateness) and objectivity. People have invoked the supposed purity of science and of technology to shore up authority for particular scientific and technological projects for more than one hundred years. Think of the logical positivist movement with the Vienna Circle in the first half of the twentieth century, which argued explicitly that scientific knowledge and those speaking for it operate exclusively in the domain of rationality. Not only that, the Vienna Circle argued that those with access to this supposedly special way of knowing are and should be authoritative. A sociological account of the emergence of these ideas recognizes that they were normatively motivated; scholars in the Vienna Circle were deeply concerned about systems of thought and belief, such as Marxism and Nazism, which states were using toward destructive ends.

Yet as countless feminist science studies scholars (e.g. Haraway 1988) have said of scientific claims, they are power all the way down (see also Foucault 1977; Fuller 2018). In fact, the intellectual legacy of a view that technologies – not humans – drive societal, political, and even moral progress is wrapped up in the legacy of atrocities associated with the colonial project (Marx and Roe Smith 1994). Historians of science and technology Leo Marx and Merritt Roe Smith (1994) detail how early US Treasury Department associate Tench Coxe was a "most eloquent and persistent" proponent of the role that technology could play in "civilizing" the Americas, and they quote from his 1787 speech on factory manufacturing as political salvation in which he claimed, "It will consume our native productions ... improve our agriculture ... accelerate the improvement of our internal navigation ... and lead us once more into the paths of virtue by restoring frugality and industry, those potent antidotes to the vices of mankind" (4). Technocrats like Coxe were, of course, proved wrong, and innovation-mediated social changes in the nineteenth century facilitated not salvation but rather a variety of ills, even including exaggerated inequity among settlers. I have witnessed contemporary proponents of big data and AI operating in apparent disregard of this history of events, echoing Coxe's statements about technological development as determining the course of human events. The United Nations Food and Agriculture Organization (UNFAO) says, for example, that "it would be hard to overstate the scope for Information and Communications Technologies (ICTs) to drive agricultural and rural development, especially for the poorest smallholders and other households" (Treinen and van der Elstraeten 2018, 1). The UNFAO (2018) claims that ICTs in agriculture will "bridge the rural divide ... support smallholders and family farmers, fishers, pastoralists, and forest-dwellers ... increase productivity and profitability, improve consumption of nutritious food, empower youth and women access to information, technology and markets and ensure that agriculture practices are environmentally sustainable for future generations" (Treinen and van der Elstraeten 2018, 11). Here we see digital tools positioned not as instruments capable of influencing agriculture but as agents "driving" positive social transformations. This is the immaculate conception of data being put to work.

Interestingly, while science and technology have long been positioned as unmuddied and thus authoritative, this bid for authority has never gone completely uncontested (Harding 2008). Indeed, science studies scholars have used careful case studies to reveal that the technical site representing twined objectivity/authority has changed over time in part due to the influence of social pressure against the regressive impacts of the sciences and the illegitimate "rule of experts" (Mitchell 2002). Ann Morning (2008), for example, describes how biology pedagogy shifted from a focus on phrenology to genetics under public awareness that phrenology was ideologically inflected with racism. Under genetics, Morning shows, the root arguments about racial hierarchy remain intact even though the locus of scientific expertise changes, becoming increasingly specialized, dependent on elite training and expensive equipment, and thus shielding domains of practice from wider interrogation. One of the outcomes of the immaculate conception of data is similar in that ICD has the potential to shield an industrialized approach to food production from reform because ICD obfuscates the politics of technologies that stand at its centre by abstracting these technologies from the social means of their production.

From Seeds to Data: Hegemonic Approaches to Food Systems Over Time

Three technological pillars have buttressed the hegemonic "industrial food regime" or intensive food production practices and the global capitalist actors benefitting most from them (Friedmann 1987): chemical fertilizers and pesticides, genetically modified seed systems engineered to work with these chemicals (Bronson 2015), and now big data. In this book, I examine the reformulation of the specific technological solutions underpinning the industrialized food regime – from chemicals to chemical-seed systems to a focus on emergent digital tools. I understand these shifts as responses to at least one decade of serious questioning about the industrialized approach. For example, in 2002, the World Bank and the UNFAO initiated a study at the request of agricultural biotechnology companies who sought advice on the future of genetically modified crops in developing countries (Stokstad 2008). In the end, a range of institutions sponsored the study, including the United Nations Environment Program, the United Nations Development Program, and the World Health Organization. An inclusive governing body, consisting of thirty governmental representatives and thirty representatives from civil society (notably, consumers, nongovernmental organizations, and private companies) assembled the study. Modelled after the International Panel on Climate Change, the study included hundreds of experts as authors and reporters, and many governments and organizations participated in the peer-review process (IAASTD 2009, viii). The resulting report from the International Assessment of Agricultural Knowledge, Science and Technology for Development (IAASTD), titled "Agriculture at a Crossroads" (2009), quite surprised many people, perhaps most of all those who had commissioned the report. The report blatantly critiqued the dominance of modern western scientific knowledge and political authority over food system change. Then, five years later, another high-level policy report, the International Panel of Experts on Sustainable Food Systems, similarly critiqued dominant, modern, western ways of knowing and doing for their role in producing unsustainable production. Again, these critiques were at once epistemic and political, in that they highlighted the highly politicized nature of dominant approaches to agricultural knowledge and practice.[7] The report states, "IPES-Food's first report proposes a new analytical lens for food systems, and makes the case for reaching beyond the traditional bounds of the scientific community in conducting this analysis" (IPES Food 2015, 2).

The past decade, exemplified by these reports but not limited to them, has thus involved increasing public critique of industrialized agriculture's social and environmental consequences *as they connect with* political economic power *and* received notions of expertise (see Clapp 2021). Said differently, critiques of technologies like genetically modified seed systems and chemical fertilizers are at once critiques of the powerful interests wrapped up in the production and use of these tools. In fact, the development of the concept of food regimes represents an attempt to trace the connections between epistemologies and the politics of food production, to highlight "links between international relations of food production and consumption to forms of accumulation broadly distinguishing periods of capitalist accumulation" (Friedmann and McMichael 1989, 95). Chemicals are bad for the health of the environment and all who inhabit it, to be sure, but they also grow the oligopoly power of transnational agribusinesses, which threaten rural social structures and livelihoods as well as political sovereignty around the globe (see Clapp 2012). As such, critiques of chemicals represent a threat to powerful interests.

In my view, the site of power in the food system has more recently moved from seeds and chemicals (or seeds genetically paired to be useful only with chemicals) to data. Agricultural authorities are now positioning farming as requiring not just broadband access and the incorporation of digital tools but also the use of a host of digital skill sets that have not historically been a part of the farmer's training or approach. As with the relationship between the genetic sciences and race (Morning 2008), big data approaches to agriculture are relatively esoteric and require elite training (or expertise) in order to engage with them, including critically. In this context, one may feel disempowered from questioning a digital agriculture approach or subverting it in the absence of comfort and skill with big data and computing. Moreover, like the genetic material underpinning genetic seed systems (Biddle 2014), most commercial big datasets and AI are closed and proprietary, and thus obfuscated from interrogation, even to those holding the expertise. In *The Immaculate Conception of Data* I argue that while precision agriculture appears to be strengthening power for large agribusinesses and food system actors located in the global North, and reproducing material wealth for the already wealthy, these political and economic interests are shielded from critique in part because of the nature of the technology but also because of the imaginative framework surrounding it. This imaginative framework is the central focus of this book – in it, big data and AI are described as standing outside of politics and interest, as immaculately conceived, and thus as all powerful.

The Chapters of this Book

The first several chapters of *The Immaculate Conception of Data* are linked in that they present ideas about what the digitized future of food production will look like. The idea of the future presented in chapter 2 is coherent and dominant, and it links to hegemonic food system players, such as powerful agribusinesses, as well hegemonic values or ideals, like the belief that good farmers maximize production of commodities. The vision of the future outlined in chapter 2 is one that exists in farm trade journals, newspapers, corporate advertisements and campaigns, a prominent scholarly journal, and at conventions and trade shows. Chapter 3 presents a different, even oppositional, future of digital agriculture, one furthered by historically marginalized food system actors like agro-ecological farmers and their heterodox thinking and practices. This alternative digital farm of the future exists in the minds of activists working on data projects in Canada and the US and within a forum for dialogue called the Gathering for Open Agricultural Technologies or GOAT. While chapters 2 and 3 are descriptive, they are conceptually linked in ways that become clear in chapter 4. Having set up what seems to be a stark dichotomization between industry and activists, in the chapter that follows (chapter 4) I highlight that actors within these two ideologically distinct social groups have something in common: a way of imagining and describing data as "driving" a "revolution" in food production and delivering good food and a good society. In this "immaculate conception of data" a datum is "raw" and untouched and this gives it – especially when it is aggregated with other data – a kind of power; so construed, ICD is a useful framework for those actors speaking for it, helping them garner support for their particular projects. In chapter 4, I unpack the ICD and tell stories about how the framework gets animated in social settings. While useful, ICD is also hazardous because it depoliticizes digital agriculture by reifying the tools produced by both industry and activists. The presence of ICD therefore at least partly explains why the critical interests that circulate vocally around GM seeds and organisms have not yet done so around agricultural big data. In the final chapter (chapter 5), I attempt to re-politicize agricultural big data and AI; I detail the particular interests guiding the collection of big agricultural data and the development of data-based decision platforms. Dispensing with ICD, I draw on a science studies theoretical starting point and treat big data and digital technologies as always already "partial." It is people who decide which data are collected from all that are possibly available in the world, and it is people who help decide which datasets a computer program or algorithm is going to use to generate information on any phenomenon. It is also people who write the algorithms that draw on big datasets, and it is people who use "data-derived" advice to implement social policies and to motivate social action. Using this anti-ICD framework – one we might call technopolitical – I expose in chapter

5 the entanglement of personal history, economic interest, and technical and societal goals with the design and use of big data and decision platforms. Private industry scientists and engineers developed two of these platforms, while activists using open source development created the third.

FarmCommand is a platform in the former category. It is a data repository and decision platform for "farm management" developed by Farmers Edge, whose CEO Wade Barnes describes the platform as universally liberating, stating, "What this platform does is use the power of big data analytics and machine learning to implement these strategies to make huge changes to anyone's farm. These tools can be used anywhere wherever you are. Fifteen years ago, farmers couldn't leave the farm. Today they can be out at the lake fishing with the kids and they get an alert that a field, or even parts of that field, need 20 pounds of nitrogen because of rain." Despite Barnes's promise, FarmCommand does not provide a god's eye view from nowhere (Haraway 1988). For one, FarmCommand is only useful if one is farming corn, wheat, canola, barley, oats, peas, sunflowers, soybeans, cotton, winter wheat, lentils, sugar cane, sugar beets, beans, desi chickpeas, or flax. Just as with GM seeds (Welsh and Glenna 2006), precision farming industries (not just Farmers Edge) are focusing only on a selection of major agronomic commodity crops. Agronomic crops are typically planted on extremely large acreages and on farms specializing in one crop. These crops are typically transported long distances, as these farms often lack direct access to markets. We can see with this one example the partiality of commercial big data platforms used in food production – a partiality that works to service food system actors entrenched within the industrial food regime.

I learned about big data platforms like Farm Command in part from reading about them or attending "webinar" tutorials for users but mostly from hours and hours of conversations with scientists and farmers. A thick empirical bedrock supports the arguments I make in the book. I have spent many hours at technical, social science, and government conventions as well as at academic conferences organized around the topics of big data and artificial intelligence.[8] I have read farm newspapers, agricultural trade journals, and corporate website descriptions of platforms that farmers can use to deposit their big data and to ultimately help "drive" farm-level decisions. I have participated in webinars on digital technologies and scrutinized their privacy and access agreements. I have spent the most time in conversations with people involved in some form or another with digital agriculture, some of which were in their sites of research and making like laboratories or fields. It is really the ideas of others that make up this book.

I purposefully embedded the stories of this book within a history of scholarly thought stretching across the typically distinct domains of critical data studies, food studies, and science studies. My hope is that this book allows for epistemic brokerage among these often-disparate fields, motivating people to think about big data and AI alongside food systems and food justice. Living well together – with humans, amongst technologies, and in environments – into the twenty-first century requires working together in interdisciplinary scholarly assemblages. If you primarily identify as a data studies scholar, you may be interested in the book because it deals with big data in a domain that has received much less popular and scholarly attention – agriculture. As I make clear in the book, there are data practices and consequences which are quite particular to the agri-food sector but from which we may draw wider insights at the same time. If you are a food studies scholar you may be interested in this book for its focus on an emergent set of agricultural technologies and the ways these technologies, and the promises made about them, intervene into ongoing knowledge–power struggles over food sovereignty. If you are a science studies scholar you will likely appreciate the ethnographic and symmetrical attention to both dominant and activist groups' ways of thinking about big data or their shared "socio-technical imaginary" (Jasanoff and Kim 2015). In the final chapter of the book, I draw on a history of science studies work, which has helped to reveal the situated and context-specific conditions in which scientific knowledge and technologies are produced (rather than simply discovered), in order to detail domain-specific practices around big data in agriculture in corporate and activist contexts. In this way, the book hopefully illustrates that bringing a science studies inflection to critical data studies means attending to how data are always mediated by the people who work with them in specific historical, political, and economic circumstances. This work opens possibilities for data studies scholars to trace the practical, institutional, and political–economic differences among domains as they may lead to different forms of "big data" and multiple big techs. Monsanto may be a Facebook but, in some ways, it is not.

While I do not take a normative position on big data in agriculture, my intent is to invite critical reflection on the practices of imagination and articulation that are reproducing food system relations, especially those of inequitable power between farmers and agribusinesses.[9] And, more broadly, my intent is to invite reflection on what Donna Haraway (2016) calls "futurisms" or orientations toward the future that prevent us from "staying with the trouble in real and particular places and times" – from focusing on today's injustices and here-and-now possibilities for engendering hope and kinship and beauty. In her 1988 book *When Old Technologies Were New* Carolyn Marvin does a radical thing and asks what stays the same rather than what is novel via innovations. Inspired by Marvin, I deploy a similar reversal heuristic in this book: amidst conversations about digital agriculture bringing radically new futures, I am interested in what is left intact by these so-called innovation-led shifts, particularly the relations of inequity that have come to characterize food systems the world over. The focus is on stories of big data and AI, yet the stories themselves are not what matters. Rather, the broadest take-away is about the importance of attending to lines of thinking and evaluation through which power is produced and reproduced, conceptualizing which itself becomes embodied in particular technical forms. These technological forms have received attention in the literature; this book is my invitation to a more inclusive conversation in the hopes that it might move the moral compass and the site for intervention further afield from and "upstream" of technological development and use. Big data and AI in agriculture are still taking shape and have yet to stabilize into a well-entrenched and difficult-to-reverse socio-technical system.

Two of the tools I analyze in this book (FarmCommand and Climate FieldView) are in their current configuration clearly favouring the interests of agribusiness and large-scale commodity farms (and indeed an industrialized food regime), while the activist platform farmOS potentially supports an alternative food system trajectory. It is tempting to run these two models for the realization of a so-called digital agriculture revolution against one another. Food studies scholars have done so when describing "productivist" assumptions – for example, that farming ought to be a rationally managed business (Kneen 1995, 69) – as having furthered an industrial food regime that competes with its alternative: a nonindustrial regime. Productivist ideas do support the materialization of digital agricultural forms, which feed the hegemony of the industrial regime, as other historical agricultural innovations have done. In other ways too, the terrain of digital agriculture is uneven. Commercial as opposed to activist data scientists are institutionalized with tremendous monetary support; historic momentum lies behind productivism within agricultural policy making; and productivist digital agriculture enjoys the support of a significant promotion engine that includes advertising, targeted marketing, and lobbying. And still, after having spent years in conversation with designers, funders, and people involved "on the ground" (including on the farm) with agricultural big data and intelligent machines, I came to see that regardless of the context of production, and regardless of how differently actors perceive agricultural success, they talk in similar ways about data and the future: a line that sees big data offering a simple techno-fix for a global food system rife with issues.

In hinging the book's detail around an exploration of the immaculate conception of data, I aim to illustrate what can happen when novel technological forms, or innovations, become caught up in pre-existing arrangements of power, including economic power but also hegemonic ways of seeing and knowing. Agricultural technologies (and all technologies for that matter) gain stability because of powerful political and economic forces and also because of culture: modes of thinking and talking that direct human action. Systems of belief can be a tremendous resource. My aim, especially in the last chapter of this book, is to peel back the curtain and deliver a more sober and complete view of contemporary innovations in food production – a less immaculate rendering of agricultural big data – in order to enable contestations of hegemonic food system relations. In this way, *The Immaculate Conception of Data* is intended to link to politically engaged scholarship that works toward food system reformation away from the dominant, industrial system. If each of us becomes more aware of the normative dimensions surrounding big data and AI, this may enable us to stay with, and attempt to seek redress for, today's troubles in the food system and beyond. An early theorist of the politics of technologies, Langdon Winner (1980), asserted in a now-canonical essay that technologies are not only used to advance social and political interests (e.g., dictatorships controlling hearts and minds via information technologies), but their very design encodes consequences for the arrangement of power and authority in society (see also Bijker, Hughes, and Pinch 2012). Technologies are not magic, and societal shifts that accompany technical ones happen only because of human decisions taken. Each of us – not just engineers and designers – has the power to shape food system futures, which we ought to see as not yet written.

2

Revolutions, Disruptions and the Future of Farming

In August of 2012, John Deere, the corporation responsible for selling the "big green tractor," released a video on YouTube titled *Farm Forward.* It is an odd kind of text – it visualizes not-yet-available technologies and runs with credits like a Hollywood film. By the corporation's own description, they intended the video to be a cinematic forecasting exercise, asking, "How will technology change farming in the future?" The movie narration answers, "The only certainty is that technology will continue to change how we farm. John Deere offers one vision on how farmers might control their operations in the future."

If you play the video and watch the first six minutes, you will see a panoramic scroll over grain fields in what appears to be a prairie landscape. An early morning sunrise reflects off of an ultra-modern, all-white house. The video cuts to the entryway of the house wherein the viewer sees, in close-up, figurines of John Deere tractors, presumably from a bygone era, when tractors were mechanical, with no authorizing software or USB port. Cut to a fridge that, unlike these old tractors, digitally communicates – in this instance with a "smart" coffee maker that begins to brew just now, at precisely 6:00 a.m. The farmer who lives in this house arrives in the kitchen in time to receive his coffee. He stands at a computer projected onto the kitchen wall, its contents protected by a fingerprint scanner that recognizes "Terry" and opens to him a wealth of visual informatics. Terry swipes to a screen displaying weather data being collected by his John Deere equipment, which advises him today is the day to irrigate. An intelligent personal assistant warns Terry of an impending storm set to hit field #511 where his son is riding a GPS-led tractor. The son exits the machine, leaving the farm all on its own.

John Deere, like many proponents of agricultural digitization, forecasts that this process will catapult farmers from their muddy boots into the creative economy. Corporations like John Deere predict that digitization will include the replacement of farm labour by automation but also the replacement of human decision-making. Instead, remote sources like satellites and "smart" farm equipment will collect data and aggregate them into big data, thereby delivering "insights" and competitive advantage, which is the phrasing from John Deere's "Precision Ag Technology" website. *Farm Forward* contains within it many of the themes I will discuss in this chapter, including the shift agribusiness has made towards investing in the development and marketing of "smart" technologies, the pressure on farmers to adopt them, and the way that promises of a digital agricultural "revolution" reproduce historic productivist thinking even as they are positioned as value neutral. I will also situate these moves toward agricultural digitization within anti-productivist resistance, where we might view the corporate messages about the neutrality and power of big agricultural data as an attempt to respond to critiques against the very real material impacts of industrial agriculture.

Agricultural Automation

While the images of completely unoccupied tractor cabs and farming from the comfort of one's living room pictured in *Farm Forward* are not today's reality, John Deere's visual narrative embeds a truism: North American farmers have been automating features of their food production operations arguably since the beginning of the modern, industrial food system with the industrial revolution. Today's automating innovations applied to agriculture ostensibly improve the efficiency of farms, but they also put the companies producing these technologies in control of large stores of data, which are of considerable benefit to agribusinesses. Social scientists have studied agriculture as a key site for the consolidation of power and the displacement of human labour since the beginning of mechanization in the industrial revolution, long before the digital age. Since Karl Marx (1889), political economists have argued that industry has taken a leading role in "appropriating" human labour and in shaping the farm environment (including its social environment) through market power, whether exercised upstream (e.g., chemical supply companies) or downstream (e.g., food processors) from the farm (for contemporary analyses, see Clapp 2015; Howard 2016). Some argue that the whole history of technological change in agriculture has been defined by appropriationism or the commodification of on-farm labour and biological processes (Goodman et al. 1987). Many food studies scholars continue to puzzle over the family farm as a site of resistance to appropriationism, focusing on the unique obstacles to a fully capitalized agriculture, which include the unpredictability of farm environmental variables (Friedmann 1980; Mann and Dickinson 1980, 498). Farms, it turns out, do not behave like widgets. In this context, scholars have argued that, unlike other spheres where corporations gain dominance via displacement, companies largely control farmers via the sale of inputs. Automated decision tools and other digital technologies are the current inputs that fit into this historic pattern. Corporations market these tools to farmers as devices that will bring efficiency or productivity gains to farmers and "make the farm pay" (Kneen 1995), while describing to other corporate actors, shareholders, and investors a "race" among companies to "control" the new market by solidifying a digital relationship with farmers (Cosgrove 2018).

Just like the mechanization of agriculture at large, automation via the digitization of agriculture is also not a new phenomenon. In fact, farmers have been at the vanguard of digitization, using sophisticated computing to replace farmer labour for a long time, and it is partly a lack of regulatory oversight on farms that has fuelled this innovation. It has widely been imagined that farms minimize the number of uncontrolled variables – or at least variables believed to be of consequence – compared to urban environments with their crowds of people; farms have thus been considered, in the minds of regulators and litigators, to require less oversight and risk governance than city streets. While in Canada, for example, guidelines for autonomous agricultural systems are "in-scope" for vehicle registration, driver training/licensing, and enforcement of traffic laws, there are no classifications for farm vehicles and no specific guidelines for autonomous agriculture vehicles (Garvey 2018). I talked to Brent, the global field operations manager of a multinational digital agriculture corporation, who pointed out some interesting tensions among visibility and regulation and innovation. Brent's expertise is in aerospace engineering and he demonstrated a farm drone for me – one equipped with "spectral" cameras that image a farmer's field according to wavelength specifications, which he anticipates can be used to indicate plant health. He spent a good deal of our conversation attempting to separate what he and his corporation were doing from what "hobbyists do with drones," which, he told me, "is not at all the same thing." In fact, Brent was careful not to use the term "drone" and opted instead for UAV, or uncrewed aerial vehicle, because, he said, "drone is a dirty word." Brent said that his corporation was presently lobbying for stricter regulations in order to gain social legitimacy for what he was doing for agriculture and what other corporations were doing for the mining sector. But even though the corporation would benefit from stricter oversight on the industry, they had benefited in the earlier days of innovation development from what he called a "lax" regulatory structure in Canada. "In the beginning," he recalled, "this was really nice for businesses like us, we do a lot of testing ... and before we were the professionals that we are today in the same level we enjoyed a lot of freedom in terms of getting access to air space and using these drones and testing different things." In the United States, Brent told me, regulation on UAVs was stricter, and this "impeded a lot of businesses." Formal legal assessments confirm Brent's assessment of the regulatory environment for digital innovation in Canada versus the US (Office of the Privacy Commissioner 2013).

John Deere claims in its corporate storytelling to have been leading farms at the forefront of digital innovation through investment in what is now called "precision equipment." The company's leadership position in precision agriculture today builds off of its historic expertise in automatic guidance equipment (John Deere 2015). In the mid-1990s, John Deere started linking its equipment with the US-based satellite navigation system, the Global Positioning System (GPS), when this was still a new technology. Initially, John Deere worked with a navigation company called NavCom, which they later purchased, to develop GPS receivers on its farm equipment that would gather data from both the farm field and from global imaging systems. In the early days of this sensing equipment, systems were not accurate or reliable enough that the GPS could guide the tractor. However, scientists at the National Aeronautics and Space Administration (NASA) were simultaneously working to stream satellite tracking data in real time via the internet – rather than collecting it intermittently by phone lines – and to develop software to correct for data errors, thereby enabling GPS navigation. While the imagined end users of this navigation tool were pilots, not farmers, the technology was ultimately applied to various "use cases" (as technology developers call them), including food production. Yoaz Bar-Sever, who was supervisor of a key group at NASA's Jet Propulsion Lab (JPL) in the 1990s and early 2000s, says the result of engineering and data science efforts during the 1990s represented a "breakthrough capability": the enabling of accurate GPS navigation almost anywhere on the planet (see Anderson 2018). In 2001, NavCom licensed the software from NASA and also contracted with JPL to receive data from the centre's global network of reference stations. While JD was testing the JPL system in the field, in-house engineers and scientists continued to work on the company's own technology for correcting GPS signals, and in 2002, JD released its GPS-based guidance system for tractors, AutoTrac, in North America and Australia. By 2004, the company officially released what they called StarFire receivers to tap into NASA's global network of ground stations and incorporate JPL's software, which it had licensed. StarFire was accurate down to four inches, which for the first time, at that time, allowed automated steering that worked for farmers. From my conversations with farmers using auto-steer systems, this kind of precision is especially important for farmers managing large acreages where turnaround at the edges takes longer and where economies of scale are so immense that shaving moments off of each task – for example, dropping a seed in the ground – amounts to significant gains.

Dan spoke with me over the phone about the differences in digital farming technologies as they relate to land size. A middle-aged man and the fourth generation of his family to farm his parcel of land, which sits next to the picturesque Saskatchewan River, Dan said with pride that he had adopted new techniques, such as the "green" farming practice of leaving the land mostly undisturbed between crop rotations. He had also adopted innovations like digital technologies. "We've been using auto-steer for years," he told me, "so all our tractors and combines, well, we don't steer 'em, we run in parallel lines up and down the field." Dan and other farmers told me about how they go to farm trade shows and technology exhibitions in order to "stay current." Indeed, there is social pressure on farmers to adopt innovations; social and political forces such as subsidies, crop insurance programs, and market concentration steer farmers toward using technologies that (further) intensify their operations and allow them to capitalize upon economies of scale (Rotz and Fraser 2015). However, increasingly capital-intensive production has paradoxically led to lower commodity prices because of overproduction, which puts a "squeeze" on Canadian farmers (Rotz, Fraser, and Martin 2017). In response to this squeeze, many farmers take on debt in order to continue adopting the newest technologies, hoping that in doing so they will outperform other farmers and stay in business. According to Dan, adopting auto-steer was a "no-brainer" because "as soon as we could have something like a seed drill steer parallel straight lines up and down a field, you know there was no overlap … so you have savings where you're not overlapping, you're not over-seeding and you're not over-fertilizing." Dan, whose 2,500-acre farm represents the median farm size in Saskatchewan, said that auto-steer is worthwhile for farms like his because the efficiency gains of doing tasks guided by GPS accumulate. He illustrated his point, explaining, "Say, you're overlapping by two feet every time, it doesn't take very long before you start to add up quite a bit of overlap." And besides, he added with a sigh to emphasize his exhaustion, "It's much easier on the operator."

In 2018, at a harvest fair near Ottawa, the capital city of Canada, I met a John Deere representative who was hawking the company's tractors at a stall located right beside the fair's noisy midway. "It's been a big year for tractor automation," he told me over the din of games and small, rickety rollercoasters. About fifteen years after corporate investment in GPS-led coordination began, John Deere introduced their 8R/8RT series machines, which use numerous sensors to automate various aspects of the tractor operation. In the mid-summer of 2019, I got to sit on one of these machines, the Autonomous 8370R Row Crop Tractor, and I experienced its automated features first-hand at a farm (Figure 2.1). "You're sitting in over half a million dollars," Jack told me as I stepped into the tractor he had rented from a fellow farmer for use that day. I felt dwarfed by both Jack, a wiry, six-foot eight-inch man in his thirties, and the tractor, whose treads alone were taller than me. The metal staircase I needed to climb in order to get into the cab was nerve-wrackingly narrow and steep. But the atmosphere inside the cab was calming: quiet, air conditioned, and remarkably clean. This was a hot and dry summer day and the field, due to water drainage issues and a long, wet winter, was not planted with crops. Outside of the cab it was dry, dusty, and noisy. But inside the cab it was so pristine that Jack took off his shoes. "This is the display you use?" I asked, pointing to what looked to me like a tablet propped on the dashboard. "And this machine has a bunch of GPS receivers?" "Yes," Jack told me, "it has a bunch, but the ones we care about today are the ones up here." He pointed to the top front of the tractor. "That's steering for me, and there's one on the

2.1
Photograph of the author standing next to an expensive precision agriculture tractor, which she got to ride on a hot day in June 2019 in southern Ontario. Photo taken by author.

blade there … it's gonna allow me to slope the field so the water runs away from the road and into the ditch right there." I learned later, in talking with a salesperson at a JD dealership specializing in "precision equipment" like the 8370R, that the machine has many other less obvious sensing devices. There is a trademarked invention that uses sensors and feedback to maintain a consistent engine speed and which, without farmer intervention, micro-adjusts or precisely controls the engine, even when the load on the tractor varies. The corporation markets these sensors and feedback systems as tools that help farmers save money on fuel.

Automation of farm machinery is inextricably linked with the collection and use of large amounts of data – or what is called "big data" (boyd and Crawford 2012) – not least because auto-steer technology innovation happened alongside innovation in satellite data collection and environmental monitoring, which were some of the first big datasets in existence before the term "big data" entered into wider circulation (Cox 2002). Every one of John Deere's tractors sold today is fitted with sensors that continuously collect data: about the soil, about crop conditions, about labour, and about the equipment itself. Just as with social media companies, the tractor corporation harvests "digital breadcrumbs" (Miller 2010); anything a farmer does on a modern tractor, beginning with opening the cab door, generates messages captured by its main onboard computer, which uploads the signals to the cloud via a cellular transmitter located, in most Deere tractor models, under the driver's seat. The software used in John Deere's "precision equipment" is proprietary, and the farmers ultimately need to pay to access useable and useful data collected by the tractor they own.

What we now refer to as big data are distinguished not just by their volume but also by their inherent connection to sophisticated computing technologies, especially to sets of instructions called algorithms. Computer scientists write algorithms that will recognize and synthesize patterns in large datasets in order to generate insights or information; often scientists and engineers use the term "machine learning" to refer to programs they design to "learn" from big datasets during use, sometimes with no *a priori* anticipation of results. In the context of agriculture, datasets are assumed to only generate useful information once they are aggregated across millions of precision equipment users and/or integrated with other big datasets (e.g., satellite weather data). Moreover, data experts translate the data from its "raw" state into useful information. Alvin, a key information and data scientist at Bayer/Monsanto, said over the phone, "I realized that the heart of any great algorithm is the analysis and processing and preparation that data has to go through to make any great algorithm even better. And there is a ton of fun to be had in engineering data as a product." Data scientists like Alvin work behind the scenes within agribusinesses using big data and algorithms to generate information that will guide farmer decision-making on, for example, when to seed, spray chemicals, or harvest.

Today, corporations like Bayer/Monsanto not only sell chemicals and seeds (or chemicals paired with genetically modified seed systems) but they also now trade in data. Other leading corporations in this business of selling advice include Trimble, Farmers Edge, and even the historic computing hardware corporation IBM. Farmers pay these corporations for use of an "automated decision system" (also called "automated technology platform"), which use various degrees of machine learning to make data relevant for farmers and which visualize aspects of the farm. A notable visualization is the "field map," which might indicate to farmers those areas of the field in need of extra chemical inputs or those areas so consistently unproductive that they might ultimately be taken out of rotation. Most corporate data scientists predict that in the future, data-driven advice will be delivered in "real time" to "smart" farm equipment, which will use data mining to make micro-adjustments to farm tasks. Data collected by agribusinesses are also circulated to "third party" corporations (not all of whom are agricultural), though we can know very little about which corporations may be using these data and for what purposes. This information is not specified in the privacy policy and terms of service agreements, which are moreover difficult to understand (Obar and Oeldorf-Hirsch 2018).

The realization of the vision of a radically digitized future of food is hamstrung by the currently lacklustre response among farmers to the use of sophisticated computing and big data in agriculture. Unlike their success with genetically modified seed systems, corporations are having a hard time achieving even and widespread adoption of both their automatic decision platforms and their most expensive precision equipment – "variable rate equipment," which makes good on field mapping. Indeed, several of the tools which fall under the rubric of digital farming came onto the market alongside the first agricultural biotechnologies in the late 1990s. Partial adoption is influenced somewhat, but not entirely, by the cost of these technologies which are more accessible to commodity growers. The US Department of Agriculture predicts that up to half of all corn and soybean farmers in the US use precision equipment, with fewer farmers paying for the advice and data platforms. Canadian studies show lower levels of adoption of the platforms – though one study on midwestern grain farmers showed that 79 per cent use GPS auto-steer guidance equipment (Steele 2017).[1] In general, several studies have found that large farm size is positively correlated with precision agriculture (PA) adoption and that large commercial farms are more likely to benefit economically from the adoption of PA (Daberkow and McBride 2003; Jensen et al. 2012; Lambert et al. 2014; Reichardt et al. 2009; Roberts et al. 2004).

I found my ride in a precision tractor somewhat surreal and totally unlike any of the tractor experiences I had some fifteen years earlier when I studied organic farmers who mostly used older, repurposed machines, all of which were mechanical. In 2019, Jack and I cruised along in the JD tractor, grading the field without doing any physical labour, instead letting the tractor lift and drop the blade seemingly on its own or according to a series of steps that had been programmed by Jack into the machine at five o'clock that morning. As we drove the irregular two-acre plot, the tractor pulled dirt from here to there and the display beeped a few times, which Jack mostly ignored. "While I'm doing this grading," he said to me, "it's keeping track of all the data I'm collecting from the field. So I've programmed how I want to grade to within an eighth of an inch … and this is the same machine and auto-steer I would use to do anything … planting … elevation, and it collects data on all that." When I asked him why he was interested in collecting all of this data, he said to me, matter-of-factly, "To measure is to know."

The collection of agricultural big data is also being crowdsourced, gathered by individual farmers using smart phone applications – or apps – that deliver the farmer one service while they collect data that are more broadly relevant. In June of 2018, at a field school on smart farming in Alberta, a digital farming specialist demonstrating a weed identification app called Xarvio Weed Scout told me that each user helps to "amass photos for the database of all types of weeds in all stages of development." These photos, he said, "teach" the intelligent machine to predict weeds. Although the application was still in the testing phase, he was confident that "between the algorithms we've built and the farmers who take pictures for us, we can make it pretty sure-fire." Ultimately, he declared, the tool would "give an on-the-spot recommendation for a chemical, a product associated with a particular weed." Bayer/Monsanto Corporation offers a suite of digital software for collecting and analyzing farm data, which the corporation suggests farmers use in order to minimize risk and streamline decision-making. One of their offers is a type of digital agricultural app that is programmed to work with big data called Weed ID, which was one of the first digital agricultural offers from Monsanto (before it was bought by Bayer). Like Weed Scout, Weed ID borrows from facial recognition software and uses machine learning to help farmers identify weeds and digitally map weed pressures.[2] I saw Weed ID in action in eastern Canada in 2017, when a fruit grower demonstrated the use of the app for me. She opened the app on her smartphone and used her touch screen to answer a series of questions, prompted each time by the previous answer she gave. The process reminded me of the one time I called a telephone service for help making a medical diagnosis, the questions moving from general to particular. I also thought back to the two summers I spent employed as a field biologist in my early twenties. I was paid just above minimum wage to don hip waders and trudge through wetlands in southeastern Ontario, identifying invasive species (another name for weeds). The ex-biologist in me was immediately struck that Bayer/Monsanto's tool not only "puts weed ID at [the farmer's] fingertips," as it advertises, but it also may help scientists identify new chemical needs and potential areas for investment in research and development in a cost-effective manner.

Crowdsourcing weed data across thousands of farmers using an app is even less expensive than hiring an undergraduate field technician. Prior to apps like Weed Scout or Weed ID, agricultural businesses had to pay in-house agronomic scientists to conduct field trials, which are time-consuming, costly, and necessarily quite particular to the region in which they are conducted. Using crowdsourced data, businesses can scale up the collection of information with economic efficiency. As with social media data being sold to marketing firms (or to agencies like Cambridge Analytica), there are clear and potentially incommensurate benefits for the corporations collecting and selling agricultural big data compared to those using the platform or application. Moreover, the most power likely accrues to those controlling the data because precision agriculture (and other analytics businesses) present a scale-driven business proposition that tethers success to control over large reservoirs of data. One leading Microsoft data scientist said to me when we spoke over coffee about precision agriculture, "AI is only as good as your data." IBM has spent billions of dollars buying a handful of companies with vast stores of medical and environmental data because, as their head of research labs puts it, "AI machines are only as smart as the data you give them" (Lohr 2016). We have seen this with the power big data has given companies like Google and Amazon, who have been in the business of collecting personal data for more than a decade, which has enabled the development of AI systems like Google Search and Alexa. Rick, a public relations person with a leading precision agricultural corporation, told me, "Our biggest competitor is no longer Monsanto, it's Google."

Controlling a Digital Farming Market

In 2013 Monsanto declared data analytics "agriculture's next major growth frontier," estimating it to be worth US$20 billion (Monsanto 2013) and that same year a financial analyst projected that the "precision farming" market would grow by 12 per cent annually to be US$18.45 billion in 2022 (Michalopoulos 2015). There appears to be various ways to access this market. Mayer-Schonberger and Cukier (2014) put forward three of these ways: being a data holder with the capability to access farm data; a data specialist with capabilities to "mine" big data for insights that can strengthen their competitive position in the data market; or a data strategist, which is a firm powerful enough to flexibly orient their corporate practices by extending data insights to novel applications that are not yet defined.

John Deere had a head start in commanding the agricultural big data market as a data holder, the primary way of accessing the digital agriculture market. As ETC Group (2016) puts it, Deere is powerful in the digital agricultural innovation landscape because "they own the box [tractor] that GenChem [the fertilizer companies] have to put their products in" (3) – and also because they have been collecting agricultural data via their machines for almost twenty years. However, since 2013 Monsanto has arguably been transitioning from being a seeds and chemicals company to a data specialist, with in-house data science expertise such that they can work with data to offer putatively "data-driven" advice to farmers. In 2013 Monsanto purchased The Climate Corporation, a valuable software developer, for US$930 million (Kanaracus 2013). The Climate Corporation itself had previously acquired a number of start-up companies that develop tools for collecting and using farm data. While food producers have used computers, satellite monitoring (e.g., of weather), and global positioning system technologies for decades, the digital tools that The Climate Corporation offers are different. Namely, they involve sophisticated computation which is used to "mine" aggregated big datasets – those built from data collected via "precision" equipment – for generating information or advice that can then be sold to farmers. In 2014, Bayer acquired Monsanto, and thereby The Climate Corporation (though the full corporate acquisition was not complete until 2018 in part due to a legal decision about whether it breached US anti-competition law). Online, Bayer describes their corporate strategy as built around three "key elements": innovation, sustainability, and digital transformation. In this digital transformation, a representative said at the time of this acquisition, Climate Corporation "plays a key role" (Bayer 2018, 30).

Despite not having direct access to farm data, like John Deere, Monsanto has gained access to these data via legal agreements with CNH and AGCO – John Deere's top rivals – that put The Climate Corporation's FieldView mobile application on their tractors. By 2016, Climate FieldView had already become a popular data storage and analytics platform used on 92 million acres in the US (Monsanto 2016). While John Deere initially appeared to be set for a competition with Climate Fieldview, choosing to sign data transfer agreements with rivalry seeds chemicals suppliers like Dow/DuPont, since 2015 their machinery has linked to Climate Corporation. Cory Reed, senior vice president of John Deere's intelligent solutions group, described their logic, stating, "We'll connect to everyone" (Vogt 2015). Or, as Dow Chemical's Andrew Liveris put it, "Everyone is talking to everyone" (Newman and Bunge 2016).

An advantage for the seeds and chemicals companies like Bayer/Monsanto comes via their historic relationships with farmers. Seed and chemical companies have historically used restrictive licensing agreements around GMO systems to solidify commercial relationships with farmers, tying farmers to the use of specific firms' commercial offerings (see Bronson 2015). And due to its sheer market share post consolidation, Bayer/Monsanto has the capability to access data from a vast number of farmers, at least in North America. Because Bayer CropScience joined with Deere in 2015 to develop digital tools (a corporate move their employees described as "precision to decision"), they are data holders, data specialists, and, due to their dominance, likely data strategists. Tom, a program manager at a tech investment firm who described his talent as "bringing investments to life," told me that historic computing companies like Microsoft and even Nokia have access to computations expertise, which gives them an advantage, but "the real advantage is in access to the data." He went on to talk about how technology companies have a problem in that they are missing both a way to gather the data and, more problematically, a means to get digital technologies to farmers in an agricultural inputs market dominated by oligopoly corporations.

Indeed, Microsoft has paired with Land O'Lakes as a means to solve this market access problem. According to their website, "With 150 million acres of productive cropland in its network, Land O'Lakes is deeply connected to rural America and has a unique understanding of farmers' needs and the communities where they and their families live and work. Combined with Microsoft's trusted cloud technologies and AI capabilities, the companies will deliver solutions that help farmers' profit potential and adoption of sustainable agricultural practices." Thus, in the agricultural context big agribusinesses like Bayer/Monsanto have the potential to lead. One journalist writing for *Mother Jones* in 2014 predicted, somewhat inflammatorily, that Monsanto was gearing up to use its historic dominance to "take over the world" (McDonnell 2014).

The promising market value of big agricultural data was an explicit topic of conversation at most of the big data conventions I attended, which in themselves were dominated by people interested in advancing business interests. The keynote speakers at these conventions were almost entirely people from the private sector: commercial technology firms like Intel or IBM, banks, consulting firms like Ernst and Young or Deloitte, and insurance companies like Blue Cross. One business sector keynote speaker at Big Data Congress talked about the data "gold rush" mentality, saying, "When we first started capturing big data, we were so enthusiastic, we collected data on everything, it was ridiculous ... but then we realized there was some value in figuring out what [our] questions are before we start collecting a bunch of data." At this point, it appears that companies like Bayer/Monsanto are well on their way to figuring out the questions that generate value from farm data; as of 2020, they have been reporting revenues from Climate Corporation in the hundreds of millions.

Visions of a Sustainable and Productive Digital Future

One gets a sense of the enthusiasm for digital agriculture not just from what agricultural technology supply firms do – the purchasing habits of Bayer/Monsanto, for example – but also from what these firms, investors, and agricultural experts say. While these firms tend to emphasize the potential monetary profit to be gained from big data when they are directing communications to investors, with farmers and others they emphasize the utopian potential that big data has to contribute to food production while reducing chemical inputs in agriculture, making farms greener and the world a better place.

Alvin, a high-level information scientist for Bayer/Monsanto, told me "long-term, there isn't agriculture without big data." In 2016, chief scientist at Monsanto's Climate Corporation, David Fischhoff, predicted that "in the not-so-distant future, we will have discretely measured and digitized every activity and condition that drives mankind's conversion of natural resources into food … bringing farming from an era of intuition to an era of analytics-based decision making." That same year, Robert Fraley, Monsanto's chief technology officer, projected that the agricultural sector was ripe for a digital revolution (Burwood-Taylor 2016), and he urged investors to get involved. The message appears to have been received. Only one month after this prognostication, an agribusiness reporter encouraged investors to capitalize upon the coming "disruption" to the sector, saying, "Sometimes we only know there was a revolution by looking in the rear-view mirror. That is not the case with the disruption in agriculture today" (Estes 2016, para. 1). A similar message to investors came in July of 2016 from the financial investment firm Goldman Sachs, which released a widely circulated report on digital agriculture as part of an "equity research innovation series" (Goldman Sachs 2016, 1). The report painted a very positive picture of digital agriculture, declaring "agriculture offers fertile ground for a confluence of technology trends, from sensors and the Internet of Things to drones, big data and autonomous driving. We see the potential for Precision Farming to lift crop yields 70 per cent by 2050 and create a US$240 billion market for farm tech, adding to agriculture's long history of holding off a Malthusian crisis." While the report pitches the benefits of digital agriculture as social goods (notably, growing enough food to feed an increasing global population), it centralizes the economic value proposition on the sale of technologies by large supply corporations. This is not surprising, given the audience this report is addressing. Take, for instance, a graph given on page five of the report, which visualizes statistics on the growth in US corn yields accompanying agricultural technology innovation through history. The graph extrapolates to 2050, when it predicts that because of big-data-informed planting and spraying (among other factors), US farms will yield 281 bushels per acre of corn. Interpreting this graph in terms of the economic logic of supply and demand, or through the lens of historic farmer experience, makes it clear the message is not primarily aimed at farmers, who face low commodity prices on corn (which is oversupplied in a competitive global marketplace). Elsewhere the report even admits explicitly, "If history is a guidepost, over time farmers should benefit from higher sales, but margins are likely to remain as deeply cyclical as they have been for the past 40+ years of reliable data." The report also explicitly indicates that the real profit from digital agriculture will be had from the sale of the farming technologies like sensing tractors. Its authors advise, "In a gold rush, sell shovels." But it delivers a third, subtler message: that there is economic value to be gleaned from the collection and control of farm-level data themselves. The report asks, "Data is everywhere, but who can harvest it? ... For all of the yield improvement benefits in the knowns, the critical underlying assumption is the processing and integration of data for access. This might be done by existing players (Trimble, Deere, Farmers Edge), startups, or large-scale existing players (IBM?)" (8). These comments indicate that there exists another likely audience for whom Goldman Sachs prepared this report. In the context of agriculture, potential buyers of farm-level data might include crop insurance companies or chemical manufacturers – for whom predicting crop performance and the need for chemical inputs could be a helpful marketing tool – and investment firms who facilitate global land-grab investments (Fraser 2019). There is a large market for farm data, just as there is for personal data "harvested" (Zuboff 2019) from participation online. And just as with social media, where corporations rather than individuals trade in data, only two firms – one in Minnesota and the other in Alberta, Canada – have developed business models where farmers may sell their data on a per-acre basis. BIXS, or Business Info Exchange System, pays a rancher on a per head of cattle basis for their data in their "Gate to Plate" third-party food traceability and sustainability information (data) platform.

Looking from the ground level, at the messages about digital farming technologies aimed at farmers rather than firms and their investors, we become privy to a similar-but-not-quite-the-same perspective on this innovation landscape. This is not surprising. Farmers have a different set of interests from agricultural technology corporations. Moreover, farmers have pressing concerns that are not shared by others along the food chain. Notably, unlike the major suppliers of inputs such as tractors and chemicals or the corporations who buy, process, or sell farm commodities, farmers do not exist in an oligopoly situation (Qualman 2019). Rather, farmers operate in a fierce global competition with each other, and this is paradoxically especially true for the large, resource-rich corporate farmers that grow commodity crops that they then sell on the global market. Promotion of digital agriculture to farmers, then, unsurprisingly, emphasizes the advantage a digitally managed farm will have over other farms – an advantage achieved via productivity gains, efficiency, and access to superior insights about how to manage farm operations.[3] Take, for example, an article from farmforum.ca, an online "source for up to date information on technology, business development, production and the community side of the agriculture industry" (Figure 2.2). The image that appears at the top of the article shows a canola field stretching endlessly in all directions under a grey sky, implying that the impending storm will not disrupt productivity (Nadler 2017). As with the messages from agricultural technology corporations on GMOs (Levidow and Tait 1991), this image shows a neat and tidy crop, conveying the ease with which this technological product enables the farmer to achieve what large-scale farmers call a "clean" (homogeneous) field. There is a road in the photograph, which stretches ahead and up to the right of the frame, pointing, as do classic statues of political leaders, towards a bright future under the new rule.[4] The metaphoric forward-facing gesture of this road signals a utopian vision of the future under data-driven farm advice, which is the subject of the accompanying article. The article itself discusses big data approaches to weather monitoring, and its text and images make palpable farmers' fears of crop ruin, increasing indebtedness, and enduring sweat and toil in attempting to render controllable the unpredictability of nature. The article's title reassures farmers, "Weather Monitoring Means Less Guessing and More Knowing."

As scholars who study expectations and promises of "the future" indicate (see Konrad et al. 2017), these expectations are "rarely presented as neutral, value-free statements, innocently referring to a range of possible developments but instead can be read as promises or concerns and warnings, implying a positive or negative valuation" (468). Over a six-month period, starting in May of 2017, I carefully read newspapers, magazines, and trade reports geared towards farmers, agricultural advisers, and others working in the agri-food sector looking at the claims around digital agriculture and attending to their normative valence. A systematic word frequency search across hundreds of articles and dozens of advertisements dealing with digital agriculture revealed a story – one describing an inevitable revolution in food production practices that will deliver power to farmers to better predict and manage risk. Indeed, a simple search and find revealed that the two most common words used in the articles were "forward" and "innovation." The normative contours of the commercial

PRODUCTION

Weather monitoring means less guessing and more knowing

BY ANDREW NADLER | AGRICULTURAL METEOROLOGIST

2.2
Article from farmforum.ca from January 2017.

messages on a digital agricultural revolution aimed at farmers were overwhelmingly positive – the articles I read not only described inevitable technology-led improvements in financial management and productivity but they also discussed wider social and moral gains that purportedly attend the adoption of digital technologies. Indeed, "progress" was also a very common word used in advertisements on digital agriculture, closely followed by the words "efficient," "productive," and "sustainable." The website for Trimble's guidance equipment is titled, "The Future of Agricultural Intelligence," and the page describes how the corporation's "innovative, user-friendly precision ag technology solutions help farmers connect their entire operation so they can make data-driven decisions in real time that drive productivity, profitability, and sustainability." In this way, corporate marketing attempts to sell farmers technologies, but it also supplies them with hope, which is as necessary for farming as fossil fuel, water, or sunshine. Almost every farmer, no matter their size or access to capital, operates with chronic economic losses and under situations of extreme uncertainty about environment (e.g., weather) and the social infrastructures surrounding farm business (e.g. commodity prices).

But according to corporate messaging on the future of farming, the promise of new digital technologies extends beyond the individual farm: Bayer/Monsanto's web page for their "smart fields" digital farming strategy leads with a paragraph describing the double economic/environmental win-win and global food security gain that digital innovations will bring, stating, "The world's population is growing, but the amount of farmland available per head is shrinking. Agricultural *productivity* will have to increase if we want to *safeguard our food supply* in the long term. Digitalization in farming can help us deploy our resources *efficiently* and *sustainably*, enabling farmers to get the best out of their fields with *minimal environmental impact*" (2020, emphasis mine). An employee for a precision agriculture service corporation which supplies advice to farmers on digital technologies told me over coffee at a trade show that "precision agriculture is be defined by five 'Rs': the *right rate* in the *right place* at the *right time* using the *right source* done in the *right manner*." Intel claimed in 2016 that their big data analytics efforts would "safeguard a sustainable future for all," and Tobias Menne, head of Bayer/Monsanto's Global Digital Farming Unit, argued that digital innovations represented an altogether new way of doing business – one focused on selling information instead of the chemical inputs the company's business formerly depended upon. He wrote on the subject in a blog post celebrating World Food Day in 2018, prognosticating, "Before, selling more products meant more business for a company like Bayer; whereas in future, the fewer products we sell the better, because we're selling outcome-based services. With sensor devices, we can learn a lot more about what is and is not helping crops and livestock and create a better way of doing things" (Strubenhoff and Parazat 2018, para. 8).

Interestingly, corporate optimism about the ability of digital innovation to replace material inputs appears to be shared among many academics studying digital agriculture (c.f. Bronson and Knezevic 2016; Carbonell 2016; Carolan 2017; Driessen and Heutinck 2015; Eastwood, Klerkx, and Nettle 2017; Wolf and Wood 1997). A key site for academic publishing on this topic is the *Journal of Precision Agriculture*, which has been in print since 1999 and bills itself as "an international journal on advances in precision agriculture." The tone of work published in the journal is noncritical, and the bulk of publications are "scientific" or technical in orientation.[5] Social science pieces published in the journal are largely survey studies of farmer adoption. In an early paper published in *Precision Agriculture*, Bongiovanni and Lowenberg-Deboer (2004) advanced a prediction very similar to Tobias Menne's claim, arguing that precision agriculture "will substitute environmental information and knowledge for physical inputs" (359). Another early study similarly described digital agriculture as "an approach" to agricultural decisions that uses continuous data collection and monitoring of farm-level variables in order to specify and perfect agricultural decision-making (McBratney et al. 2005). Indeed, the idea of the 5Rs of agricultural big data comes from academic papers, one of the most highly cited being Delgado (2016), who discusses the 7Rs for nutrient management and conservation: (1) the *right* product; (2) the *right* rate; (3) the *right* method of fertilizer application; (4) the *right* conservation practice; (5) the *right* place; (6) the *right* scale; and (7) the *right* time of the application of fertilizer and the establishment of the conservation practice (see also Delgado et al. 2019).[6]

The specific argument that digital tools applied to agriculture will bring sustainability to food production practices is widespread in the academic literature, which infers that because algorithms drawing on huge datasets will make decisions about the use of water and agrichemicals, they will result in precise, targeted, and thus judicious use of these scarce or harmful inputs (Poppe et al. 2015; Sonka 2015; see also Burwood-Taylor 2016; Ghaffarzadeh et al. 2017). An early (2004) literature review of academic work on the sustainability gains from digitization "confirm[ed] the intuitive idea that PA should reduce environmental loading by applying fertilizers and pesticides only where they are needed, and when they are needed. Precision agriculture benefits to the environment come from more targeted use of inputs that reduce losses from excess applications and from reduction of losses due to nutrient imbalances, weed escapes, insect damage, etc." (Bongiovanni and Lowenberg-Deboer, 2004). As indicated by the word *should* here, studies evaluating environmental impact have done so only indirectly, by assuming that a more targeted application of chemical fertilizers and pesticides would equate to a reduction in these inputs and, moreover, to overall environmental gain (see Gebbers and Adamchuck 2010; cf. Akhtman et al. 2017).[7] While the original definition of "sustainable agriculture" from the academic literature focused on incorporating what agricultural economists call "best management practices" such as conservation tillage, crop rotation, and diversity, the emergent conversation in this literature centres on a technology-focused sustainable agriculture. It has also moved away from a site-specific management focus to the notion of global sustainability, where automation and the use of big data and AI are predicted to serve the basis for a global shift in food systems. As one Canadian agricultural economist named Phil told me, "If we are to feed ten billion people by 2100 while preserving our environment, the next green revolution must incorporate the virtual world."

The link between precise information gleaned from big data and environmentally sound management dominates the literature on PA, which increasingly treats PA as a "paradigm shift" from production-based agricultural goals to global sustainability:

> Last century, during the "Green Revolution," the use of synthetic fertilizers contributed to increased agricultural production. However, their use did not reflect local soil and water conditions because recommendations were developed for larger agro-ecological zones. They only focused on increased productivity, neglecting any adverse environmental consequences … Using soil sensors in agriculture can fundamentally change this approach by allowing innovative "bottom-up" approaches that characterize local soil and environmental conditions in space and time, improving the efficiency of production to maximize farm incomes and minimize environmental side effects. (Rossel and Bouma 2016, 71)

In these descriptions, just like those given in corporate advertising and promotion like the *Farm Forward* video that began this chapter, precision agriculture is a project of abstracting information from the material. It is also a temporal project characterized by an inherent orientation towards the future where the system is putatively data-driven and anticipates, predicts, and predetermines the best course of action: when to spray herbicide, when to hire and fire labourers, or when to purchase extra insurance. In this way, scholarly definitions of precision agriculture follow the larger discourses about big data, wherein material things "always seem to be disappearing" (Chun 2011, 11) and where emergent digital technologies are thought to so vastly outstrip human capabilities – in searching and cross-referencing in particular – that they represent a paradigmatic or "scientific revolution" (Anderson 2008). One academic researcher who also works with Microsoft told me "we have achieved everything we can [environmental benefits] using conservation tillage," and now it is through "data that we will unlock the power of the soil." What emerges from looking across the visions, the marketing, the promotion given by proponents of big data and AI in agriculture is a clear picture of a utopic digital future.

New Technologies, Old Promises

Despite the rhetoric of revolutions, paradigm shifts, and novelty, dominant corporate and academic discussions of current agricultural technologies are very similar to the nearly one-hundred-year-old message that has been used to sell agricultural inputs from the earliest tools like the seed drill which were billed as necessary for agricultural modernization.[8] As Santos and Kienzle (2020) put it "traditional agricultural mechanization, characterized by the use of tractors and engine power, will be matched and even surpassed by automated equipment and robotics and the precision they can provide in farm operations" (iii). The message that digitization is necessary for advancement is even more exaggerated when applied to smallholder or peasant farming. As example, one call for papers in the journal *Frontiers* titled, "Agile Data-Oriented Research Tools to Support Smallholder Farm System Transformation," claims that, "a transformation is needed in order to deliver food security and decent incomes for the farmers themselves and at the national level" (Hammond et al 2021, n.p.). The claim that farms and farming are central to industrialism and development is so canonical it is referred to as *the* agrarian question (the question being: what role can and should farming play in national industrial development?) and was asked even before Karl Marx.[9]

More broadly, the message that current technologies are necessary for agricultural development are connected to a particular model or "regime" of food production for which these inputs are necessary (Friedmann and McMichael 1989). Today's advertisements and corporate messaging on digital agriculture pair moral and political order with the effective application of new technologies to labour, a "technological progressivist" discourse that historians of technology trace back at least to the Enlightenment (see Marx and Roe Smith 1994). Such messages also echo what food studies scholars call the "productivist" vision that agricultural technologies not only contribute to efficient and productive farming, but they also contribute to food security and societal stability. Agricultural researchers, government funders, and advisers have used productivism to encourage farmers to adopt agricultural innovations throughout history, from Jethro Tull's seed drill to GMO seed systems (Levidow and Carr 2007; Tannahill 1973).

There is a host of cultural and political assumptions embedded in productivist logic. Productivism turns on an assumption about the central place of food production in maintaining a postwar social and political order (Cloke and Goodwin 1992; Marsden et al. 1986). Bishop and Phillips (1993) have argued that productivism is rooted in societal memory of wartime hardships, when farmers were considered (at least by settler rural residents) to be the best protectors of the countryside (Newby 1979). In this way, some have described productivism as backward-facing, interested in the maintenance of "traditional" agrarian institutions such as the "family farm" and viewing urban, industrial development as a threat to these institutions (Halfacree 1999). But there is arguably a contemporary manifestation of productivist logic as it intersects with digital innovation. If we think back to John Deere's *Farm Forward* video, we can trace this neo-productivist line of influence, wherein the visual representations of existing and not-yet-real technologies presented in *Farm Forward* support its textual message that digital tools will extend the North American farm into the future, ensuring its survival via innovation-led modernization. The promissory rhetoric of precision agriculture thus arguably responds to widely held fears among farmers today (and others working in the agri-food sector) of an income "crisis" (Qualman 2019). The widely reported trauma among farmers who are making abysmally low incomes (see Purdon and Paleja 2020; Weingarten 2018) is not an anxiety shared by the rest of society, who in a global food system are seemingly (at least in the immediate term) independent of the success of farmers. Many people in Canada claim to not have any connection to a farmer today (Statistics Canada 2016). Scholars have traced productivist messaging in advertisements for pre-digital farm machinery and also in expert advice from agricultural "extension officers," or farm advisers, who have for years suggested to farmers that they risk becoming financially obsolete unless they adopt innovations to capitalize on minor efficiencies (increasing returns on investment) and "make the farm pay" (Kneen 1995; Qualman 2019; Scott, 1998). Despite being culturally conservative, productivism imagines farming as highly industrialized: an "efficient" and "productive" "business" enterprise rather than a livelihood. Productivity and efficiency in this framing involve maximizing crop output by using technology to replace people and diminishing time spent farming (Kneen 1995, 69) with the ultimate aim of maximizing national agricultural exports. In the contemporary context, this messaging is made to relate to today's context by reframing the need for productivity in terms of a wider global ethical responsibility, claiming to harness the power of technology in response to a growing global population. Indeed, productivist discourse suggests that the goals of the farmer – expressly articulated in economic terms – are synonymous with those of global community. According to Frederick Buttel (2003): "The essence of the predominant 'productionist' ideology was a doctrine that increased production is intrinsically socially desirable, and that all parties benefit from increased output" (11).

While productivist logic predates the expansion of world food trade and a global market for food commodities that became entrenched in the second half of the last century,[10] it arguably rooted itself firmly in public and political discourse on farming during the course of these large structural changes to the food system and economy. Corporate globalization ushered in an era of agricultural "development" based on monocropping and the notion of "competitive advantage." Under the goal of national self-sufficiency for agricultural commodities, combined (at least in Canada) with the role of agricultural exports in the national economy, government programs since the early twentieth century have supported – both culturally and materially through subsidies and other support programs – the increasing adoption of technology and the intensive use of farmland as a means to boost production of commodity crops (Cloke and Goodwin 1992; Muller 2008, 396; Wilson 2001). From the 1969 *Report of the Task Force on Agriculture*, for example, the Canadian federal government described the policy goal of supporting those farms that are "rationally managed, profit-oriented businesses ... units that are large enough to afford better management" (Government of Canada Federal Task Force 1970). In the late twentieth century, similar productivist recommendations also emerged from organizations like the Western Canadian Wheat Growers Association, which since the 1970s has suggested that farmers will only be able to achieve the efficiencies demanded by the global food system by increasing the size of their machinery. Some farmers took up these recommendations, able to do so because of their farm size and access to credit, while many others went out of business, their land bought up by the remaining farms. Henry

Ford famously said that the biggest problem with running a factory is that you had to hire whole people; in agriculture the productivist system requires fewer farmers to meet its goals (Cochran 1979). Between 1936 and 1996, Canadian farms got progressively fewer and bigger, such that a four-hundred-acre farm in 1936 is now more than five times that size (Statistics Canada 2016). According to productivist logic, this is good and "rational" management of a system that prioritizes economy over "irrational" biological and social considerations such as malnutrition or equity among farmers (Kneen 1995). As we can see, the promise of a digital agriculture revolution to keep competitive farmers in business is not all that revolutionary.

Two articles published in *National Geographic* forty-six years apart serve as an illustration of the persistence of productivism and technological progressivism related to agricultural innovation. In 2018, a special issue of *National Geographic* positioned emergent digital tools within long-standing productivist promises of global food security and well being in the twenty-first century. One article, titled, "This Tiny Country Feeds the World," described the increased yields resulting from the use of precision farming technology:

> In a potato field near the Netherlands' border with Belgium, Dutch farmer Jacob van den Borne is seated in the cabin of an immense harvester before an instrument panel worthy of the starship *Enterprise*. From his perch 10 feet above the ground, he's monitoring two drones … Van den Borne's production numbers testify to the power of this "precision farming," as it's known. The global average yield of potatoes per acre is about nine tons. Van den Borne's fields reliably produce more than 20. That copious output is made all the more remarkable by the other side of the balance sheet: inputs. (Viviano 2018)

The themes in this more recent article nearly mirror those laid out in a *National Geographic* article published back in 1972 but this time focused on innovation in US agriculture.[11] "The Revolution in North American Agriculture" discussed an agricultural innovation in seed breeding: hybrid seeds. A plant science invention of the twentieth century, hybrid seeds are produced by crossing two inbred plant strains that display well-documented phenotypes or outward traits such as high yield. Although they yield very high and sometimes under adverse conditions (such as dry soils), they require large quantities of chemical fertilizers and herbicides. The article is framed by productivist goals, discussing how "tailor made grains for hungry lands [of the Global South]" may be a "major weapon on the battle against one of the gravest problems in the world: the population explosion" ("The Revolution" 1972). The article profiles several American farmers, including Earl Blaser, a successful "farmer-executive," pictured with his sons, pointing purposefully across a long desk – an object of totemic significance in his role as farmer-businessman. The hyphen is telling, drawing a direct line between the farmer and business practice with nothing in between – not the land, not his family, not other farmers who form a community. By the 1970s, successful North American farmers did less farming, aided by computers ("the progressive farmer's almanac"), airplanes, and transient farm workers ("75 hands"). While not visible unless one brings these two articles together across time, there is an evident link between the predictions made in 2018 and in 1972 about the future of agriculture: despite technological and societal shifts over the decades, a sustained focus on productivism circumscribes our imagination of what is to come and what ought to come.

Agriculture: Immaterialized Beyond Reproach?

Despite the general trend, some farmers have actively resisted transitioning into a "successful" business according to productivist logic, and it is possible to make sense of the new push among many agricultural actors for digitization, at least in part, as a response to this resistance. As a neoliberal transition toward hands-off governance weakened older political associations between farmers and government (and among farmers) in the 1980s, some turned toward social movement networks of environmentalists and consumers (Mooney 2000). Farmers gathering in the late twentieth century around extant environmental and anti-capitalist politics collectivized to explore "alternative" food system strategies, like organics and direct-to-consumer marketing. Qualitative research has revealed that some early alternative producers held *a priori*, countercultural leanings, while others were practically motivated to reduce expensive and immediately (as in, personally) harmful chemical herbicides and pesticides (Muller 2008). Minimal inputs and decentralized forms of marketing run counter to the ideology at the root of the productivist system (Goodman and

Watts 1994; Pugliese 2001) but they also reduce costs by bypassing retailers and input manufacturers. Because organic practice is more time consuming and labour intensive, a single organic farmer cannot farm the acreage that a conventional farmer can; therefore, alternative farming operations have tended toward small-scale and human capital-intensive. In the 1960s and 70s, alternative farmers were at the forefront of a non- (even anti-) productivist agricultural "movement" (Muller 2008, 403), which included alternative research, working against an "eclipse of community" (Newby 2008, 95) and a "one-dimensional knowledge … constructing a similarly narrow agrienvironmental policy" (Harvey and Riley 2005, 20). Qualitative research has revealed that farmers who identify as ideologically wedded to organics often care less about producing food and more about re-embedding community and human–non-human animal bonds (e.g., by strengthening local relationships through direct trade or marketing; see Heaton and Brown 1982; Reif 1987).

Alongside "alternative" farmers, social scientists – notably environmental historians and critical food studies scholars (see Cronon 1991; Fitzgerald 1993; Kline 2000; Stoll 1998) – have long questioned the environmental and human welfare effects of farm technologies. The focus of critique has changed from descriptions of "disruptions" caused by the introduction of the steel plow to discussions of the social and environmental effects of nitrogen fertilizers introduced in the nineteenth century. In the twentieth century, the objects of scholarly critique were hybrid seeds, chemical pesticides, livestock growth hormones, combine harvesters, and then GMOs (Berlan and Lewontin 1986; Goodman and Redclift 2002; Kloppenburg 2005). Nonetheless, a common thread within this scholarly critique was that the application of technologies to food production played a part in generating chronic surpluses of particular commodities, subsequently lowering commodity prices and triggering periodic debt crises among farmers. These critiques suggested that agricultural technologies have thus led to rural depopulation (Qualman 2019; Weiss 2007) and trapped farmers in a "technology treadmill" where they become dependent on adopting the newest technologies and on the moneylenders who finance the purchase of these expensive tools (Cochrane 1958; Schnaiberg 1980).

Academic critiques of industrial agriculture suggest that the model has intensified food system inequities (Federici 2004; Patel 2007; Perelman 2003), given unprecedented control over food systems to financial entities (Burch and Lawrence 2013; Clapp and Helleiner 2012; Isakson 2015), and brought into question the influence of market forces on governance and policy at the expense of public interest (Friedmann 2005; McMichael 2012; Tansey and Rajotte 2008). It has also presented new challenges to human health (Lang and Heasman 2015; Patel 2007), food security (Clapp 2012; Lawrence 2017; Zerbe 2019), and environmental sustainability (Altieri 2009; Cribb 2010; Qualman 2019; Weis 2007).

Critiques of productivist agriculture have arguably intensified in academic work but also among activists and high-profile policy institutions (Albritton 2009; De Schutter 2015). A landmark report in this regard was the International Assessment of Agricultural Knowledge, Science and Technology for Development (IAASTD), which was published in 2015 and titled "Agriculture at a Crossroads." Hannah, a scientist who authored IAASTD, told me that its history is linked to the Millennium Ecosystem Assessment of 2003, which she described as explicitly connecting agriculture to "the environmental problems of soil degradation and climate change." Within an ecosystems framework, the IAASTD team were able to consider social factors. Robert Watson (who had headed the Ecosystem Assessment) assembled a team of scientists and social scientists to answer the question "How can we reduce hunger and poverty, improve rural livelihoods and facilitate equitable, environmentally, socially and economically sustainable development through the generation of, access to, and use of agricultural knowledge, science and technology?" Behind the scenes, according to actors who sat on the IAASTD, there was pressure from agribusiness, in particular corporations like Syngenta and Monsanto, to endorse the adoption of GMOs as crucially important in meeting global poverty reduction and global food security targets. Ultimately, however, the report argued that the only way to confront some of the "major challenges" of our time was by "combining local and traditional knowledge with formal knowledge" (2015, 2). Hannah explained to me the importance of the leadership of Robert Watson, who "surrounded himself with 'no women'" like her. She stated, "He designed a dialogue process that made room for different kinds of knowledge and was able to change the organization's view on ecological knowledge, Indigenous knowledge. He included ecologists, entomologists, holistic thinkers, sociologists and anthropologists instead of just economists or agronomic engineers ... people who were able to see outside of the dominant paradigm." In the end, Hannah said frankly, "IAASTD changed the focus from one about corn yield and efficiency to a broader set of ecological and sociological concerns."

Then in 2016, the International Panel on Environmental Sustainability released a report titled, "From Uniformity to Diversity: A Paradigm Shift from Industrial Agriculture to Diversified Agroecological Systems," which not only endorsed alternative approaches, including small-scale and agro-ecological farming strategies, for their contribution to climate mitigation, biodiversity, and food security, but explicitly critiqued industrial agriculture. Since 2016 the Food and Agriculture Organization of the United Nations (UNFAO 2018) has recognized the importance of small-scale farming, suggesting that "small farms produce a higher share of the world's food relative to the share of land they use, as they tend to have higher yields than larger farms within the same countries and agro-ecological settings" (2014, para. 13; see also Global Alliance 2020). It also recognized agro-ecology as a pathway to achieving sustainable development goals and stated that some national governments were offering supports for farmer-to-farmer networks to share knowledge and propagate low-input agroecological approaches (2018). The UN has also come out with highly critical reports on the negative implications of agricultural chemicals on humans and non-humans. In January of 2017, the Special Rapporteur on the right to food presented a report to the UN Human Rights Council severely criticizing the global agribusinesses that manufacture pesticides, accusing them of the "systematic denial of harms" and "aggressive, unethical marketing tactics" which have obstructed governments and individuals alike from assessing the "catastrophic impacts" pesticides have had "on the environment, human health and society as a whole." Since the summer of 2018, Bayer estimates that there are currently more than 42,000 plaintiffs alleging that exposure to Monsanto's Roundup and its other glyphosate-based herbicides caused them or their loved ones to develop non-Hodgkin's lymphoma (Gillam 2019).

In the context of widespread critique against industrial agriculture, there is benefit to a corporation identifying itself as a data company as opposed to a chemicals company, a resignification we witnessed when Monsanto's Tobias Menne claimed that the company was now selling information instead of chemicals. In 2017, a sales associate at Bayer named Bev talked to me about the corporation's literal divestment away from seeds and chemicals, which was happening in the context of the merger with Monsanto. She explained, "Most of the chemical and seeds assets that we have to divest are going to BASF. They are German and they don't have a very large seed portfolio, but they have a significant chemical portfolio ... BASF was judged to be a good house." While

Monsanto is a clear public enemy, Climate FieldView, though owned by Bayer/ Monsanto, can more easily escape the gaze of environmental activists and others who critique the effects of pesticides and GMOs. Climate FieldView not only has a different corporate profile, it also promotes putatively non-material and thus non-toxic precision technology as non-obtrusive and therefore helpful to both individual farmers and society at large. John Deere, as a machinery – not chemicals – corporation, has an even lower profile than Climate FieldView, and thus there is little scrutiny over what data their machines are collecting, with whom those data are shared, and for whose gain.

In my conversations with people working for agriculture technology firms, it became clear that productivism through precision technology was a dominant ethos they held (many of them spoke to me in terms of pro-productivity), yet the arguments were neo-productivist in the sense that they also included pro-sustainability claims regarding big data and AI applied to agriculture. Against mounting criticism of the societal and environmental fallout from industrial agriculture, it is logical that corporate actors would emphasize the moral contribution that intensive food production practices, supported by tools like chemicals and now big data, might make – for instance, boosting production and theoretically ensuring a sufficient global food supply. An argument I heard even more frequently suggested that these tools would reduce the environmental impact of agriculture. Take for example Wade Barnes, CEO of Farmers Edge. Wade is stocky and self-assured, distributing his wide grin indiscriminately. He grew up on a Canadian family grain farm of average size for western Canada (thousands of acres) and trained at university in agronomic science. He started what he now considers a precision agriculture company, Farmers Edge, in 2005. Similar to the origin stories of many companies who trade in big data such as Facebook or Amazon, Farmers Edge lore has it that Barnes started the company in his basement with his best friend, amidst staggering doubt that a service offering scientific advice to farmers would succeed. At the time, Barnes said, "We were agronomists," or agricultural scientists, whereas "today we are a huge crew of software engineers and electrical engineers and data scientists." Barnes explained that he had always been guided by the intuition that "good farming needed good information," and his sense of a good farm was deeply conditioned by his upbringing. Like his father, Barnes viewed a good farm as one where innovation in both practice (technique) and technology helped to manage financial risk and where the goal was keeping the farm, the rural community, and the agri-food sector viable. The moral goals for Barnes, therefore, were entangled with technical goals focusing on increasing productivity, and they went beyond the societal value of rural community sustainability to include environmental stewardship.

Judging from outward-facing communication, it appears that the corporate mission of Farmers Edge is environmental as well as economic. In a video it released on social media in 2016 entitled "Empowering Farmers, Improving Sustainability" Barnes says, "Farmers face lots of different challenges … they are truly managers, and they need the same type of tools and data that other industries have to make good decisions … We believe that Farmers Edge can make huge changes by using ag technology, by using big data … we know that we can grow more food, with the same amount of acres, with better management practices that will reduce the environmental footprint." Barnes's message acts as a kind of response to those who are critical of productivism or industrial agriculture.

It is difficult to parse genuine moral goals from strategic public relations and marketing. In the spring of 2019 I sat down with a stakeholder relations representative from Farmers Edge who told me without a hint of self-consciousness that his job was to "tell the sustainability story" – to industry associations, governments, and farmers – "about what our growers are achieving by optimizing fertilizer use … the positive environmental impact of that." The representative continued, "I tell the story of variable rate and what that means from an environmental perspective." Doug, a semi-retired soil scientist working on contract for Farmers Edge, was even more candid, disclosing to me that his research and personal investment into precision agricultural technologies was at least initially motivated by a desire to boost productivity. "I've worked on variable rate since 1991," he told me, "when the technologies were pretty clunky … no big data then." He continued, speaking for the company and saying their primary motivation was as much economic as environmental: "We knew yield potential across fields was uneven … we had significant anecdotal information about that … we were interested in exploring the idea that with new technologies we might vary the fertilizer rate to optimize the yield potential and profit on farms. That was the driver. We weren't all that interested in sustainability at that time. But as things developed it became obvious that there are some sustainability and harm reduction benefits." Given Doug's soil science expertise and his many years working in the domain of precision agriculture, I asked him to help me understand the connection between the kinds of recommendations given to farmers on a platform and sustainability gains. Was it, I asked, that by using a platform that draws on big data and sophisticated computing, farmers are able to only apply chemicals to those area of the field in need and thus reduce overall input? Not exactly, he told me, stating, "What we have found is that the actual reduction in total fertilizer … the concentration in effort R&D is on total nitrogen and phosphorus. We reduce the total amount very little, but we have found by redistributing it within the field, the value per unit of input goes up and so the ROI on fertilizer dollars comes in." Thus, while sustainability/economy may be connected in discourse, in the material practice of precision agriculture, the results tip toward gains measured as increases in yield and economic return.

Regardless of the veracity of the claims about digital farming's larger societal benefits, the neo-productivist message appears to circulate, moving across the high-level policy and funding documents, across trade journals, corporate websites, and conventions, and onto the farm. Many farmers I spoke with who are using some form of digital technology (from GPS and auto-steer to the decision support platforms) were easily interpellated into the technologically progressivist corporate messaging. These farmers are already entrenched in a productivist logic and they justified their investment in digital tools as a way to make data-informed decisions relevant to productivity (e.g., optimizing chemical input). Many farmers also spoke to me about their use of digital tools to gauge risks arising due to production, weather, market, or climate variability. One public sector data scientist told me that mid-sized grain farmers who had adopted some level of precision agricultural technologies were looking for relief through the data, explaining, "Farmers work so hard at the peak seasons of the year, and it's exhausting. The one thing that the technology has brought to them is peace of mind. So once they get engaged and they start measuring everything, just in the very basic level. I'm not even talking about *big* data analytics. If they are using a guidance system, and they know how much product, it puts their minds at ease. There is less on-the-fly decision making, and they are less tired at the end of the day." At the same time, according to this public servant, farmers were still "looking to [provincial government agricultural unit] to also demonstrate the economic benefit of going down this path." Micheels and Nolan (2016) surveyed roughly 500 prairie farmers managing livestock and commodity crop operations in North America and they found something similar: farmers expressed willingness to adopt precision agriculture if they could see a clear economic efficiency gain. However, they also indicated that social capital, in the form of neighbouring farmers or government experts they know, heavily influenced adoption. The yet-realized widespread adoption of digital agricultural tools thus clearly depends on their proponents demonstrating success, notably among so-called "early adopters."

But those farmers using digital tools to boost productivity, manage financial risk, and reduce uncertainty also spoke to me about their social duty to contribute to feeding a growing global population by maximizing the productivity of their farm and/or to contribute to economic and food security in Canada. I heard the twined productivity/sustainability rationale from every farmer I interviewed who currently uses digital technologies. Moreover, it became clear to me that many farmers gathered their neo-productivist understandings of digital agriculture's benefits from farm newspapers and trade shows; farmers appeared to first learn about digital innovations and then adopt them because of marketing. One middle-aged grain farmer, Hof, described his first encounter with the Lightbar guidance system at a tradeshow. Using a tone of voice that almost indicated a mystical experience, he said,

> I first saw it at farm shows where they were displaying them … As soon as you saw it you had to have it because, you know … you had a GPS antenna that you mounted on the front of your machine or on the roof or on the hood of your tractor. The Lightbar system was inside! What it did was it allowed you to set an A–B line in your field, and then set the distance to the next pass, and then the Lightbar would tell you when you are on the right spot. Then a few years later, the next component to that was made so that the machine would be steered according to that … it was a very big step.

Like Hof, Andy also grew interested in GPS guidance through marketing at a trade show. Generally soft-spoken and seemingly introspective, Andy told me that the new technologies "grabbed" him. In fact, he attributed his decision to enter farming as a middle-aged person (without a family history of farming) to his enthusiasm for farm innovation: "I quite like the machinery and so it was the machinery part of farming that really attracted me to begin with, and so, that's sort of how we drifted into farming. I enjoy buying a new piece of machinery and then using it."

Most of the participant farmers who were using precision equipment and automated decision platforms explained that they were at least partially motivated by finance. For example, despite the near religious reverence Hof used to describe his first encounter with this digital farm tool, later, he talked in more pragmatic terms in the same conversation, describing Lightbar as a simple device that saved him money, explaining, "What the Lightbar did was it saved me time and money because it cut down on my overlap. In order to make sure that you cover the whole field, you know you might be overlapping a few feet of your machine ... so if your machine was say, 50 feet wide and you're overlapping two feet, well that's four per cent. And, so it saved right away four per cent in time and costs ... and, you know, input costs have risen." Some farmers said that they invested because of the cost of *not* investing – the possibility of "falling behind" their competition or their farmer neighbours. A soft-spoken farmer managing a mid-sized operation, Joanne, told me that she had "no doubt that smart farms will come," in part because big data platforms were already in use and farmers were on the technological treadmill:

> Farmers will have to take advantage of it in order to remain competitive. If all of your neighbours farm with this kind of technology and gain some kind of an economic advantage then, probably you will be just left behind in the race. And that's what we've seen in history here. People that farmed four parcels of land made a very comfortable living back in the 1950s. And if you stayed the same, if you didn't change, everything just moved right past you. Costs went up and you couldn't make enough money to live. If you did nothing wrong but you stayed in that same place.

Others I spoke with were like Joanne in their matter-of-fact resignation about the necessity of adopting digital technologies. The farmers' discourse mirrors the prognostication of corporations about our inevitable smart agricultural future. Jan, a horticulturalist from Canada's temperate and fecund west coast, told me "robotics is the future."

> The small robotic idea, I suspect, will come just because of the labour issue. It's hard to get enough people to run the machines right now. And it's so seasonal. We need a lot of help at seeding time, which lasts about one month, and we need a lot of help at harvest time, which lasts about six weeks, maybe two months, and the huge need for help goes away after, to some extent. So, it's very hard to manage your labour around that kind of seasonal demand. Robots will solve that.

It is not just farmers who are banking on a digital agricultural revolution; international development and philanthropic organizations are also investing in a presumed inevitable move toward a smart farm of the future – one that delivers on the productivist promise and takes us away from material harm. From its beginning, the World Bank membership has imagined its intervention to be political and social, a mid-twentieth century project of world reform "elaborated in powerful corridors of post-WWII Washington, London and Paris, and at the Bretton Woods conference of 1944" (McMichael 2001). Formerly, the organization invested in seeds and chemicals as a way to secure global political stability in the global South because, as then-President Truman put it in 1948, "The economic life of the poor is primitive and stagnant … Their poverty is a handicap and a threat both to them and to our more prosperous areas" (quoted in Escobar 1995, 3). Today, the World Bank frames its investments into digital agricultural innovations in similarly moral terms, as an inevitable process of technology-led positive social change. They frame smart phones, big data, and computing as the answers to long-standing food system problems, such as food shortages exacerbated by ecosystem pressures, because they will increase the productivity and decrease the environmental harm of food production (World Bank 2013, 2016, 2017). One recent World Bank document, called "The Future of Food," asserts that "digital technology is transforming the way farms and agribusinesses are operating in developing economies" (Nielson et al. 2018, 30). The World Bank has also argued that there is a need to fund "transformational and high-impact solutions driven by innovation and technology" (World Bank Group and China Development Bank 2017).

Governments in developed countries are also investing heavily in large-scale big data projects. For instance, the European Commission has made broad commitments to digital innovations for the collection of farm-level data across member countries. As an example, the Internet of Food and Farm 2020 project (IoF2020) explores the potential of the "Internet of things" – or machines working together putatively without humans – for European farming. IoF2020 has a stated goal of building a lasting innovation ecosystem that fosters the uptake of precision agriculture as one "vital step towards a more sustainable food value chain." The funding announcement states that, "With the help of IoT technologies higher yields and better quality produce are within reach. Pesticide and fertilizer use will drop and overall efficiency is optimized." One example of a project furthered under this funding is RHEA, which is developing ground and aerial robots equipped with sensors for collecting data on chemical use; their goal is to reduce harmful agricultural inputs by 75 per cent (see Vieri et al. 2013). In Australia, the Commonwealth Science and Industrial Research Organisation (CSIRO n.d.) has developed a digital platform for aggregating and mining data from PA equipment. The project, called Digiscape, aims to "solve multiple knowledge shortfalls in the land sector simultaneously … by building a common big data infrastructure that will support next generation decision making and transform agricultural industries and environmental action." Neither the United States nor Canada has anything as comprehensive as IoF2020 or Digiscape, although the US National Institute of Food and Agriculture has tracked the adoption of PA since the late 1990s, and the US Department of Agriculture continues to invest in a variety of digital agriculture extension – or advice – services to farmers as well as research and development activities related to precision agriculture in particular. In Canada, a much-celebrated recent federal budget flagged agriculture as an area ripe for investment in digital innovation and the potential development of a common analytics platform (Advisory Council on Economic Growth 2017, 10).

Big data and AI enthusiasts celebrate state-level investment in these technologies. "Agriculture really is at the cusp of a new industrial revolution … This is Canada's moment to take advantage of a huge opportunity," said Dr Evan Fraser, the head of the University of Guelph's Arell Food Institute, on Canadian public radio in 2017 (Tunney 2017). Fraser applauded the government's 2017 economic strategy for a focus on agri-food exports and digital innovation in the sector, and he dramatically sketched a scene for the radio journalist: "Imagine a tractor … driving through a field, and the tractor itself senses where it is on the field, and plants the right seed at the right time and gives it the right amount of fertilizer. Or a robotic dairy barn that tracks the life and wellbeing and welfare of the cow in real time and tailors the inputs that cow receives, the diet that cow receives."

I was asked to perform similar imaginative exercises at every big data and AI convention I attended. At Data Congress in 2016, I attended a "Next Economy" session about the data-mediated economy of the future. When the panel began, the moderator asked the audience to close our eyes and picture "perfect profiles of customers so that firms forecast not just what customers want, but what they will want and they improve profitability." The moderator continued, "There is a broader transition in the entire global economy from tangible to intangible, big data are a resource that can't be depleted." It was often the same keynote speakers who appeared at these conventions which to me emphasizes the near-religious (or occult) soothsaying nature of these messages about the future. Sandy Pentland of MIT Media Lab spoke at two of the conventions I attended, and at another convention, one speaker responded to a question by talking at length about what Sandy Pentland *would* have said in response had he been present, saying, "Sandy Pentland has really interesting things to say about this, about bias and preventing bias and the importance of bias-free datasets, and there are all sorts [of] ways of doing this, including by making sure there are checks and balances on those who are supposed to be keeping the checks and balances over the use of data."

Sometimes the forecasting was stated in the form of a rhetorical question, such as when Bill Gates asked on his blog (2018), "Can the Wi-fi chip on your phone help feed the world?" Given his significant corporate investment in digital agriculture (Lohr 2016) and into the IBM AI named Watson, it is easy to infer that the answer, according to Gates, is "yes." Yet while the neo-productivist discourse touting big data appears to address productivism's discontents – notably critiques of its environmental and social impacts – the discourse actually keeps intact fundamental elements of the industrial food regime, notably the strategic role of agriculture in the construction and development of capital accumulation and corporation power and thereby inequity between agribusinesses and other food system players and the non-industrial approaches which they often try to advance.

Looking at the dominant vision for the future of farming in a broader historical and critical context, we can see that claims about the radical novelty of big data in agriculture belie the reality. North American farmers have been using technology to replace human labour since the Industrial Revolution, and indeed elements of the farm have been automated for decades (long before the existence of any "smart" city). While it has yet to be realized, agribusinesses project that the future "farm 4.0," as envisioned in John Deere's *Farm Forward*, will prove lucrative for lenders as well as for farmers, in part because data are envisioned as perfecting on mere human insights about farm management. In this way, the faith in data as a tool of progress and of productivity is part of a trend that exceeds agriculture – a faith that divorces data from humans and human fallibility entirely. Yet there are elements of the promises and uses of big data that are unique to agriculture. For example, unlike social media data, agricultural data are captured by farm machinery, which means companies who make this machinery, such as John Deere, stand to gain from agricultural digitization. Those agribusinesses with established relationships with farmers – even more so than companies with data science prowess – have an advantage in the market establishing around the processing of the data themselves and in the commodification of data as a resource that can be sold to third parties. Some farmers have concerns about this data use, but many farmers share elements of the corporate vision by believing that data-driven farming will help secure them better – even perfect – knowledge of their farm. Omniscience and powerful predictive capacity are compelling promises for producers who operate under increasing amounts of uncertainty about climate and commodity prices. Many farmers are content to envision themselves operating a future farm from the comfort of their living room, reducing their chemical use, saving the planet, and saving money – or at least outcompeting their neighbours.

3

Appropriate, Open, and Alternative

If the dominant vision for the future of digitized food production is characterized by a conspicuous absence of the farmer, whose hands-on labour and insight have been replaced by automation and "intelligent" machines there is an alternate vision: one where farmers drive innovation, in local contexts of production, as part of an agriculture *qua* community-building social movement. This chapter describes this alternative vision of a digital agricultural future and the groups furthering and coalescing around this vision. While the activists described in this chapter share the agribusiness faith that data are "driving" us toward a utopic agricultural future, they hold an altogether different societal, technical, and agricultural ethos in their commitment to open science and appropriate technology and in their practices of insubordination against the industrial food regime.

Calvin, a self-described "technophile," helped to start the Gathering for Open Agricultural Technologies, or GOAT, which he understands as a community-born and community-building activity that includes "various different people: people involved with the farm hack community and various other open source agricultural related projects like farmOS." At the 2018 GOAT, researchers like myself, farmers, and food and technology activists were all abuzz about the development of a community-built big data repository and decision tool called farmOS. FarmOS is built upon Drupal, which is a very popular web content management framework (similar to WordPress). Drupal is itself free and open source. Like the wooden framing of a house, Drupal is the infrastructure upon which farmOS is built, and GitHub is where the platform is hosted or, to continue the metaphor, where the house is built. GitHub is a version control software based upon the open-source Git package, and it is used to facilitate groups of coders who can write code, correct for coding or logical errors, and test lines of code before adding them to the main platform. Farmos is then run on the server called Farmier.

The farmos digital platform is supported by a loosely organized and transient group of people engaged at different levels, from the state to public bodies to the business community. These supporters hold views across the political spectrum, though they seem to share a desire to enhance citizen participation and empowerment with respect to state or corporate power via digital innovation. The exact tentacles of farmos are hard to isolate, trace, and describe, in large part because of its open and shifting nature and because the development of farmos is not housed within any one institution but rather on the popular open software development platform GitHub. Those participating in farmos include individual public-sector researchers from government (e.g., US Department of Agriculture, Extension and Conservation), academia (e.g., University of Vermont, Tufts), non-profit organizations (e.g., National Center for Appropriate Technology), as well as a variety of farmers, most of whom are what food studies scholars might call "unconventional" (e.g., market gardeners, permaculture farmers). One prominent institutional presence affiliated with farmos is Wolfe's Neck Center for Agriculture & the Environment in Freeport, Maine. Wolfe's Neck is run by a square-faced man named Dorn Cox, who always has a smile on his face and who figures prominently in the GOAT and farmos communities. Wolfe's Neck is a working farm and educational centre whose endeavours are united by a commitment to "regenerative" agriculture. Indeed, building or regenerating technological, food production, and wider social systems appears to be the guiding ethos behind the development of farmos. Anja, a volunteer coder in her early thirties, talked to me about the entanglement of technology and wider social values in her involvement with farmos. Anja is a highly skilled and credentialed programmer, with a PhD in computer science from a top US university. But more than this, she identifies as someone who cares deeply about the environment and social justice. Anja is a bit of an outlier within GOAT, whose local network instantiations (like individual chat threads on the discussion forum) are socially mixed but still dominated by white males with significant social privileges. Anja made time to have a phone conversation with me the day before she was to get married, and she spoke at length about the importance of environmental resilience, where "a key piece of creating resilience is having systems that are decentralized.

Everything is interconnected … My hope is that we can both have our tools and our communities reflecting each other." Anja's views are typical of those held by GOAT members and those volunteering to build farmOS. FarmOS represents an alternative to the dominant industrial and productivist forms of agri-tech in its focus on open data and an accessible and open source farm platform; its decentralized forms of data gathering and volunteer labour organization; and its commitment to empowering the citizenry.

Agri-Tech as Social Movement

GOAT and its signal technology, farmOS, alongside similar groups like a Canadian agri-tech cooperative called Autoconstruction, are clearly situated within wider mobilization and activism – notably the appropriate technology and open technology movements, as well as "alternative" agriculture movements such as organics. While historian of technology Carroll Pursell was already writing off the appropriate technology movement as a thing of the past in 1993, a number of GOAT participants and farmOS volunteers referenced this movement in their conversations with me in 2018. Pursell describes appropriate technology as a broad countercultural assertion of doubts about the role of technology on society and the environment (1993, 685). Often misunderstood as an "anti-technology" movement, appropriate technology activists instead subvert attempts at technological universalism, casting doubt that all technologies work well for all users in all places at all times. Alternative technologists are committed to an understanding of technology as antihegemonic and locally contextualized. The birth of the appropriate technology movement stretches, like many countercultural movements, back to the 1960s and 1970s when groups such as the New Alchemy Institute in Massachusetts and the Farallon Institute in California advocated for "self-reliance, local autonomy, and respect for Nature," as the latter codified in a manifesto. These original appropriate technology groups were partly responding to the funding patterns for scientific research and technology development programs from the US government, which ostensibly aimed to have all countries following the same pattern of industrialization as the global North: large factories, industrial agriculture, and the development of engineering infrastructure (especially large electrical power projects).

The concept of appropriate technology gained real currency as applicable in the global North after the publication of economist Ernst Schumacher's ([1973] 2010) book *Small is Beautiful: Economics as if People Mattered.* Schumacher critiqued "crude judgements as to whether or not technology should be developed," arguing instead for an approach that judges technologies based upon their context of development, application, use, and governance. In particular, Schumacher and his followers critiqued large-scale capital-intensive technological projects because they tend to be "controlled by large corporations and/or bureaucracies, which seldom give priority to human needs. Being large scale and usually resource intensive, they tend to have a massive impact on natural ecosystems. Their scale and mode of organization similarly militate against creativity and meaningful participation by workers. These technologies often are very complex and poorly understood by the public, so that crucial decisions may be made by a small group of technical experts. In addition, the centralized character of a technology and the magnitude of the risks involved encourage hierarchical organization and the centralization of control" (296).

Early appropriate technology activists critiqued large-scale and centralized technological efforts as ignoring or misunderstanding local environments, both natural and cultural, and consequently privileging the already powerful. These early appropriate technology groups were equally ideological and pragmatic, also recognizing in their writing that a failure to build locally appropriate socio-technical infrastructure leads to dead ends: machinery lay idle because while useful in some contexts like Northern or "donor" countries, it was useless in different places and circumstances. The key texts of these mid-twentieth century instantiations of appropriate technology offer a group of tenets: that technologies ought to be cheap enough to be accessible to nearly everyone, simple enough to be easily maintained and repaired, and suitable for small-scale application.

These tenets circulate today among farmOS volunteers, though they are largely divorced from the wider global justice context of the early appropriate technology movement. According to Michael Stenta, a farmOS founder, the platform started as a "side project," when Stenta got "hooked" on the problem of representing the environments of "small diversified farms," whom industry and public sector research and innovation had underserved. In a phone conversation in early 2018, Stenta described how agricultural research in both the public and private sectors has been geared toward a very narrow set of industrial agricultural problems that food studies scholars might call "productivist" (Buttel 2003; Kneen 1995): how to grow more food on less land, with less people, and less money. Dominant agricultural technology proponents from the private and public sectors often focus on the goals of productivity and efficiency even though, as we saw in chapter 2, a narrow focus on these agricultural "problems" has in turn led to different problems; intensification of farming systems has driven up yield but also led to the degradation of the soil, for example. So, as someone principally concerned with environmental sustainability, Stenta told me that he started farmOS because he wanted to bring visibility to those non-productivist problems facing small farms aiming toward higher-value – both economic and environmental – products. Stenta (2018) described the scientific challenge of representing the relative complex environments of such farms, asking, "How can we represent all of the detail? On these farms there is a lot of things going on – it's often more complex than on larger farms ... As I was harvesting and working on these farms I was thinking about how to track what was happening. And I got hooked on this problem: how to represent enough aspects of farming in a generalized way and how to include information from cheap sensors and public data."

Stenta's comments demonstrate how members of this activist community frame agricultural problems as requiring particular technical solutions and processes of scientific knowledge-making, not unlike agribusiness proponents of digital agriculture (Hecht 2011). The dominant agribusiness, academic, and even governmental framing suggests the problem is productivity and maintaining the agri-food system's aggregate contribution to economic growth (subsequently leading to an increase of social welfare, including nutrition improvement), which is to be achieved by technological innovation, happening largely in the private sector but supported by public funding.[1] Actors in this epistemological camp use top-down, quantitative (largely economic), and reductionist approaches to knowledge production and innovation. Alternately, members of GOAT frame the problem in terms of food sovereignty and supporting communities' access to healthy and culturally adequate food, which they argue can be achieved through a democratization of agricultural data and science – enlisting and empowering farmers and using other forms of bottom-up knowledge approaches (see also Vía Campesina 1996). Participatory narratives frame agro-ecological and regenerative alternatives, understanding science and technology as an element in society and politics (see Thompson and Scoones 2009).

Farm Hack, a kind of analogue predecessor to GOAT, is a whole community of people (many of them from GOAT) who "build and modify" farm tools precisely for small-scale and unconventional farmers, for whom, as Dorn Cox puts it, "good farm equipment is often too expensive." Different countries have their own Farm Hack groups who assemble worldwide under the farm activist organization La Via Campesina or the International Peasant's Movement. The rural sociologist Michael Carolan (2017) has described Farm Hack as exemplary of "collective benefit ontology," aimed at "improving the livelihoods of all farmers, and future generations of farmers" through peer-to-peer education (see also Bauwens and Pantazis 2018). The initial Farm Hack community has now developed a well-stocked set of resources for running do-it-yourself workshops, and this "wikilist" continues to grow through online crowdsourcing of knowledge (see Farm Hack n.d.).[2] Unlike GOAT, or those working on farmOS, the majority of Farm Hack members are practicing farmers. A series of hardware unite the work of Farm Hack, GOAT, and farmOS. One is DIY aerial drones, which are rigged to feed data back into the farmOS platform. Dorn Cox describes "aerial imagery" as "a non-destructive way to collect a tremendous amount of environmental info about the farm on crops but also on other systems (water health)." The Farm Hack community also developed a DIY "raspberry pi" sensor for collecting data on moisture and temperature, which can be fed into the farmOS platform through a framework developed by farmOS coders for receiving data and linking it to areas of interest, or farm "assets." These are mini-computers built from basic materials one can acquire for US$50 and make by following tutorials on the Farm Hack website.[3]

There is a French Canadian group resembling Farm Hack, called Autoconstruction. Autoconstruction is situated within an agricultural cooperative (of the French tradition) called Coopérative pour l'Agriculture de Proximité Écologique (CAPÉ) or, roughly translated, "an agricultural cooperative for local and organic food." I met with the leader of CAPÉ, Reid Alloway, alongside two volunteers who run its DIY tool-building workshops, in the fall of 2018 in Montreal. We were all presenting on a panel during the annual meeting for the food sovereignty non-profit Food Secure Canada. CAPÉ member Sam Oslund had organized the panel, titled "Addressing the Shortage of Appropriate

Farm Technologies Through DIY." Sam knew about me because he had responded to my call for interview participants on the GOAT forum, and we had spoken on the phone months earlier. In fact, both Sam and Reid were involved with GOAT and were at its inaugural meeting. Sam is a quiet and earnest person with an anthropology degree and a passion for food justice and environmental sustainability. Like other GOAT activists, Sam told me he was angered by the fact that most agricultural technologies are developed for those who farm large amounts of land and thus have access to more capital. "Autoconstruction," he said, "addresses the technological gaps." Sam had invited Reid onto the panel to talk about the Autoconstruction tool-building workshops, which are intended to be a mechanism to help farmers who cannot afford commercially available farm tools and implements but who want to "innovate" their operations. Reid presented on DIY workshops, many of them following the modules developed by Farm Hack members, but he also spoke about his seventeen-acre cooperative farm, Tourne Sol, which was then in its thirteenth season. Reid, curly-haired and energetic, talked to a relatively small audience with pride about Autoconstruction's most popular DIY workshop, which taught participants to build a "hacked," homemade tractor three-point hitch, onto which farmers could attach other implements, like a universal bus. Commercially available hitches are expensive, running hundreds of dollars each. Reid was running workshops where farmers could make a hitch in one afternoon for US$50.

Also on the panel was Jenna Jacobs, a farmer and CAPÉ tool-builder, who spoke about their farm, La Ferme Coopérative aux Champs qui Chantent, which at 114 acres is relatively small for a meat farm in Quebec. With the help of a few volunteer labourers, Jenna was working a farm of 2.6 acres of organic veggies (sold locally), 100–500 hens, and two dairy cows. Jenna told the panel's audience that "this becomes about problem solving from a cost effectiveness background – even scale-appropriate technologies are out of price range for farms like mine … so this leads to home-grown innovations." Jenna detailed the particular use value of a thermostat they had built following the Farm Hack wikilist instructions – an Arduino-based greenhouse climate controller (CAPÉ's version is called the Otomoate), which "micro" controls the internal greenhouse temperature, turning devices on and off like a home thermometer does. Jenna said that this tool and the DIY hitch were the most popular among Autoconstruction members, indicating that "market gardeners in particular have the problem of [a] finite number of tractors and many implements, and so they need to alleviate danger and reduce time wastage on changing tools."

The Autoconstruction website describes the group as a gang and a "joyeuse tribu" or tribe, clearly signalling the activist dimensions of their work; one farmos participant from the US similarly described their group as a "rebel society" working on collaborative design and community-building for alternative agriculture (organics in this case). Reid told the panel audience in Montreal that collectivizing was part of CAPÉ community members' broader social goals, but it was also pragmatic. He told a story of how in sourcing steel for the three-point hitch, the community was able to "get together and pool interest, and we then became an interesting customer for manufacturers when we got big enough and organized enough and we got the steel for less." After our panel, Reid, Jenna, and Sam talked to me about the difficulties in facilitating collective action among small farmers already marginalized in the global food system. They said that Autoconstruction had to use "distributive prototyping," or email exchanges among CAPÉ farmers, to vet tool-building instructions because "otherwise, you can build a tool just using something pulled from the Farm Hack website but then it doesn't always work for every farm and if someone you know from around here has used a similar tool, you can get feedback before you start building" (Reid). Jenna in particular talked about the difficulties in doing any kind of agricultural research as a lone, small, and diverse farm, explaining, "There are government grants for small farmers, but I don't even have the time to apply for them and I'd much rather farm." Jenna told me that, like many Autoconstruction members, they are interested in automation and in developing tools that "interface" between high and low technology. But at present, Jenna was completely maximized in terms of the hours they could devote to farm innovation and the priority was "working with the 50–60 farmers in Autoconstruction to develop their needs into basic farm implements … making technology more accessible and appropriate." Autoconstruction members not only build useful tools in the workshops but, according to Reid, they are empowered through the education experience; when it comes to the digital tools, Reid described to me the importance of digital and data literacy for farmers at a time when it seems "a transition to the digital is inevitable."

Under an ethos emphasizing locally appropriate tools, GOAT organizer Calvin started an innovation project called Open Pipe Kit, which, he says, "was designed as [a] sort of general-purpose net of things … [a] data collection sort of library to make it easier to connect sensors of any sort to databases online. Our focus was on, sort of, small scale agriculture … We were mostly interested in data collection on those farms." Most commercial plant databases are not operable for small and diverse farms, and the tools fail to work on a range of personal computers with varying levels of performance (read, older machines). Many farmers, Calvin told me, use old machines that are functional but obsolete by their manufacturers' standards. Calvin said that while Pipe Kit had made strides in serving diverse farmers and farms, designing systems to work with both older and modern computers and software was a substantial challenge.

Bret, a developer working on farmOS, talked to me about the politics of the epistemic imbalance in agricultural knowledge that is weighted toward large-scale and globally facing operations. He called them the "blind-spots" of national scientific efforts to collect farm-level environmental data around "local food economies," and he told me they exist because these smaller farms simply do not make significant money. "It's insane," he said, "the lack of data and thus our understanding about local food systems." The science studies scholar Scott Frickel (2010) and his colleagues have written about what they call "undone science" or areas of research that get left untouched – research questions never asked, knowledge on people or places never created. What knowledge gets created or not has less to do with the whims of the individual scientist than with larger political forces like activism or the market for technologies. According to GOAT members, another layer in this story of knowledge/power is that the results of whatever publicly supported research does exist have been tightly controlled and closed, rather than democratized.

Made obvious by Stenta's (2018) comment above about wanting to "include information from cheap sensors and public data," farmOS is more than simply a digital platform collecting and making use of big data; it is seeking redress for closed and inaccessible agricultural science and technology. Dorn Cox told me that with "farmOS, we're able to have democratized access to environmental data so that anybody has access to high quality, high resolution data at very low cost, and has high participation." FarmOS is developing its platform in close connection with the farmers using it, not just because some (though not many) of those farmers are also writing code but because the data and computer scientists doing the coding are explicitly seeking user feedback. For Anja, notions of appropriateness and user feedback figure centrally in the openness of the knowledge production. She explained, "What we care about is this idea of shared common, whether it's things like shared information, shared resources or community building. There is a sense of collective action. There is a sense of responsibility, not just to yourself but the environment that you're working in. And tools that we build are responsive to needs." Anja's vision of a future data and agri-tech commons was something I found shared among all of the people I met who are involved with farmOS, Farm Hack, and Autoconstruction, and it differs markedly from the technical goals I heard among industry scientists who spoke pridefully about their unique expertise and the need for businesses to translate data into something useful for farmers.

Open Source for Societal Progress

Clearly, those working on farmOS share a set of values with broader open source and science movements, notably the values of shared knowledge and freedom from the commercialization of knowledge. Like appropriate technology, the open source movement stretches back to the countercultural 1960s, when early computer enthusiasts were building machines in their garages, motivated by the democratic potential of understanding a machine on its terms (what Sherry Turkle [1985] describes as the value of "technological transparency").[4] According to one of the "fathers" of the movement, Eric Raymond (2001), today's open source developers are "heirs of the real programmers of the immediate post-war period, who came from the engineering and physics fields ... [and] programmed in FORTRAN and another half-dozen languages that have now been forgotten" (3). Community building and membership are key values held by members of open source communities; indeed, my interviews with open source programmers working on farm data platforms verified a phenomenon the wider literature on open activism has identified: that volunteer coding can be thought of as necessary for membership in open source as an elite social group (Lohr 2001). During an interview with *First Monday*, another well-known open source figure Linus Torvalds declared that "making Linux freely available ... was a natural decision within the community that I felt I wanted to be part of" (Ghosh 1998).

There are arguably other aims of the open data, information, and science movements that current digital agricultural activists like Anja share. Anja told me about the work of the Open Knowledge Foundation to dismantle technical and legal restrictions on data access and circulation, such as restrictive licensing agreements. But she also told me that the goals of people involved in open data were to enable wide participation with data and empower people like farmers to be a part of data collection and data science. Science studies scholar Philip Mirowski (2018) enumerates some of the aspects of open data and open science, which include open access to existing scientific knowledge (e.g. open publishing), open and transparent peer review (e.g. non-blind review processes), and open production of scientific knowledge (e.g. citizen science). All three of these aims appear to motivate those working on farmOS and are captured by what volunteers call their "development methodology": a broader approach beyond software production and farming to wider societal organization. FarmOS is open in the sense that all of its code is visible and freely available; anyone can install the platform on their computer, tablet, or smartphone, and anyone can host the system. Moreover, anyone can contribute by writing code and developing novel features or directions for farmOS; Michael Stenta considered this kind of participatory technology development as a "big picture goal."[5] Stenta told me that "open" for this community is not just about a collective contribution of code but "also trying to build a *community* around the software" (emphasis mine). Similarly, Cox stated that public participation in science, environmental improvement, open hardware, software systems, and organic farming are all "expressions" of the same community. At the 2018 GOAT meeting, a self-described "junior coder" said to me, "My vision is that there are more open, transparent agricultural organizations and that those words are applied to organizations themselves so that people involved with it have a fair share of it and understanding what's going on [with the tool]." Open agricultural data thus emerges as one specific initiative that draws on a wider and longer-standing logic of seeing socially progressive potential behind "open" models of information production and sharing (Bates 2012; see OKFN n.d.).

Critical social scientists have noted an asymmetry in the efforts of organizations like Open Knowledge Foundation to open data, where public versus privately collected data are more frequently made accessible (Kitchin 2014). Take for example Open Data Charter's "Agriculture Open Data Package," which aims at "achieving food security and sustainable agriculture" through open governmental data:

> Data that anyone can access, use or share – can help shape solutions by enabling more efficient and effective decision-making at multiple levels across the agricultural value chain, fostering innovation via new services and applications, and driving organisational change through transparency. Large amounts of data are collected and generated by governments to develop and monitor policies and stimulate developments. By publishing this data as open data and stimulating the use and uptake by the sector, we can improve different areas: empowering farmers, optimising agricultural practice, stimulating rural finance, facilitating the agri value chain, enforcing policies, and promoting government transparency and efficiency. (n.d.)

This asymmetry partly results from the fact that governments collect large amounts of data in an effort to surveil and manage populations (Cheney-Lippold 2011), and they have done so since the beginning of computing, through survey data from the national census and environmental data from weather stations, satellites, and other observational equipment (Kamilaris, Kartakoullis, and Prenafeta-Boldú 2017). Bernie, a GOAT activist, told me that if the United States Department of Agriculture's data related to crops and climate were made widely available, "There is the possibility to significantly reconfigure modes of understanding and food production that have previous been guided by dominant interests." In the mind of activists like Bernie, then, agricultural open source community efforts emerge into historic contestations between institutions (like the state) and modes of production and citizenship that potentially challenge key parts of its logic (like productivist agriculture).[6]

GOAT activists and farmOS developers are advancing their work through the support of other, more resourced and highly visible institutions calling for opening agriculture data, like the United Nation's Global Open Data for Agriculture & Nutrition (GODAN), which claims, "Global challenges [exist], including food insecurity, health crises, climate change, poverty and more. Open agriculture and nutrition data can play a role in solving these challenges. Numerous advantages of open data have been identified. Open data can facilitate collaboration for faster and better innovation. It can be a platform for entrepreneurship and new economic activity. And it can increase transparency, accountability and efficiency across organizations" (GODAN and de Beer 2016, 5). Another prominent and well-resourced organization,

ISRIC World Soil Information (n.d.), aims to tackle the issue of soil degradation using open data. According to its website, ISRIC aims for "a world where reliable and freely-available relevant soil information is properly used to address global environmental and social challenges." Activists describe organizations like ISRIC as "data custodians" who gather, store, and manage huge volumes of data. These organizations also provide information through their in-house analytics services, composed of both people and intelligent machines (for examples of agriculture-related biodiversity loss, see Debinski, Kindscher, and Jakubauskas 1999; Turner 1989; Urban et al. 1987). In addition to being public and governmental, the bulk of the data concerning open activists tends to be quantitative (OKFN and Access Info Europe 2011) because environmental information is largely recorded as quantitative and because these data present less technical and ethical difficulties in their merging than the "unstructured" kinds. At the same time, the technical and design challenges associated with bringing disparate quantitative datasets together is not small, and many, many open agricultural data proponents are working to develop shared standards, languages, and protocol to facilitate this task.

I had a long coffee with a leader at GODAN whose time was largely devoted to bringing together different publicly available datasets. Callum, a computer science professor with an initial degree in agriculture and environmental science, worked for years on bioremediation from agricultural pesticides, where he "fell in love with" the bacteria involved in bioremediation. This love affair sent him into upper degrees in microbiology and bioinformatics, which was how he developed expertise in computer science. Callum grew up in the UK and talked to me through a thick Welsh accent about the important role that "data providers" like Environment Canada have in releasing their data as a public good. Between the loud noises of a milk-frothing machine and gaggles of chatty university students, Callum went over the technical details of this work with incredible patience shown toward me, a social scientist without any computer science training. He described how his invention, an intelligent machine he named HYDRA, moves beyond the model where someone in need of information can access data via a website using a precise input and output description. HYDRA, he told me, "performs a complex search query that finds existing publicly available data from a variety of datasets across the internet." Callum stated that his commitment to using open data is at once a commitment to making "raw" data useful for what he calls "knowledge users." He elaborated:

> Knowledge users could be a lawyer, an innovator, a farmer, really anyone who needs to make decisions based upon knowledge. They know what knowledge they want but they don't necessarily have the technical expertise to find the data themselves. One approach is to develop services around this data processing, but my goal is to empower the knowledge worker themselves so they don't have to lean on a technical team ... They should be able to invoke that data selection process themselves. Data searching and use should not be about my idea, I'm not the domain expert, but I work with people who have domain expertise in soil science, for example, and using this tool, it's a better route to success.

Callum likened this kind of next-level big data usage to the democratizing potential of early computing, before graphical interfaces. He told me that current big data was as disempowering as the graphical interfaces of today's personal computers, where "someone else is making a decision for you." He explained, "With most big data use right now it's the same – someone else is deciding instead of the farmer, and that's a shame, because the limitations of the data querying then drive the kinds of questions being asked. With tools like HYDRA, we will have more creative questions and can solve big environmental problems." Callum did say that the kind of work he was doing was difficult to fund through the public sector mechanisms available to university researchers, and thus he received funding from the Bill and Melinda Gates Foundation and GODAN. GODAN has a significant project in which Callum has been involved, whose report title, "Government Open-Up!" reads as an injunction; the document is meant to help governments identify and publish quantitative environmental datasets relevant for the agricultural sector. On their website, GODAN makes big claims that this big data initiative "could catalyse sustainable agricultural production in support of Sustainable Development Goal 2: Zero Hunger" (n.d).

Even though the focus of open data initiatives – including those of GODAN and partnering groups such as GOAT – is on governmental data, participating activists like Cox argue that private corporations, who increasingly collect agricultural data through precision equipment but fail to share it, hamstring the sustainability potential in widespread data collection. Michael Stenta told me that open sharing of farm knowledge is necessary for "farmers and innovators to build upon," and he imagines that the information gleaned from farmOS – whether the source code, the data, or the advice the platform offers – may be useful not just for farmers but also researchers and service providers. Stenta saw farmOS as working in contrast or opposition to the commercial data platforms, which use various techniques like user agreements to close access to datasets. Therefore, Stenta told me, "Data and knowledge ownership is also an important piece of this ... a lot of the commercial software systems don't give access or control over farm-level environmental data. You basically sign that away. But with farmOS, the goal is that you share what you want to share in order to contribute to a larger knowledge base."

Calvin pointed me toward the GOAT mission statement, which he described as being "about wanting our food system to be in an open place where data can be ... not really data specifically, but like the things that you can learn from data shared openly to make our food system better as opposed to proprietary system." Cox was more philosophical. To him, nothing short of the history of human betterment was at stake in the opening of all data – not just commercial datasets. Science, he told me, was founded upon wide knowledge sharing, and we could not make progress without it. He said that agriculture, like science, was a "shared human endeavour," where "open source, open science hardware and software systems and also the farming itself" were expressions of "public participation in science and production through environmental improvement." Anja put it to me this way: "There is a lot of shared values between the types of agriculture that I'm interested in and types of computer science I'm interested in. And I think we're beginning to realize that centralized systems, whether technological or environmental, just aren't adaptive or resilient." In this way, data scientists working in activist and industry contexts, like those described in chapter 2, share a steadfast commitment to developing big agricultural datasets, even as activist efforts to "open" agricultural data are antithetical to industry efforts to render environmental data proprietary.

Quotidian Insubordination

Calvin informed me that participants in GOAT, farmOS, and Autoconstruction came to the community primarily because of an interest in technology or in farming, but not both equally; he placed himself in the former category. "I'm more of a technologist and less an agriculturist … less farmer," he said. However, the dichotomy between the two groups is somewhat false. Reid Alloway was quick to point out that small and organic farmers are just as "innovative" and high-technology as the biggest and most corporate operations, claiming for himself the identity of both a designer and a hacker. Dorn Cox is emblematic of this dual identity. In addition to working at Wolfe's Neck, he runs Tuckaway Farm, a working farm in New Hampshire that grows more than one hundred different crops. While farming, Dorn uses inexpensive sensors and drones to simultaneously collect and share environmental data on farmOS because, as he puts it, "I believe every farm should be a research farm that shares its data globally. The more data the better … With huge amounts of data, over time, at really high resolution, we have the opportunity for a very, very different kind of science. Instead of this deductive … this drive towards specialization … we don't have the sort of observational bias … it can be decoupled from our own bias."

For people like Dorn and Jenna Jacobson, technology building – whether it is coding farmOS, running a steel welding workshop, or farming organically – is a form of everyday subversion or what scholars have called "quotidian insubordination" (Scott 1998; see also Franklin 1999). By avoiding many conventional farming "inputs," such as herbicides and pesticides, organic farmers undermine the current industrial food and agriculture system in refusing to support those large agribusinesses who supply these inputs and subsequently wield tremendous power over food system directions. Instead of a focus on efficiency and productivity – the central ethos of industrial agricultural operations and institutions – "alternative" producers work towards independence, self-reliance, and feeding local communities, both literally and figuratively. Political scientist James Scott (2014) describes "quotidian insubordination" as relatively low-risk, anonymous, and obscure because it "flies below the archival radar, waves no banners, has no officeholders, writes no manifestos" (12). For GOAT and farmOS participants, the subversion is not just in what they do but what they refuse to do; most of the farmers I met through GOAT refused (or were reluctant) to buy new farm equipment or even seed. These acts have a flagrant anti-consumerist overtone, and while they are self-serving in that they reduce capital dependency, they also cut out those fed by this dependence or what food studies scholars call the "treadmill" of consumption inherent to industrial agriculture (see Cochrane 1958). GOAT farmers buy second-hand or used materials, and they trade goods as well as services instead of using money.

The resistant food politics performed on an everyday basis by members of GOAT, farmOS, and Autoconstruction are supported by a set of shared values that drive members' attempts to make positive contributions to the food system and beyond. These values circulate among members via canonical texts on agriculture and the food system, which members reference as they converse with one another, with extra-community actors like me, and with the larger public. Even though I never met a permaculture farmer connected with big data activists, nonetheless, many activists mentioned David Holmgren's text on the agricultural practice as influential on their technology design. In *Permaculture: Principles and Pathways Beyond Sustainability* (2002), Holmgren lays out twelve principles of agro-ecology including "apply self regulation and accept feedback," "integrate rather than segregate," "use and value diversity." Another of the seemingly canonical texts for GOAT activists is Bill Mollison's *Permaculture: A Designers' Manual*, published in 1988. In this book, Mollison describes permaculture not just as a type of food production but as a design ideology and associated social movement, aiming for "integration of landscape and people providing their food, energy, shelter, and other material and non-material needs in a sustainable way" (1988, ix). Mollison also argues for a reframing of agriculture as an intertwined natural and human system, what is now typically called an agroecosystem (Altieri 2009; Cleveland et al. 2014; Conway 1998; Conway and Barbier 1988; Gliessman 2015; Mollison 1988; National Research Council 2010; Nesheim, Oria, and Yi 2015; UNFAO 2014, 2018). According to scholars, the agroecosystem operates on the local (ground-level) scale but also expands to include national and international systems, such as international trade regulations and practices (see Conway and Barbier 1988).

While considering the broader food ecosystem at the supra-national scale, most GOAT participants I met were primarily local-facing in their efforts toward food system transformation, working on the ground every day toward the change they imagine will be ushered in via alternative farm and technology design practices. One member told me that only by transitioning to local agriculture and food systems could we address the root cause of many food system ills: people do not have power over the food they eat or over the methods by which it is produced, processed, and regulated. American political economist Gar Alperovitz (2017) argues that the dissolution of labour unions and cooperatives in the latter part of the twentieth century enabled an individualization of societal problems and gave those who were already powerful further mechanisms to maintain hegemonic authority. GOAT members talked to me about the importance of gathering and community as a means to seek redress for societal individualization and systematically design and construct a collectivizing institution that supports longer-term transformative food politics, particularly on a local scale. Many GOAT participants appeared to belong to additional local and sustainability-oriented agriculture institutions, including grassroot cooperatives, "permaculture guilds," and local farmers' organizations. Some of these institutions, such as community-supported agriculture programs (CSAs), double up on localizing efforts by literally supporting the local economy through exchange of goods.

Activists also described a common set of consciousness raising texts that appear to motivate their insubordination efforts. More than one person referenced Frances Moore Lappé's *Diet for a Small Planet*, first published in 1971. The book is on one level about the environmental hazards of meat eating but also builds awareness of "humanity's power to unmake our living environment" through industrial agriculture (1991, xvi). Pulled almost directly from Moore Lappé, the core agricultural values held by the GOAT community members are: care for the Earth by rebuilding or regenerating natural "capital"; care for people by looking after one another and local community members; and set limits to consumption. They believe these values contribute to the long-term food system goal: food sovereignty or what one GOAT member defined for me as "equitable access to food and the opportunity to grow food." Attached to this goal of food sovereignty is the image of a "regenerative" food system, which Cox described as "growing anew … not just with food but with community and renewable and non-renewable resources." Community members, perhaps especially those who farm, are pragmatic, but they're also borderline utopic in their optimism about the future of farming. In light of the vast potential of new digital and open technologies, they see the achievement of their food system and political goals as entirely possible. Dorn Cox put it perhaps most eloquently. He spoke over the phone about "Enlightenment science" or "modern science" as having an "insufficient understanding from a systems level of how things are all interoperable to understand the potential damage," he went on to talk about the environmental sustainability and social justice promise embedded in informatics and digital technologies. He continued, "So, I feel like it's only been in the last decade with the bio-tech revolution and newer, lower cost measurement and satellite imagery, and really looking … systems science that have come along so far that's enabled us to really start to uh, instead of just to count off all of those negative externalities, we can actually start to pull some of the values in to our decision-making process and start to incorporate that in to human values that are used for day-to-day decision making." Quotidian insubordination and data science are intertwined in unexpected ways for farm and food activists like Dorn who see data as a tool they can harness to build their version of a better world.

GOAT and its signal technology farmOS are clearly situated within wider mobilization and activism – notably the appropriate technology and open technology movements, as well as "alternative" agriculture movements like organics. Despite being open source, the functioning of this decision support platform is premised upon the collection of big data, just like commercial platforms such as Monsanto's Climate FieldView. And yet, the volume of farm data "feeding" farmOS is many magnitudes smaller than the commercial platforms, which have the advantage of the seed and chemical supplier's historic relations with millions of farmers and access to their data. Like industry scientists, activists describe "data-driven" agriculture as exceeding what is possible in the material realm. And yet the activist coders or hackers gather data and feedback on their design from direct personal relationships with organic, agro-ecology, and regenerative farmers. Many activist coders actually go out into the fields where quotidian insubordination and data science intertwine in unexpected ways. Activist innovation spaces, at least those I visited, are themselves messier and less formal than commercial or government labs and are more gender-diverse (in these spaces I met a woman coder and a trans woman farmer). Activist data and computer scientists talk about sustainability in reference to digital agriculture just as much as industry actors, yet what they mean by the word differs greatly; while the dominant vision for a future farm 4.0 uses less farm inputs like chemicals and water (but also farm labour), the activist vision of the future engages farmers in local production practices centred on biodiversity and feeding into local community, as opposed to global, food systems. As I explain in the next chapter, what these activist movements and organizations share is a preoccupation with data and a faith that digitizing agriculture will build a better world. As the next chapter will make more explicit, this faith is rooted in a conception of data that has links to long-standing ways of describing technology as separate from and better than society – a framework I call the immaculate conception of data.

4

The Immaculate Conception of Data

While activists who build open source agricultural technologies (like Dorn Cox) and corporate proponents of precision agriculture (like Bayer/Monsanto's Tobias Menne) do not agree on what the future of food production will look like, they share an epistemic commitment to algorithmic ways of knowing and improving agriculture. They also share a way of speaking about big data that I came to realize is so widely shared that it might be considered a "social imaginary" or a "common understanding that makes possible common practices and a widely shared sense of legitimacy" (Taylor 2003, 23; see also Jasanoff and Kim 2009). The notion of an imaginary is rooted in sociological studies of beliefs and claims about the future, specifically ones that are collectively versus individually held (see Durkheim 1912), and that then comes to affect individuals. Rather than referring to purely ideational concepts, however, I draw on science studies scholars Jasanoff and Kim (2015) and use "imaginaries" to grapple with the co-production of ideas, interests, and the materialization of technical projects (4). Science studies treatments of expectations, visions, and imaginaries have investigated the *performativity* of future representations, where "these studies show how future-oriented discourses, practices, and materialities shape the way society makes sense of science and technology, adjust how actors create strategies, and contribute to the shaping of technologies, as well as the development of entire technology fields" (Konrad et al. 2017, 469). Science studies scholars have predominantly used the concept to underscore how scientific and technological projects are intertwined with sociocultural elements that differ across national contexts (Felt 2016; Kelleher 2015) or subcultures (Lakoff 2015; Tidwell and Smith 2015), and scholars have largely focused on representations of the future related to nano- or biotechnology (Chiles 2013; Selin 2007; te Kulve et al. 2013; Väliverronen 2004). I extend this research by describing a sociotechnical imaginary around data – one wherein big data are "raw" and subsequently provide truths about the world as it really is. In this imaginary, the human is simply a shepherd of a big data way of knowing (or what data scientists call "insight") and arriving at a utopic future. The corollary of seeing data as untouched by the human is seeing the knowledge drawn from the data as all-powerful. In this chapter, I detail the circulation of a powerful sociotechnical imaginary around big data as it operates in specialist domains of expertise on emergent digital innovations and in intimate spaces of data production and use. I also connect these stories that are presently in circulation to long-standing ways of thinking about science and technology as isolated from their biological and cultural context and as omnipotent. Karl Marx described this process of social isolation as reification, Donna Haraway calls it fetishism; in the context of agricultural big data I call it the immaculate conception of data (ICD). In this chapter, I will outline how ICD gets used by actors working with big agricultural data, for example, in a "pitch" to government funders for a possible technoscience consortium necessitating a large injection of funding (in this case from public money). I will also show how ICD gets used even as those using it labour away in messy human–machine relationships. I explain why, despite or perhaps because of this messiness of reality, ICD is both useful and hazardous.

A common expression of ICD is "data-driven," a phrasing I heard in interviews with engineers, in farm fields with activists, and at conventions with venture capitalists. "Data-driven" connotes that data have agency apart from the humans who select and organize them. I heard the phrase at the very first big data and artificial intelligence convention I attended: Big Data Congress, which in 2016 was hosted on the east coast of Canada, in Saint John, New Brunswick. The organizer, Geoff Flood, took to the stage at the beginning of the day and greeted two hundred people (the majority of whom appeared to be men in suits) by saying, "We have terrible problems, such as how to produce enough food and global warming … Our mission is to build a better world by leading data-driven society in Atlantic Canada." As Flood left the stage and the room waited for the keynote speakers (including the well-known Sandy Pentland of MIT Media Lab), Bob Dylan's "The Times They are a-Changin'" played in the background. To me, the song's message supported Flood's opening remarks: data are in the driver's seat of positive social change, and all humans need to do is set up the automated systems and step out of the way of the moving train of inevitable progress. Data scientists and others at this conference spoke to me about algorithms and computer programs not as human-made tools to be put to human use but as capable, in and of themselves, of delivering essential services. One data analytics firm employee described how "the algorithm can successfully isolate all the images that have this anomaly in it, [and] can then generate a map that can say, 'here are your insects and here is your virus, here is your disease.'" The algorithm in this phrasing is an agent capable of analysis and speech. Quite frequently data were described as not just driving analysis and the generation of insight but also broad social, even global-scale change. Ren, for example, a leading data scientist with Microsoft, talked to me about the power of digital technologies to revolutionize peasant farming in the Global South from something "primitive" to something "innovative." Bright-eyed and whip smart, Ren told me "data driven farming makes farmers grow more."

Data-driven does not just connote agency, but it pulls from prior metaphors used in reference to early computing and the internet, like "information superhighways." Al Gore coined this latter metaphor when he was the US vice president, apparently to soften members of the public to the early web by downplaying its technical features and connecting its use to an everyday activity – driving – well-understood by Americans (Wyatt 2004, 251; see also Markham 2003). A near "total reliance on metaphors to think about the emerging telecommunications infrastructure in the late 20th century" (Sawhney 1996) was evident in the public discourses of this time, which described complex communication structures as "digital thruways," "pathways," and "highways" (e.g. National Telecommunications and Information Administration 1991).

But ICD's symbolic and semiotic history stretches even farther into the past. In fact, the history of the word "datum" animates the cultural force of ICD. Daniel Rosenberg (2013) describes how the definition of the term data has shifted significantly over the past 300 years. Originating from the Latin *dare* or "to give," datum was something that was granted as given in an argument. Even today, within Euclidean geometry, data are the items from which one begins a mathematical proof, like raw minerals awaiting mining and manufacturing. The idea of data gradually shifted from a description of that which precedes argument to that which is pre–analytical and thus *beyond* argument, as always existing just as it is.

As Konrad et al. (2017) describe in their review of sociotechnical imaginaries scholarship, setting expectations around particular imaginaries of the future requires effort – the "strategic voicing and dedicated promotional efforts of actors" (467). In this sense, I came to see that people enact the etymology of data when using the phrase "data-driven" today in order to convey the inevitability of technology-led social change, or what science studies scholars call "technological determinism." I witnessed a bold expression of this determinism at a "partnering for success" meeting in western Canada in 2017. Agricultural industry "stakeholders" had assembled to strategize about how they might compete as a "smart agriculture supercluster" for significant funding from Canada's Ministry of Innovation, Science and Economic Development. An agricultural economic consultant, who had organized the event and convened those organizations comprising the nascent "cluster," said to the room in an opening address, "The federal budget is nine hundred million dollars set aside for innovation over five years … This here [smart agriculture supercluster] is an Alberta-led national-in-scope cluster that involves ag and food and ICT suppliers and the idea is to leverage across the value chain the power of data."

As he spoke, he pointed at a slide that displayed a high-level visualization for the proposed supercluster. On the visualization, data were at the root of an economic revolution in the agri-food sector; positive outcomes started with data and finished by delivering applications, decisions, and tools. The slide visualized what were described as "pinch points" that might stall this future via big data and automation: "lack of access to data" as well as "lack of digital skill among farmers." In other words, the genesis of the project and everything it would bring was "data" with human elements outside of (or getting in the way of) these processes. A similar message was given at a meeting organized by Asia Pacific Economic Cooperation on the theme of digital agriculture; senior economist with the World Bank, Ghada Elabed, a soft-spoken woman, offered an efficient list of "no regret policies" that would lead to social good: "strengthening access to data; reviewing regulations that constrain adoption of data technologies; supporting digital entrepreneurship; and investing in transformational digital and development."

Data Democracy

Arguably since the early internet, assumptions about technological inevitability have motivated significant efforts toward technological skilling and re-skilling, such that worries about lack of access to internet technologies have completely circumscribed conversations about the social implications of digital technologies. The now popular concept of the "digital divide" is used to describe how early internet access opened up spaces for participation for some, while lack of access created new social exclusions and aggravated old divisions, notably along the lines of gender, race, and socio-economic status (Smith and Magnani 2019; Gorski 2003; Wong et al. 2009). Just as the broader "digital divide" scholarship has typically focused on particular societal actors' lack of access to ICTs or lack of digital skill (Haight, Quan-Haas, and Corbett 2014; Sciadas 2002), similar problematics have driven both academic research and government conversations about the social impacts of digital agriculture (Aubert, Schroeder, and Grimaudo 2012; Batte and Arnholt 2003; Bramley 2009; Daberkow and McBride 2003; Fountas et al. 2005; Reichardt and Jurgens 2009; Stafford 2000). The Canadian Ministry of Agriculture contracted a study of farmer engagement with digital agriculture, which showed that the number one "barrier to adoption" was price, followed closely by internet speed or cellular data coverage. Indeed, data coverage is a major technical element that the dreamed-about "smart farm 4.0" will rely on, given the scale and complexity of anticipated data streaming. While some large-scale farms already run their own networking infrastructure, most farms face the typical challenges of rural connectivity: unreliable, poorly maintained communication networks with slow, spotty connectivity and inconsistent or sometimes absent sources of power. Farms require networking both within their physical boundaries – for example, from field sensors to a central farm computer – and from their boundaries to the cloud – for example, for integration with remote sensing such as satellite images.

Following from this study, the Canadian Ministry of Agriculture contracted an academic researcher, Dr Helen Hambly from the University of Guelph, "to determine to what extent broadband connectivity, or lack thereof, impacts precision agricultural adoption and productivity of agricultural operations and the economic growth of the sector" (from the statement of work/contract agreement). A public sector scientist who "builds algorithms, software and scripts" for environmental monitoring told me, "The Internet is becoming a basic human right, whether people like to hear that or not ... People would argue against you, people would say, "No, no, no, Internet's not a right, if you can afford the Internet you should pay for it, but it's not a basic human right." But you know weekends weren't a basic human right before unions came in and stuck ... It got us the five-day workweek. So, the change is inevitable." One can only assume that Dr Hambly's work and her mobilization of findings under the rubric of digital access has been incredibly influential, given the enormous federal government investment that has followed from it. The Universal Broadband Fund, which launched on 9 November 2020, is investing C$1.75 billion in order to "bring high-speed Internet at 50/10 Megabits per second (Mbps) to rural and remote communities" (ISED Canada 2021b). The Department of Innovation, Science and Economic Development is investing CA$585 million by 2023 in the Connect to Innovate program, which aims to meet the "challenges" presented by "geography and smaller populations" that "present barriers to private sector investment in building, operating and maintaining infrastructure in [rural and remote] communities" (ISED Canada 2021a). These are just two of at least eleven similar government programs.[1] There are similar efforts south of the border, led by the US Department of Agriculture and also Microsoft Corporation, whose digital agriculture program, FarmBeats, is aimed almost entirely at the issue of access. According to an academic publication on FarmBeats, "Data-driven techniques help boost agricultural productivity by increasing yields, reducing losses and cutting down input costs. However, these techniques have seen sparse adoption owing to high costs of manual data collection and limited connectivity solutions ... FarmBeats, an end-to-end IoT platform for agriculture, enables seamless data collection from various sensors, cameras and drones" (Vasisht et al. 2017, 1).

The very act of this significant research investment can be read as an expectation of, or strong commitment to, a particular future (Konrad et al. 2017). The assumption underpinning all of this research and government intervention is that full digitization is inevitable and human intervention need only harness the change for the good of everyone. Indeed, several months after that first smart supercluster meeting, I happened to see the letter of intent that went forward at the first stage in this funding competition. It defined the network of actors as "a consortia [*sic*] to catalyze systems for data-driven solutions across the supply chain." The phrasing to me implies that the change is there, ready to be, with humans acting not in the driver's seat of this change but merely as a chemical agent spurring catalysis.

But behind all of this effort to build access to the so-called digital revolution in agriculture also lies a long-standing presupposition that equates internet-based communication to democratic participation and thus purports that all citizens ought to have the "freedom to connect" (Clinton 2011). Famous early developer or "father" of the internet Vint Cerf has the actual job title of Internet Evangelist with Google Corporation, where he travels worldwide, lobbying governments and the private sector to invest in internet infrastructure as a means to democracy. Since 2010, Cerf has further promoted this message as commissioner for the Broadband Commission for Digital Development, a UN body which aims to make broadband Internet technologies more widely available. Scholar of the internet Clay Shirky (TED 2012), drawing from the Canadian historian of communication Harold Innis, has argued that the internet is inherently democratic because it is "flat," a decentralized network of power and knowledge and thus a perfected "public sphere" for open, free dialogue among all citizens. This vision was perhaps a better fit for the original mid-twentieth century internet, which located information on millions of servers all over the world, connected with one another via server-based networks. This early system was non-hierarchical not just in its spread but its governance, where the computer servers anchoring the system were both large and small, public and private, and managed in a somewhat ad hoc variety of ways. Today, however, this global socio-technical system involves massive data storage centres, each containing tens or hundreds of thousands of linked servers, operated by highly controlled and centralized private corporations and government military and surveillance authorities (Mosco 2015). Indeed, these data centres are so tightly controlled they are only visited in person for maintenance or repair and as a consequence the interior spaces are usually not lit. The black box is literally a black box. But breaches in public trust, like Cambridge Analytica, give us some inkling about the anti-democratic things corporations are doing with data behind closed doors.

Despite the current political economic realities of data control, immaculate conception of data puts a fresh face on – and thus keeps in circulation – myths from the end of the last century around computing as delivering an end to history, annihilating geography and transforming the body and the body politic for the better (Kurzweil 2010; Polyani 1967). As we know, myths are not judged based on their claims to truth, but whether they live or die (MacIntyre and Emmet 1970).

The immaculate conception of data also relates to the commonplace phrasing "raw data"– a phrase which, if put into the big data-based algorithm called Google Search, garners almost eight hundred million returns. The phrase "raw data" naturalizes data, suggesting they are like natural resources pulled from the ground like oil or minerals (Crawford 2015). One popular book aimed at marketers is even titled *Mining the Social Web* (Russell and Klassen 2019), and more than one data scientist described their career to me using the passive phrasing "data capture" and the work purportedly done by algorithms on these data as "processing." Like early colonialists intent on grabbing natural resources to build up empire, representatives from agribusiness were quite candid with me that they found themselves in the midst of a "rush" to "capture" data because data were currently lucrative (in their resale, for example). At one big data convention, as I wandered the swag tables, I noticed a glimmer coming from one data "mining" agency's stand. The source turned out to be hundreds of shiny metallic USB keys stacked in a pyramid for give-away, each shaped like a gold brick. The intended message was that data are like gold and this company helps extract riches from this resource, whose full value is hidden from those without the data science or computing expertise (or access to voluminous data).

People involved in digital agriculture frequently described data to me in terms that connoted data as agential, and they almost always described the systems that are designed to use big data in anthropomorphic terms. Tim, a salesperson working for a corporation selling "predictive data analytics for agriculture," talked to me about how Monsanto had bought into his business, saying, "They've invested large sums of money into us." Despite occupying a prominent position in his company, Tim is young-looking and otherwise fits the profile of someone working in a creative economy characterized by Silicon Valley tech firms like Facebook, where the median age of employees is under thirty (see PayScale n.d.). Tim said that after Monsanto invested in his company, he went to their head offices in St Louis: "I've been to St Louis and met other companies invested in by the agribusiness." It was after this trip that he got the impression that "they want to make sure they know what is going on. You see, the big piece, especially in a system like agriculture, is the more data you have, the smarter your system is."

Like Tim, many of the data or computer scientists and engineers I met talked about their technologies as "smart" and agential. When I was in the early stages of learning not just about digital agriculture but also about big data and sophisticated computing, I asked Steve, a programmer who worked on open source tools, to explain what exactly an algorithm was. Steve paused and faltered. "Uh it's hard to say … but," he explained, resting on yet another metaphor, "it's what happens when a computer *runs* software." Yet it is computer programmers working in companies like Tim's, not computers by themselves, who play a decisive role in shaping the machine learning decision systems they sell to farmers and agricultural consultants, not least because most of these systems encompass a number of models that are implemented in the computer code of the system. Models can be neural networks, decision trees, or logistic regressions, among else and they are moments of human–machine cooperation where the human crafts the manner by which the computer selects categories. And while the choice of model is conditioned by the complexity of the dataset that will be "fed" into the machine, it is also dependent upon socio-economic factors like computational resources. Of course, humans construct the data "fed" into the machine, and humans decide on the problem the machine is meant to inform. Tim and Steve's way of thinking and speaking is not idiosyncratic, and indeed ICD is built into their disciplinary history; programmers like them parse today's AI programming from an older relationship with machines, which were built "by hand" by humans who explicitly outlined a logic of decision-making about the categorization of data. This historic process is also referred to "Good Old-Fashioned AI" (Winograd 2006) because it once dominated the field but has now fallen out of favour (and is blamed for the twentieth century "AI winter" or the period of disciplinary underperformance).

Even if data are commonly described as a natural resource, it is a fact that "raw data is an oxymoron," as Geoffrey Bowker put it cleverly and succinctly in 2005. No datum is untouched. Rather, human decision-making marks each data point, beginning with the work of determining what counts as a possible variable that will be used to measure a particular phenomenon. Furthermore, someone decides how to collect data on that variable, as well as how to organize those data and then analyze them. In the case of an automated decision support system for farmers, humans have, for example, chosen the "inputs" (the host of data points on variables like soil and seed). And if the system "learns," then a human has decided which data will "train" it. A human has produced a matrix of weights that the classifying machine will use to determine the classification for new or future input data. Each stage of this process is an epistemic move that involves categorical judgment, a fact that seems to disappear when viewing data in a repository, as though they were there all along (Bowker and Star 1999).

Critical data and communication studies scholars have worked toward denaturalizing data by studying big data and algorithms "in the wild" (Burrell 2016), or as they interact with real human lives. Scholars have called out the pernicious ways that putatively "data-driven" decisions (mediated by putatively objective algorithms) have reproduced societal disadvantage, not least because many of the big datasets that "feed" algorithmic decision tools are biased. Take for example Virginia Eubanks's *Automating Inequality* (2018), which directs attention to the role of digital technologies in social institutions like medical insurance provision decisions and affordable housing policy. Eubanks writes against the common assumption that, given access to massive volumes of data that are analyzed via sophisticated predictive analytic tools, service providers can make decisions based upon objective truths about populations, research subjects or consumers. Through detailed ethnography, Eubanks shows that data-based systems categorize people for a range of non-technical reasons that map onto historic racial and socio-economic biases, and which result in the rejection of applications or cessation of benefits – decisions which have real import in real people's lives. Kathy O'Neil's popular book, cleverly titled *Weapons of Math Destruction* (2016), lays out impacts of consequential and opaque automated systems that are designed to derive insights from big data. O'Neil worked herself as a mathematician at a time when artificial intelligence and automation were first being implemented to drive financial forecasting and investment. Like Eubanks, she focuses on a few sites where algorithms drawing on big datasets are being used to make decisions – for example, in school administrations hiring and firing public school teachers, in insurance companies awarding and denying benefits, and in legal boards deciding on whether to grant parole. Like Eubanks, O'Neil also shows how the models in her case studies are not free from human bias, but rather built on flawed assumptions and partial data at the expense of the already poor and vulnerable.

O'Neil calls for transparency in the use of algorithms and a retreat from the socio-technical value of efficiency in favour of policy-making guided by the principle of justice (see also Pasquale 2015). Similarly, Safiya Umoja Noble (2018) argues that algorithms, influenced by advertising influence, embed systemic racism and reproduce harm for people of colour. The empirical basis for Umoja Noble's scholarly exploration in *Algorithms of Oppression* are search returns from Google – a learning algorithm that draws on internet data. Umoja Noble uses analysis of returns from a variety of words and concepts such as "black girls," which, Umoja Noble reveals, returns pornography disproportionately compared with "white girls." Likewise, the concept "beautiful" returns mostly images of young, white girls leaving young women of colour without a subject position in reference to societal norms. Other scholars look critically at less politicized uses of big datasets and algorithms, such as Tarleton Gillespie's (2014) work on search, trending and other content filtering and ranking. Given that internet-derived data clearly exist in concert with human values and decisions, for instance about what counts as beautiful, phrases like "raw data" are highly inappropriate.

Science Studies and the Power of Objectivity

Immaculate conception of data is intended as a meeting ground between this critical data scholarship and science studies scholarship and can help us unpack the link between data's perceived rawness – the perception that data are untouched by the human hand or immaculate – and its social force. The common or received view of data as immaculate is a lot like the received views of science and of technology, both of which are now shopworn figures in the field of science studies. Since the latter half of the twentieth century, science studies scholars have pointed out that the "received" dominant view of the scientist is someone who simply holds a mirror up to nature, following an exceptional method that allows for "discovery" of the world as it really is, without human interpretation. Facts, in the dominant western view, are thus found not made (Latour 1988), with scientists merely delivering this "mechanical objectivity" through superhuman-like powers of self-restraint which allow them to divorce themselves from their interests and beliefs (Daston and Galison 2007). In 1942, the sociologist Robert Merton codified science as "certified" knowledge that looks nothing like harmful ideologies such as Nazism or fascism; science, he argued, is value-free because the scientist is "disinterested." This view of science thus makes a clear distinction between science and other ways of knowing the world. Also, according to Merton, scientific knowledge emerges from direct empirical observations, which sit outside of the theories these observations confirm or disprove. Due to its supposed disinterestedness, universal scientific knowledge is thought to accumulate over time, leading to better facts and ways of intervening in the world (Hacking 1992, 1–2). Similar to views about science, a steadfast dichotomy between humans and artifice has dominated modern western thought, both popular and philosophical, such that technologies are thought to be value-neutral. The National Rifle Association, a US gun lobby group, famously captures this view of technological neutrality in their slogan, "Guns don't kill people. People kill people." Here they imply that guns are merely inert things with no inherent risk or value.

Science studies scholarship has worked against this received view, detailing the ways in which science in practice or "in action" (Latour 1987) is contingent, and they have advanced a culturally and historically located understanding of objective knowledge (Daston and Gallison 2007). Science studies scholars have also revealed how scientific knowledge and technologies reflect the context-specific conditions in which they are produced (Winner 1986). Actually, scholars have shown how values are a necessary part of productive scientific knowledge formation, not least because every scientist comes from a "social location" which informs how they are in the world and in their scientific practice (Haraway 1988). Historian of science Thomas Kuhn (1962) argued that extra-scientific elements are an important part of the production of scientific knowledge; scientists would not solve puzzles in any given field without sharing a common set of basic theoretical premises and vocabulary or a "paradigm." Drawing on a series of historical examples, Kuhn revealed the "theory-laden" quality of any scientific observation and its contingency both historically and disciplinarily. He claimed that the fundamental assumptions driving inquiry had changed over time and the sciences were overwhelmingly not unified in their representations of the world. However, he believed that these representations allowed for productive intervention. Similarly, contemporary philosopher of science Kevin Elliott (2017) has said that knowledge is woven within a "tapestry of values," which play a crucial role in identifying research topics, choosing research questions, sorting sometimes conflicting evidence, and communicating results.

If the theory-ladenness of observation is productive in practice, in parlance or in public messaging, advancing a view of science and of technology as outside of human values has proved a winning strategy. The received view of science has persisted in part because of its broader functioning within arrangements of power and authority in the world outside of the laboratory – what Langdon Winner (1980) calls "politics." Within the received view, the knowledge produced by the scientific method and held by credentialed experts is not just widely considered different, but it is considered superior, evidence upon which to build better technologies and also societies. The scientist or the person speaking for nature has historically occupied a position of power (Sarewitz 1996).

Take, for example, the "father" of modern Western science, Francis Bacon. Bacon was made famous by his public assertions that the most noble human ambition was to establish "dominion over the universe" (quoted in Merchant 1990) by using the scientific method to "bind" nature into service (169). According to Carolyn Merchant (1990), this process of establishing power over nature by binding and subduing it constituted, for Bacon, "a new ideology of objectivity seemingly devoid of cultural and political assumptions" (172). Bacon also wrote about the possibilities opened by "the distant voyages and travels" that had become frequent by the time he published his *Novum Organum* in 1620. Post-colonial science studies scholar Jatinder K. Bajaj (1990) has drawn attention to Bacon's assertion of a "most intimate connection between the ways of human power and human knowledge" (144), reminding us that Bacon argued that objective "knowledge in the pursuit of power ought to be organized by the King" (45). When Bacon spoke of science serving mankind, therefore, he "meant the gentry of Britain and aristocratic groups in other societies. This was the accepted usage of the term mankind in his time" (50). Similar to Bacon, Robert Merton's aim in describing what made scientific knowledge special was explicitly to help establish scientific institutions as the rightful arbiter of social policy. As political theorist Yaron Ezrahi (2004) has observed, the "trauma" caused by fascism and totalitarianism during World War II led many liberal democratic thinkers to view objective knowledge as "the best protection against the dangers of arbitrary political power and of mass passions and violence aroused by political imagination undisciplined by reason and enlightenment" (273). Merton's 1942 book was as normative as descriptive; he argued that the "race, nationality, religion, class and personal qualities" of the scientist ought to be "irrelevant" (270), their method proceeding based upon the "temporary suspension of judgement and the detached scrutiny of beliefs in terms of empirical and logical criteria" (277). He also argued that scientific findings should be treated as "a common heritage" (273), given that they are the product of collaboration and that the scientist should never derive personal gain from their findings (276).

Today most people who think carefully about or practice in the sciences understand that "disinterestedness" is nothing more than a notional ideal; moreover, many people widely acknowledge that it is a view which can be used as a resource for stabilizing boundaries of power (Shapin 2010; Shapin and Shaeffer 1985). Actors can use ostensibly universal and neutral facts to "both discipline and democratize the uses of political power and authority" (see also Ezrahi 1990, 288). Well-known science studies scholar Brian Wynne (2011) calls this scientism or the use of the received view of science as a mechanism for shoring up support for one's tacit social, political, or economic agenda. One only has to think about television advertisements for toothpaste to understand scientism; many feature a "dentist" wearing a laboratory coat and making claims about brand X's wonderful capacity for rendering teeth whiter, healthier, and less sensitive to heat and cold. Automatic authority, trust and power attach to those people who speak for science (and who perform this conception of expertise by wearing a lab coat) because they are thought to speak without bias, to speak truthfully about the way the world really is. The view of medical expertise – or of an automated decision system drawing on big data – as inherently truthful is a palatable ideal which may have deep roots. However, this view also reflects the mood of a more recent historical moment, wherein facts and truth seem always to be disappearing and people, even those in positions of power like the past US president Donald Trump, are not committed to grounding their claims in good knowledge (or even reason). People may not be trustworthy, so put your faith in data. Think again of the farm trade report that responds directly to farmers' concerns about the unpredictability of nature and market forces with a reassuring title that reads, "Weather Monitoring Means Less Guessing and More Knowing" (Figure 2.2). Big data equal a kind of truth. The feminist science studies scholar Donna Haraway calls the assumption of decontextualized knowledge coming from the scientist the "god's eye view" (1988). She does not call it the "bird's eye view" because it is not just an alternate vantage that one gains from rising above but rather is such a superior vantage it is believed capable of delivering both omniscience and omnipotence.

Immaculate conception of data as a framework is meant to capture this aspect of power and performativity, which is at play in the received view of data and artificial intelligence. Kevin Kelly (2002), cofounder and former executive editor of *WIRED* magazine, exemplifies ICD when he writes an addendum to *deus ex machina*, or God in the machine, as "God *is* the Machine," a rephrasing he thinks more accurately describes the "transcendent power of digital computation." According to business analysts, the practice of hiding human input in AI systems remains an "open secret" among those who work in machine learning and AI – one that has proved useful when pitching one's wares to investors who appear very much captivated by ICD (Olson 2021).

In calling the imaginary discussed in this book ICD, I pull on these multiple cultural threads that bind our relationships to science and technology and also borrow directly from the Christian doctrine of the immaculate conception of Mary. This doctrine claims that Mary, the mother of Jesus, himself the son of God, was sinless or conceived by God to be without "original sin." This doctrine is aligned with that of incarnation, which declares Mary as a virgin upon the birth of Jesus. Mary's conception of Jesus was clean because God put it there, much like Haraway's supposed "god trick" of the scientist who simply finds facts as if they are gifted from on high. Significantly, Mary's purity makes her a powerful figure within Catholic religion. Indeed, her purity is the reason why the Catholic prayer "Hail Mary" refers to her as "full of grace," literally filled with the power of God. This doctrine has been useful for the Catholic Church as well as other institutions that have aligned themselves with religious doctrine. For example, Stephanie Linkogle (1998) writes that the religious discourses surrounding the figure of Mary as pure and maternal buttressed the Sandinista regime in Nicaragua because constructions of Mary helped to validate women as mothers and thus limit their potential in the public sphere. This social conditioning worked to materially support the Sandinista regime, for example by encouraging women to birth and care for children. Similarly, Giulio Girardi (1987) suggests that several South American dictatorships have "recast" religious expressions of purity to reinforce their revolutionary projects insidiously, building tacit acceptance by propagating their political aims via "seemingly apolitical or unaffiliated religious discourses" of purity (quoted in Linkogle 1998, 134).

Just as the doctrine of the immaculate conception elevates both Mary and Jesus above humans, leveraging the ICD elevates data by stripping it of its mundane, messy, and potentially sinful origins. If people perceive data as simply existing (rather than being made to exist), then they can perceive data as escaping the vicissitudes and politics that threaten to destabilize the social order. Data are positioned as immaculate and therefore "trustworthy" (Porter 1996). Sorting algorithms based upon big data are read as "authoritative" for similar reasons. Prominent digital technology scholar Clay Shirky (2009) explains the human–algorithm distance as inherently trustworthy, a process where algorithms "extract" value from information sources "without any human standing beside the results saying, 'Trust this because you trust me.'" Like ICD, the metaphor of cloud computing is a "cultural force" because it naturalizes the technology and lays the foundation for "digital positivism" or the idea that data speak truth directly (Mosco 2014). At the same time, there is a subliminal and powerful magic to cloud imagery, according to Mosco's (2014) analysis of Western art history, in which he argues, "Clouds are more than cultural evocations because they replenish the resource that is absolutely essential to sustain life, leading sorcerers and scientists over the millennia to apply their particular talents to conjure rain bearing clouds. In this respect, the cloud is transcendent because it knows all time and all space, and oversees every form of organic life" (207). And just as religious doctrine makes pure the conception of a fetus, ICD performs an abstracting function for purportedly data-driven food production by promising its separation from the human–material interface.

We can think back to the *Farm Forward* video released by John Deere Corporation, which forecasts that the digitization of food production will catapult farmers from their muddy boots into the creative economy. On its corporate website, John Deere suggests that this shift will include the replacement of hands-on farm labour by automation (Figure 2.1) and human reasoning by self-learning computer programs drawing on data gathered by smart farm equipment and satellites. In the stories told by John Deere promotional videos or technology industry associates, digital tools relieve human workers from difficult and time consuming – indeed, laborious – farm tasks, and they perfect faulty human logic and limited human capabilities. The same theme can be found in the narrative about agricultural automation coming from engineering professional associations; for example, a key source of professional advice predicts that "most aspects of farming are exceptionally labor-intensive, with much of that labor comprised of repetitive and standardized tasks – an ideal niche for robotics and automation" (Brown 2018). We then only have to think of the weight of ongoing contestations around farm labour to understand the work that an encounter with *Farm Forward* might do. The so-called "labour crisis" in agriculture – the shortage of people willing to do agricultural labour – has moved from an academic conversation to a policy problem to a popular issue debated among members of the public. The solution in Canada to chronic agricultural labour shortages, especially during times of intense labour need like fruit picking season, has been to import temporary foreign agricultural workers. But this solution itself raises contentions, not least because of the lack of legal entitlement given these workers and the impacts of this precarity on their health and wellbeing (Basok 2002; Bolaria and Li 1988; Perry 2012; Sharma 2006). Digital agriculture's promise of labourless farming appears to solve this thorny issue with a seemingly neat technosolutionism. The ethical issues brought about by outsourcing to robots those areas of labour that are unattractive to Canadians are not totally obvious. Moreover, the abstractedness the ICD also appears to answer the related but distinct problem of an aging North American farming population and the fact that there are not new farmers ready to replace them. In the farm of the future predicted by digital enthusiasts, one will viably produce food from the comfort of one's living room because farming will no longer be an embodied, physically demanding experience. Remember from chapter 1 Wade Barnes' description of the advantage the digital offers from Farmers Edge: one can be enjoying leisure time (in his example, fishing) while also farming. Boundaries between embodiment and materiality and leisure and work are seemingly erased under ICD.

Similar to promises embedded in *Farm Forward* or the promotional rhetoric of Wade Barnes, Tim told me that he got into his work out of an interest in making the messy, open-ended biological systems of the farm more manageable, in his estimation, through abstraction, modelling and simulation. Over coffee, he claimed that he remained wedded to a conviction that "simulating agriculture would, like, make [farms] more efficient." When I asked him about the destructive implications of abstracting agricultural practice, such as the potential displacement of agricultural workers, he laughed me off, saying,

"Like, I don't imagine this will ever replace the need for agronomists but it will mean that the agronomists won't need to strap on the boots and spend eight hours in the field ... Human reading [versus computer reading] of data is not scalable and that information doesn't play into the bigger picture and it doesn't speak to the other data sources it relies on, so if the system sees a viral plant, its sees all the viral plants and it knows."

The abstracting tendencies built into ICD fit within larger assumptions about our digital "era," wherein the interface between data's materiality and its social elements – the hands-on techniques for collecting data or the massive digital storehouses servicing "the cloud" – are rendered invisible (Burrell 2020). The big data storehouses of Google Corporation, for example, are situated in the Arizona desert, where the buildings and their appendages (e.g., solar panels for diverting energy pressure from the grid) exist away from the view of most humans. I heard from more than one data professional about the "DIK" (data to information to knowledge) or the idea that information is only gained from "raw" data through the use of sophisticated computing or "analytics." David Weinberger (2010) suggests that the DIK doctrine in computer science oversimplifies the causal connections between data, information, knowledge, and wisdom and that knowledge is not the result of filtering data into information. He argues, "[Knowledge] results from a far more complex process that is social, goal-driven, contextual, and culturally-bound. We get to knowledge – especially "actionable" knowledge – by having desires and curiosity, through plotting and play, by being wrong more often than right, by talking with others and forming social bonds, by applying methods and then backing away from them, by calculation and serendipity, by rationality and intuition, by institutional processes and social roles" (para. 12).

Yet I found that, in the case of digital agriculture, the transformation is commonly described by scientists and technologists as a kind of Frankenstein's monster process – one where human experts create machines that are then capable of things no human expert could achieve. Tim told me that the assets of his predictive analytics business were the "mathematicians and computer scientists coding algorithms that [pause] the algorithms look at an image and tell you what's in it based on training datasets." In response to a question about potential ethical issues associated with big agricultural data, a public sector data scientist told me that "these maps, whatever, you know they're interesting and they get distributed around, but if you really want to use that for something meaningful, then you have to take the downloaded data, and you have to build the intelligent computing to do something with it ... I always say data in and of itself is no value." A scientist working for a large agribusiness told me that his research team was so convinced about the power of AI to help "raw" data ascend to the level of useful information that they were collecting "tons of data ... but we don't really know what we will use them for or what will come from [the data]." One powerful consultant in the North American agri-food sector – someone who has the ear of industry and government – screened the slide deck for his presentation over coffee break at an agricultural technology convention in 2018; a slide illustrated his prediction that we were headed to a completely optimized farm operation he called "Agriculture 5.0" (see Figure 4.1), showing an exponential curve marked with dots indicating historic agricultural innovation, from "muscle" to "machine" to "chemistry" to "biotech" to what he ultimately predicted would be "convergence." Convergence, he declared with confidence and certainty, is where "it all comes together: sensing technology, robotics, precision agriculture, artificial intelligence, data ... and means far less work and more return." Various actors from across industry and the public sector not only disappear the role of humans at the stage when an "intelligent" machine is created but in their use of ICD they draw on age-old ideas of science, technology, and objectivity and valorize today's computing as rendering the human imperfect and thus obsolete.

The Messy Human-Machine Compromises of Digital Agriculture

Feminist critics of the technical and philosophical "transhumanist" movement have pointed out that abstracting away from the wet body, swapping it out for an entirely digital existence, is nothing more than a (largely white, male) fantasy (Shildrick 2005), and the same appears to be true for dematerializing food production. I saw evidence that today's big datasets, and the computing that is written to use them, do not constitute a human-free and pure enterprise but rather a sometimes useful but often incomplete and imperfect dance – a human–machine bumbling that includes digital architecture, data, and ma-

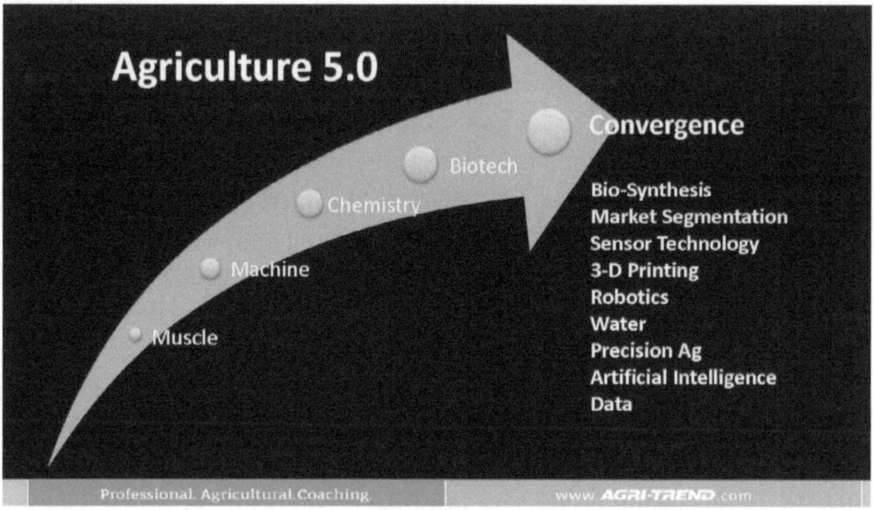

4.1
Final slide on a deck shared with the author at an agricultural technology convention in 2018.

terial things (like plants) in the world. Callum, the computer scientist who plays a leading role in the UN organization GODAN, first described his big data search tool called HYDRA as a person looking for a lost set of keys: "HYDRA looks around [gestures in a sweeping motion], dynamically building different workflows based upon the availability of any data it finds … It looks up and discovers and then asks: where are the data that are needed for this?" When I asked him about the work required to build this functionality, he said, "Well, sure, there have to be descriptions on top of the databases, people have done that … but once that description has been put on … and you know, we have also automated that task." But between the description of solely machine or solely human intelligence lies a far messier reality that came to the surface in the context of a different conversation I had with Callum. During a discussion about funding and how his work has required patient and relatively open-ended funders (like Bill and Melinda Gates) Callum told me that the road toward automated tasks with HYDRA had been and continued to be bumpy, explaining, "After the conceptual vision for HYDRA, we developed a prototype and then got $900,000 for testing it, and we had teams of researchers in each university trying to build out these service descriptions over many different use cases … and improvements were necessary, it has been slow."

Similarly, I met Martin, the "precision analytics" officer for a medium-sized agribusiness, who described a "gap" in predictive algorithms between cause and effect, which only human reasoning and intuition could currently close. A tall man with a thick French Canadian accent, Martin cut his teeth as a child working on farms, spent his adolescence receiving formal training in agronomic science, and transitioned into data science as the agricultural industry increasingly engaged in data practices. The agribusiness Martin worked for was a food processing company that was contracting most of its commodity growers to supply them raw goods. It was in this capacity that they were using data analytics, in the form of yield monitors on some farms and a combination of remote sensing methods to generate wavelength estimations of crops, analyzed by an intelligent machine for information on field "performance." Gesturing at an indecipherable (to me) image of different colour blotches – red, yellow – he told me about how various colours could be an indication of which areas of the field are "underperforming," which could in turn indicate soil depletion and that in turn could justify taking those areas, or indeed whole farm fields, out of rotation. The company gathers most of its commodity inputs from farmers who work on contract and thus presumably the information extracted from this data-reading process could also help the corporation justify taking whole farmers off contract. Martin told me that he needed to "rely on outside knowledge, at least right now, to be able to bridge the gap." Laughing, he told me that outside knowledge meant "somebody literally going out into the field to figure out what's wrong." He therefore required the expertise of a field technician, a plant expert or an agronomist who could take the advice generated with the help of his intelligent machine and translate it into something useful for the corporation, like which areas of a field were "underperforming" in terms of yield. He admitted, "At first, we assumed that all the data – on growth parameters like leaf area index, soil parameters, drones capturing aerial imagery – would tell us the truth, but it turned out the data wasn't great. Image fuzziness was an issue. Cloud cover could influence the imagery. Calibration of equipment was a big challenge. We have found that we cannot treat the outputs as reliable without verifying with human labourers."

While social science has described a shift towards algorithmic decision-making (Finn 2018), less work has described in detail what appears to be a division of labour between humans and computers (Blanke 2014; Brynjolfsson and McAfee 2011), where they are assembled within the same infrastructures, and how the different forms of reasoning and practice are brought together to establish relevance and to learn what is significant and insignificant information. Some of the people I spoke with were candid about the experimental nature of this reasoning process. The GOAT activist Chris confided in me, while fiddling with a soil sensor that was not working the way he hoped it would, "I'm not expert in the field, but I think there is also a lot of speculation about the possibilities without proof of how well it would work." At the Vermont Organics Farmers' Meeting of 2014, the digital farming activist behind farmOS, Dorn Cox, talked about the gap between the dream of AI and today's reality. He said to a crowd of people, "AI is the dream. That's what we've always wanted. We want robots to think and we will likely end up having some form of this, but if we're not thoughtful and deliberate in design of these systems, whether it's thinking about the implications on the society, whether it's thinking about what do we actually think it means to be human and how do we want to then articulate that in digital form … If we're not thoughtful about these things then we'll end up either building useless things or harmful things, both of which I think are equally terrible. Right now, we seem to be mostly building useless things."

Similar to Cox's expression of useless technology, Jerod talked about his tools as redundant. Talking on the phone and across several time zones, Jerod, an executive at an international data corporation, told me "precision equipment … just validates what I already know." Jerod, a fast-talking, seemingly whip-smart digital enthusiast, is also a Canadian farm boy with ongoing connections to farming. He described to me his experiences using precision equipment on his family farm and said that he had not learned much: "I have been over this field my whole life. I know that in such and such an area the soil is terrible and I know I get less yield. But now I have a number and a chart and a map to validate that. Before it was a gut. So, the technology was not a solution for me, but it validated an issue." In part because of the social force of ICD, such validation is not useless. In Jerrod's case, he told me that it was the only reason he had switched from high-input, intensive agriculture to a regenerative model, explaining, "So really what [precision agriculture] led me to think is that if I continue to produce this way I will not survive. So, it led me, the businessman, to think of … I can keep doing this over and over again but it will get me nowhere. So really it was mind-blowing and I would never have thought … now I'm in year three of a regenerative application on farm … and would never have done this before." Jerrod told me that he knew that his previous use of chemical inputs was unsustainable, both environmentally and economically (as in, it worked less well over time as his crops developed resistance), but he just could not trust himself to make a radical departure from what he had learned from his family and from agricultural college. He grew up on a farm that followed the dominant "productivist" logic; he had seen his grandfather and father succeed (increase the size of the farm, for example) but also struggle just to get by. Jerrod said, "I knew this was terrible. But now I can *see* it is terrible." Just like Jack in chapter 2, Jerrod found that algorithmic logic and big data provided trusted knowledge superior to that gained through his own empirical assessment.

Comments like Jerrod's reminded me of Ian Bogost's (2015) influential essay in *The Atlantic* titled "The Cathedral of Computation," wherein he describes our current culture's seeming obsession with "the algorithm," and computational ways of knowing. Though computer scientists would suggest that a transition from certainty to probability (Wiener 2007), fuelled by computational tools like modelling, characterized the twentieth century, Bogost's central claim is that people like Jerrod and Jack have lost sight of predictive analytics as probabilistic. Instead, "A supplication is made to the computers … even as they simultaneously claim that science has made us impervious to religion" (para. 2). Critical data studies scholar Kate Crawford (2015) does a wonderful job describing this same faith in relation to one's self-knowledge, arguing that a shift happened during the long durée of modernity after the Enlightenment, which "intensified the tendency to know our own bodies as a set of external numbers." "If I ask you," she suggests, "'how do you know your body?' Many people would hold up their self-tracking devices."

True to ICD, epistemologies which position big data and algorithms as superior abound precisely because they are useful; in the case of digital agriculture ICD is useful for multiple food system players, from farmers to agricultural insurance companies. Agroclimate Impact Reporter (AIR), a platform developed and moderated by the Canadian government, is exemplary of the social work ICD performs. Volunteers and farmers collect and aggregate big climate and weather data, then "feed" it to the platform. Multiple farmers told me that they use AIR (and thus contribute to its dataset) in order to help them anticipate weather risks to their farm, but more important is the access it grants them to programs and supports (see Agriculture and Agri-Food Canada 2020). Validating their assessment of drought risk through AIR gives farmers eligibility for insurance programs and subsidies, as well as tax deferral (e.g., the Livestock Tax Deferral program); many previous reporting mechanisms are no longer as readily accepted. I spoke with a data scientist named Hannah who works on the platform and uses the data from it to "monitor the crop type across Canada" by combining the crowdsourced "ground" environmental data with satellite data and artificial intelligence to predict real-time crop condition assessment. Hannah was unique as a woman in a leading data science position, but she spoke in the same terms as others. During a late-afternoon conversation in Hannah's near-windowless government office – one crowded with stacks of paper and books – she told me that today, compared to twenty years ago, the whole basis for environmental policy has changed because of an increasing reliance on data-mediated visualizations: "We know … Now we know every field in the country what is growing in it. Or it could be on the soil – whether it has been tilled, or it hasn't, or it's even in the process of being tilled and by this type of instrument … It's really powerful to know."

Yet while farmers, insurers, and data scientists talk about a seamless route from data collection to certainty, I not only heard about but also witnessed many instances of a gap: between data and meaning and between ideal and implementation. And I witnessed meaning emerging not from machines alone but from a human–machine collaboration. Ian Bogost (2015) describes how meaning emerges in this collaboration, explaining, "Once you start looking at them closely, every algorithm betrays the myth of computational purity … Think about Google Maps, for example. It's not just mapping software running via computer – it also involves geographical information systems, geolocation satellites and transponders, human-driven automobiles, roof-mounted panoramic optical recording systems, international recording and privacy law, physical and data-networking routing systems" (para. 19).

Sometimes the human–machine interaction I witnessed was characterized more by tension than collaboration. When I rode on Jack's expensive precision tractor in July of 2018, he was re-grading a field using a putatively hands-off process, yet he kept having to touch the iPad mounted inside the tractor cab because it was frequently beeping, very loudly. When I asked him about the attention he was giving the device, he indicated that there was some flaw in the machine's reading of the "site plan" that he had built earlier that morning (at five o'clock). I met one "precision agriculture specialist" who had started his own small business advising growers on digital technologies in farming in Ontario. Bute, a young red-cheeked enthusiast, drives all over southern Ontario, helping farmers solve problems that arise in the application of digital tools to food production. "Farmers" he said to me, "need someone who is willing to come in, get their hands dirty a little bit, and figure things out on the fly. If you can't problem solve on the fly, it's gonna hurt your business." He also told me the farmers who appear to need the least help problem solving are those who "know farming," whose expertise with the land helps them understand "why the systems do what they do and why it's important."

Spending time with agricultural big data and algorithms-in-action makes it obvious that, as Lev Manovich (2001) explains, "Big data do not just exist, they have to be generated." Moreover, the context in which data are generated influences the meaning produced, and whether they are considered adequate, correct, or up for contestation. When I spoke with Hannah about crop mapping in her Canadian government office, she gestured at a printed crop map and told me, "What this is doing is using satellites, and it's hard to tell at this resolution, but it's thirty metres … and every thirty metres we know what the crop is. Here are the different crop types [points at a legend] … This is an example of classification: corn looks like this, and so the computer program works to pick out corn. They train the algorithm and then they reserve data to check the validity." When I asked her who "they" were, she replied, "Hmmm … yes, well the algorithm obviously is computer-generated but there's always an accuracy assessment. Scientists produce meta data files that tell how it was produced and which determine its accuracy." Drawing insight from the data is a matter of skilled observation and human–machine negotiation, where seemingly automated actions involve normative judgments (Latour 1987). And yet the evidence of this normative work seems to disappear once the datum becomes datum, or once the algorithm appears to run, like the driverless tractor in John Deere's *Farm Forward*, all on its own.

Again, just like post-humanist fantasies about a future technological "singularity" where human bodies are replaced by machines into which we have uploaded our informatic material, the fantasy for digital agriculture is that despite *current* hiccups, it is just a matter of time before we are not needed.

"Eventually," Martin told me, "we're working on something that will basically look at a signal that the plants would give to be able to navigate diagnostics directly. But you know it takes time building the intelligence … 'Feeding the beast,' as I call it, it takes time." One government data scientist described how "the whole idea of interconnected cities and these kinds of things, I think it's inevitable, even outside of agriculture. I mean people are resistant to change, especially when it's automated change, but … I think it's just inevitable, it's just progression, we've seen all this stuff before." Anja, the activist who voluntarily coded for farmOS, described a similar future: "When I imagine the trajectory of how I see the shaking out [of agriculture's future], we start with electrons but then we start moving to organic computing. There are ways to start incorporate [*sic*] more things and have things that are self-adaptive, just as our bones themselves are in fact basically just humans. At some point the line blurs and it is still in theory highly likely that I am living in a simulation."

I am quite sure that none of the data and computer scientists, funders, or activists I met would go to bat to defend the presuppositions of value neutrality and purity laid out by ICD. Indeed, Dorn Cox's speech about the power of open data for sustainable agriculture, delivered to the Vermont Organic Farmers' Association meeting in 2014, contained this nugget, which clearly indicated his awareness of the politics of technologies: "Tools are reflection of values and the processes which are used to build them. In order to build a food system we can be proud of, it needs to be a product of sharing and a shared power, versus those who control capital and labour." But the truth value of ICD operates quite independently from the social work it is enlisted by a variety of food system actors to do. The people with whom I spent time in the production of this book used the ICD framework in large part because it was clearly *useful*. Here is where we can again draw on the combined analytical purchase of critical communication scholarship describing "data fundamentalism" and STS thought on science, values, and the performativity of sociotechnical imaginaries; doing this helps us understand why proponents wanting to win people over to digitization of agriculture regularly evoke ICD. ICD has cultural currency, and it is persuasive precisely because it makes a link between value-neutrality, truth, and power. ICD has been used to justify an urgent need for the funding of digital agricultural research projects – both industrial and activist – because it helps those "pitching" their work claim that it delivers truths about on-farm environments and farm management. It is similarly useful for generating interest in the digital agricultural market among investors. One Goldman Sachs report from 2016 described "precision farming" as "technology driving innovation," where "agriculture offers fertile ground for a confluence of technology trends, from sensors and the Internet of Things to big data and autonomous driving." The article went on to claim that precision farming would "lift crop yields 70% by 2050 and create a $240 billion market for farm tech." Martin, in fact, told me that his large agribusiness had adopted precision agricultural techniques, which now accounted for a prominent wing of the business, because its CEO "got the idea from a *McLean's* article on drones and he thought these are going to be powerful." Martin explained, "We were given a very strong mandate that we needed to drive change at the farm level, very very rapidly … [Data analytics] was more or less like a means of disrupting change and bringing change at the farm level." Industrial agricultural firms use ICD as a marketing device to generate support for their products among consumers at a time when confidence in the use of chemicals and other industrial agricultural tools is at a low; they can represent datafied agriculture as value-free, not ensnared in the tainted history of chemical companies like Monsanto. Moreover, datafied agriculture appears to move us beyond the harmful interventions that agriculture has historically made into the natural and social world. In this way, ICD is also compelling to farmers who want to be better "stewards" of those socio-natural systems they manage. One farmer told me he uses precision agricultural equipment and yield mapping because he is certain he will use less fertilizer, boasting, "I can put the fertilizer in one machine and be within an inch of the plant."

Other farmers are sold on these tools via the assurance that ICD provides. Indeed, amidst staggering uncertainty, many farmers are looking to digital agriculture to make life comprehensible, a fundamental human desire. As Umberto Eco says in an interview with *Der Spiegel*: "What does culture want? To make infinity comprehensible. It also wants to create order – not always, but often. And how, as a human being, does one face infinity? Through lists, through categories, through collections" (Beyer and Gorris 2009). It is comforting to give our trust and decision-making authority over to big data and seemingly autonomous machines (Porter 1996).

ICD also circulates as currency among academics. Data scientists use ICD to position themselves as part of an expert "in group." AI insiders like Sandy

Pentland of MIT Media Lab (who was present – in body or in name – at all of the seven data conferences I attended) police the borders of that group, claiming that big data analytics can reveal such profound truths about the world that clever scientists able to read those truths perform "social physics." Other academics also use ICD. One of the most well-cited papers on "precision agriculture" describes it as a radically different "approach" to agricultural decisions – one that substitutes computation for frail and imperfect human logic (McBratney et al. 2005). In an early paper on the subject, Bongiovanni and Lowenberg-DeBoer (2004) make a bold prediction that reads out of place in an otherwise tepid scientific article (and journal), claiming that precision agriculture would "substitute environmental information and knowledge for physical inputs" (359) and create a "paradigm shift" in food production. This academic language very closely resembles Tobias Menne's (2017) blog post, which promises a dematerialization of farming and the disappearance of its environmental footprint. In a talk titled "Open Source for Agricultural Resilience" at a Vermont Organic Farmers meeting in 2014, participant Dorn Cox also predicted a future of farming where open source technology would replace human insight, claiming, "The history of agriculture has been extractive but now we have an ability to not degrade but to share and understand. The Apollo image was the product of billions of dollars of investment, but these images [shows a slide of DIY digital sensors] are of my farm and they cost only hundreds of dollars. We are able to see beyond anything humans can see … beyond the human spectrum … this is all now accessible. And it's built on open source technology."

ICD is not only ideologically versatile, appealing to various groups, but it also shows a versatility in scale, being likely to appear in high-level policy documents as well as in local conversation. At the Asia Pacific Economic Cooperation meeting, a presenter from International Telecommunication Union (whose tag line is "committed to connecting the world") argued that a "whole of government approach" was needed to "revolutionize" the world by creating "smart cities, smart villages, and smart islands." The October 2011 cover of *Popular Science* magazine reads "Data Is Power," next to which appears a Promethean hand encircled by a corona of light. Articles inside this issue argue that data can be effectively "harnessed" to solve a wide range of societal ills, including feeding a global population in a way that responds to environmental crises. The applied data company who sponsored Big Data Congress in 2016,

T4G, attempted to persuade attendees to use their services by stating in the event's brochure that "big data = big results. Now comes the hard part – planning and preparing for major change. Let T4G guide your transformation." And ICD came up in every conversation I had with data scientists and AI enthusiasts, from industry, non-profits, and activist groups. In fact, I began to see that actors were using ICD as a rhetorical device in an attempt to convince me – the outsider – of the merits of a range of digital agricultural activities. One industry representative told me over and over about the power of computing, repeatedly saying, "The computer can do that" or, "we know how to teach a computer to do that." In a pitch to me that was surely borrowed from a recent pitch he had made to a group of venture capitalists about the value of their automated decision system, he stated, "The value is not like anything we have seen … there are a thousand possibilities you can do with a technology like this, so when you're building something for a customer and they know what to ask for, they know, based on their area, what information do I need."

Especially when engaging with the activists from GOAT and Autoconstruction, I could feel the force of ICD working on me. On a farm in Quebec one sunny day in April, when the Canadian winter wind was still biting but the fields were clear enough of snow that farmers could gather outdoors for a sensor-building workshop, I really wanted to believe one activist called Ester, who told me, "Information allows us to sort of be thoughtful and be deliberate in our engagement with food, the environment and each other. There is a powerful natural relationship between the ability to imagine things, build models, and build something … both sustainable food and resistance and that cluster of ideas." I felt pulled in by the simplicity of this vision: model a sustainable future and then voilà, an alternative system, at the centre of which stands big data, will overwrite the existing socio-technical architecture, which has been built up around an environmentally harmful, chemical-intensive food production system. The fantasy of ICD is far more alluring than the reality of working on various fronts, at various levels of resistance, against a global industrial food regime with seemingly unstoppable "momentum" (Hughes 1987).

While I certainly do not labour at the coalface of this resistance movement, I do know what an uphill battle it can be to advocate for shifts in our industrial food regime or even to raise awareness that there is such a "regime": on a government panel for which I was expert, I had to work very hard over two years to get my fellow panellists to state explicitly the link between intensive agriculture and plant health risks (like mass pollinator extinction linked to the overuse of agricultural chemicals). My attempts to shift the discourse from a listing of invasive species to one entertaining the framing of such invasions as produced by systemic and human-induced risks were repeatedly flagged as too "radical." ICD provides a workaround to "radical" critiques because it leaves intact foundational paradigmatic assumptions; one stalwart assumption is that high technologies, such as computational tools, are central to progress and another is that our dominant economic (capitalist) configuration of humans–nature–technologies is inevitable and good.

I understand why ICD works on farmers and other members of the public, for today it is not just science studies scholars who are required to confront what Steven Yearly (2005) calls the "inherent sociality of science" (181); innumerable scandals render transparent and problematic the politics and economics behind technological development and use. In this context, we might understand ICD as a partial response to what Stephen Ramsay (2011) calls the "beached solipsism" of postmodernism: the eternal regress of critique, deconstruction, and reflexivity, which can leave one unsure about how to act in this uncertain world.

Despite its allure and its usefulness, ICD is hazardous (Marx 2010). Historian of science and technology Leo Marx argues that "technology" is a hazardous concept, describing the historic move away from labelling discrete tools used for specific purposes with their precise names – like hammer or toaster – to the abstract and abstracting concept arising in the English language alongside the first complex socio-technical systems during early industrialism. Science and technology studies scholars have attempted to trouble this received and hazardous view of technology and science because it prevents us from scrutinizing the politics and human decision-making behind particular technological configurations. A common deconstructive method is to undo taken-for-granted "matters of fact" by going backward in time to moments in history when those facts were not yet accepted, before they were "black boxed" into textbook scientific descriptions, which by and large fail to mention all of the messy social processes that went into their making (Latour 1987). Feminist and post-colonial science studies scholars have called attention to the ways in which technoscience is far from neutral. They use detailed case studies to point out how knowledge projects are implicated in oppressive social and political agendas, from racism to the domination of nature and global environmental crises. It was, for example, the desire of the East India Company and British colonial administrators to "reinforce and legitimate the conceptual image of their empire" (Edney 1993, 61) that led to the financing of cartographical surveys of the region. Indeed, "science, cartography and the state had to be aligned" in order to "achieve the integrated assemblage of geographical knowledge that we now take for granted," which went hand in hand with the inequitable global concentration of wealth in the West (Turnbull 2003, 116; see also Brockaway 2011).[2] It matters, as Donna Haraway (2016) put it, what thoughts think thoughts, what stories tell stories, what knowledges know knowledges (199). The notable feminist technoscience scholar Evelyn Fox Keller (1992) has argued that she works to reveal who can know because of a commitment to the same sociological project undertaken by Robert K. Merton; Fox Keller acknowledges that the scientific method works (those of us who have taken antibiotics might agree), but an STS view on science allows us to inquire into exactly what any particular knowledge project does in the world and for whom (60–2).

In the next chapter, I begin from the position that data are cooked rather than raw (Levi-Strauss 1964). I wield this science studies perspective on technologies as always already touched and politicized to get outside of the ICD in order to ask interrogative questions. Who shaped this platform and according to which specific scientific decisions about the collection of data, the construction of models, and the machine learning they feed? And what food system problems and actors are served by these human decisions?

5

The Politics of Digital Farm Technologies

Despite its prevalence and power, the immaculate conception of data is specious; instead of untouched by the human, agricultural big datasets and the computer instructions written to work with these data are the product of a myriad of decisions and specific practices and, as such, even the biggest datasets and the most "intelligent" machines are deeply entangled with human interests and values. This chapter is devoted to detailing some of these decisions taken – regarding which data are worth collecting, on which types of farms, and upon which variables to focus data science efforts. I also trace the interests that are currently directing the production and use of digital farm technologies even though this second line of inquiry is made difficult in part because of the legal and economic infrastructure surrounding big agricultural data and algorithms used by corporations; for instance, firms use trade secrecy law to block access to datasets such that the farmers and critical social scientists alike are limited in what can be known about corporate data practices (and profit). I furthermore detail some of the implications of current dominant big data practices, in particular for food justice. Sociotechnical imaginaries like ICD can become solidified into a deterministic lock-in, fostering a continuation of historic patterns (Konrad 2006); I detail data practices in this chapter in order to intervene into the seeming inevitability of visions of *the* future given under ICD, to open space for readers to think about trade-offs, winners and losers, or unforeseen alternatives.

When Wade Barnes, the CEO of Farmers Edge, says that he is intent on supporting "good farming" with "good information," he is referring to a very particular kind of farming and very particular information technology arrangements. Barnes's sense of "good farming" has been deeply conditioned by his upbringing; Barnes describes how, like his father, he believes a good farm is "an economically contributing" farm, where the farmer manages financial risk well and keeps the farm and rural community viable. Translated, an "economically contributing" farm is one that produces large volumes of commodity crops for sale on an international market, what food studies scholars label as "productivist" (Buttel 1993; Friedmann and McMichael 1989). Though the dominant wisdom (from both institutional agri-experts and corporations) has been productivist for several generations, what constitutes "good information" has changed over time, in large part alongside changes in technical capacity. In the early days of Farmers Edge, Barnes helped farmers digitize data on their use of chemicals or farm labourers and organize that data into spreadsheets; he used simple algorithms, or computer programs, to more systematically extract pieces of information that he hoped would help farmers cut down on their costs. However, this work was time consuming and therefore expensive. Furthermore, according to Barnes, it showed unfavourable return on investment. Barnes persisted, however, guided by a belief in "data-driven" farming, and his company grew as digital innovations and social shifts allowed for greater windows onto farm-level systems. Notably, from the early 2000s, Canadian grain farms increasingly adopted "precision" farm machinery with sensors for collecting data, and weather data became more publicly available under changes in satellite regulation and use (see Davis 2007).

In 2014, Barnes decided to "revamp" Farmers Edge because "we were inundated with data – some from satellites, some from precision equipment, mostly tractors – and it was a credible resource, but farmers weren't using it to make better decisions." I heard this repeatedly during my conversations with commercial data scientists, who described a problem of too much unprocessed data without proper data systems (including human talent) for managing it and making it meaningful. Jeff, a well-connected ex-politico who was spearheading a smart farming initiative in Canada at the time of the interview, explained the situation to me. Dressed in a sharp suit and speaking quickly, he said, "You've got a glut of information and what do you do with it? We're somewhat stuck there right now. [We lack] processing power, and even being able to move the data." Barnes described one of the main technical issues as a lack of reliability in extant data. Here, he understood reliability as data that was "up-to-date … exactly when farmers need it most." Timing is of crucial importance in farming, especially under the weather variabilities that global climate change is causing. Farmers, especially those farming large acreages, need to be able to perform tasks like seeding or harvesting quickly, when the weather and other conditions are just right.

The technical reality corresponding to Barnes's vision of reliable environmental data is a network of sensors extending across more than 4,000 farms in North America, Australia, and Brazil. In order to have predictable access to up-to-date data, Barnes partnered with hardware manufacturers and data and computer scientists to develop his own, proprietary data collection devices and corporate-protected algorithms for mining corporate-controlled proprietary datasets. Since establishing this network, Barnes has described Farmers Edge as a "leader in *independent* data management" (Farmers Edge 2015, emphasis mine). The company boasts of its prowess in centralizing data, ostensibly motivated not only by a desire for reliable and dependable data but also by a pursuit of accuracy. Farmers Edge collects those data which the company's engineers, agronomists, and data scientists believe necessary for uncovering information most useful for particular farms, installing company weather stations on those farms themselves. These in-house scientists work to aggregate data collected across Farmers Edge consumer weather stations and also from Farmers Edge brand "telematic devices" or plug-in sensors installed on farm machinery. Finally, the company also collects remote environmental data from a private constellation of satellites (via a partnership with Planet Labs). "Today," Wade says, "we are in the business of *decision* ag … Right now in precision agriculture there are lots of people collecting data but fewer people using that data to make smart decisions on the farm."

While spokespeople for decision support tools like Wade Barnes attribute their commercial advantage and success to fully privatized data collection, storage, and in-house data expertise, the reality involves a more complex relationship between private and public, especially in relation to remotely collected environmental data. Anthony, an analytics officer in the Government of Canada who conducts environmental and crop mapping, described this relationship and its implications at length to me over coffee one day outside of an agricultural field research station in Ottawa, Canada's capital city. While we sipped hot coffee under the hot sun at a picnic table from which a distant cow could be heard mooing, Anthony told me that a primary characteristic of this relationship is that public and private entities share innovation unequally. He explained that while public institutions contribute a great deal of data and innovation to private enterprises, those enterprises often bar them from accessing certain advantages that private data offer, such as higher resolution data. Anthony described how scientists like himself, working in public contexts, face prohibitive costs that prevent them from accessing and using such data. At the same time, he also pointed out that public sector research and innovation is essential for private industry research and development – for example, the National Aeronautics and Space Administration (NASA) and US Geological Survey data repositories, and contemporary data sets, such as the maps he creates and openly publishes. Public remote sensing infrastructures, whose data generation capabilities have led to data archives at the exabyte (i.e., 1018 bytes) levels and beyond, have furthermore resulted in driving the public sector to invest into large data systems in order to serve a wide scientific community. These systems, while good at disseminating data, still require extensive and complex knowledge of a variety of satellites and sensors, file formats, meta data standards, and much more (Blumenfeld 2019). Not everyone has the expertise to gain benefits from these systems though many corporations – especially those data strategists with in-house agricultural science and data science expertise – are in a position to gain. While the datasets Anthony himself has created are publicly available, he was also aware of the structural biases and inequities surrounding their use, stating, "These maps … they're interesting and people will use them and they get distributed around, but if you really want to use [our data] for something neat and something meaningful, then you have to take the data and you have to use the data, download the data, and have the experience and software to do something with it. We know that industry is using these maps and data."

The Black Boxing of Commercial Digital Agriculture

The industry Anthony was discussing is largely composed of companies like Farmers Edge or even larger and more powerful ones like Bayer/Monsanto, and though we know broadly what types of data these companies collect, we cannot see how the corporation brings together, structures, and ultimately uses the data. Said differently, the datasets and computer programming behind the decision support platforms are a pernicious black box: full of assumptions that cannot be questioned or challenged by farmers or outside researchers like

Anthony and myself because none of us is privy to the data or the code. Early patent law on algorithms and digital property promoted the opening of this box via the concept of "transparency," which was leveraged by lawyers to condition intellectual property protection on publicly inspectable written descriptions of claims (Fromer 2009). Patent law requires an inventor to "disclose his invention to the public so that science can progress by building on divulged knowledge" (Fromer 2009, 539). Over time, however, the system has shifted away from transparency as a legitimation strategy, toward trade secrecy law, which allows copyright protection over the original selection and arrangement of databases, and permits companies to recover damages from anyone (e.g., a rogue employee) who discloses confidential data or code (Pasquale 2015). Corporations (and lawyers) justify these data control practices not primarily as trade secrecy but largely as part of their attempt to protect consumer data security from nefarious actors, such as hackers and terrorists (Pozen 2010). In conversations I had with these scientists, they frequently conflated commercial rationales for trade secrecy with consumer data security, what Frank Pasquale (2010) might call a kind of "security via obscurity" discourse. Corporate scientists believe that if data are tightly controlled, they can best protect farmer privacy. Ren with Microsoft told me that the corporation's data scientists take data management very seriously because, he said, "we want to make sure the data gets in the right hands." I should have but failed to ask him, "Whose hands are the right hands, exactly?"

While the centralization of data systems theoretically answers questions about the reliability and security of data, it at once reduces the end user's range of options. For instance, my close reading of license and use agreements surrounding decision platforms suggests that corporate-restricted data access currently prevents the farmers who provide the data (via their machinery, for example) from easily accessing them. Farm organizations and activist groups have made this lack of data access among farmers a fairly prominent issue. The United Nations group, Global Open Data for Agriculture and Nutrition (GODAN), funded a 2016 study to review public documentation like press releases and websites (i.e., not datasets or algorithms) for indications of how food system actors were (or were not) exchanging data and what power imbalances might exist between these actors. They found that agricultural data were predominantly shared through the publication of findings, such as the final report from an agricultural research project in academic journals whose editors encourage the opening of public research data, or through licenses, as happens through open data portals. But data shared through partnerships between farmers and corporations – governed by consent and use agreements – are largely shared only in one direction, from farmer to corporate parties or with individual farmer clients. The study states, "Despite the fact that a significant amount of existing agricultural data concerns the farmer, very little data flows to them. This issue is magnified where data about smallholder farmers is concerned … Is there a level of responsibility to share a certain amount of usable data with the farmer whose data is being collected?" (Kaminski-Killiany and Walker 2016, n.p.).

Arguably, and paradoxically, companies like Bayer/Monsanto have used privacy agreements as one tool to secure trust with farmers about the usage and potential misusage of their personal data (Newman 2017, see the so-called Monsanto Privacy Model), and to some extent large agribusinesses have engaged with their farmer clients in the building of these legal devices (though they have not engaged with farmers in the global South, even though global satellite systems collect a great deal of commercially relevant data from these environments). These engagements have been mostly uncontroversial. Compared with intellectual property around genetically modified seed systems, for example, lack of access to agricultural data, lack of transparency about its use and lack of regulation governing corporate behaviour vis-à-vis farm data has been a non-issue. In Canada, data collected via digital agricultural equipment appears to conform to the information privacy definition of personal data as that wherein it is reasonably possible for an individual to be identified through its use alone or in combination with other available information (Osler, Hoskin, and Harcourt 2018, 55), yet agricultural data is not accounted for under any of the existing legal statutes. This gap, however, only presents as a constraint if one mistrusts the corporations enough to care. In the conversations I had with farmers using corporate data decision platforms, most primarily identify as corporations themselves and share in the ethos that sees farmers as businesspeople eager to cut down on the presentational overhead and presumed cognitive work (not to mention digital skill set) required to engage with data directly. Most were happy to receive conveniently delivered algorithmic advice via the corporate platforms and indeed saw this ease and relief from labour, including the intellectual kind, as what they were paying for. A small handful of these farmers expressed interest in greater corporate transparency, though many of them conflated corporate and government ("big brother") access to data and the "intimate details of the farm" via data collection.[1] One farmer expressed his fear that "if all of these advisers have all of this information collected, and they share it amongst themselves, they'll have much more information than the farmers have and it could greatly influence marketing and just how farmers are sold on various inputs, you know?" But even those farmers voicing some hesitance were at once uninterested in gaining access to unprocessed data, even to peek behind the corporate-protected algorithms used to generate advice. This was also the assessment of Phil, a Government of Canada data scientist who estimated that farmer interest in "raw" data is low, claiming, "Farmers don't give a crap about our operational monitoring here. They want their auto-steers to work, they want the GPS systems to work, they want the services that maybe they subscribe to to [*sic*] give them the best advice and information on, 'Hey it's shaping up to be a real dry summer, how should I deal with this?'"

Good Farms Get Big and Grow Corn

Even without access to code or the datasets informing commercial decision support systems, one can still analyze what is happening at their surface, using what Ian Bogost (2015) calls the "procedural rhetoric" or the implicit or explicit argument made by a computer model or algorithmic decision.[2] One of the most dominant surface-level politics of agricultural big data and the associated computer programs is their bias toward large farms. Within the immaculate conception of data framework, analytics is a job that algorithms do. Algorithms, particularly the "self-learning" kind, parse large datasets, identify patterns, and infer meaning. But algorithms only embed human choices about what is worth measuring in the first place, as well as the selection of data that will be used by these "intelligent machines." The computer scientists and engineers who design the algorithms and build the datasets define the range and content of categories that are of relevance and thus create limits and affordances according to these choices. As Cheney-Lippold (2011) puts it in relation to gender-sorting algorithms, "Algorithms learn and change what patterns constitute manliness, but they do not change the fact that they are looking to distinguish men from women." In other words, humans build a binary model of gender into this example-sorting machine.

Similarly, company scientists design commercial tools like Bayer/Monsanto's Climate FieldView and Farmers Edge FarmCommand to include data only on a small selection of major agronomic commodity crops, those grown on large farms. Because of their low per-unit value, agronomic crops, such as corn, canola, or soy, for example, are typically planted over thousands of acres. More "minor" crops, including field crops, vegetables, and fruits (e.g., apple, tomato, and peppers), are typically planted on much smaller acreages (in the hundreds) and in areas where farmers have more direct access to markets (e.g., greenbelts surrounding cities). For a host of reasons, including cost of land and environmental variation, there is a significant fragmentation across North America in land acreage managed per farm and, subsequently, there are large disparities in the market for agricultural machinery. Prairie farms are large, with 26 per cent cultivating more than 3,525 acres on average in Canada (Statistics Canada 2016). The average farm in Saskatchewan, Canada, for example, is 1,700 acres, versus 261 acres in the eastern Canadian province of Nova Scotia (Statistics Canada 2016). Again because of the lower per-unit value of commodity crops, larger farm size does not directly correlate to higher income earnings for many prairie farms. Indeed, 57 per cent (or 70,245) of Canadian farms report an annual farm operator income under CA$49,000 (Statistics Canada 2016), though these farms require expensive machinery and in general their operators have more access to capital (and thus debt) for technological investment than smaller farms. Additionally, large acreage production systems thrive on the scale and scope of the kind of efficiencies that large tractors with data collection sensors can offer. Paradoxically, as farms in North America have grown progressively larger over the last seventy-five years, labour has become increasingly scarce and many farmers have gone out of business, one cause of the labour supply problem that has overall made larger equipment a solution to completing farm operations. As farms get bigger and fewer, so too do tractors get bigger in both size and horsepower. Ninety-foot-long seeders and sprayers are not uncommon on North American prairie farms, and such equipment can easily have a 400-horsepower engine. Companies have designed precision agriculture tractors that collect data and big data decision systems with these large, commodity crop and capital-intensive farms in mind.

The farm scale and industrial bias of FarmCommand is obvious from the visualization and mapping features of this particular platform. The maps accessible to farmers (who pay for these maps) are meaningful only if one adheres to a rigid conventional farming strategy of seeding in neat rows separated by areas of soil "cleaned" of weeds. The "crop health maps" generated via the private satellites of Farmers Edge display "variability" in growth measured as a general impression of plant density. Said differently, the maps use colour to give the farmer a gestalt view of their yield, where colour indicates areas that might require attention (increased fertilizer, for example) in order to increase the density of growth. Such environmental mapping will fail to advise an organic farmer, for instance, whose seedlings may be surrounded by plastic or mulch weed cover. Additionally, the commercial systems like FarmCommand or Climate FieldView give a kind of overview of farm machinery, labour, and crops which is only useful if your farm is so big that you cannot manage this oversight on your own (or with a few other farm workers) through direct relations with the machines, animals, and plants that populate your farm. Said differently, the commercial platforms are only worth the capital investment if you have multiple machines and a suite of hired workers you do not oversee directly, which is the case on many large farms where temporary foreign workers currently make up a significant portion of agricultural labour in North America.

That commercial agricultural big data and decision platforms are biased toward large industrial farms mostly located in the Midwest of North America is on some level inevitable, given the political economy of agricultural technology. Alvin, who was working for Bayer/Monsanto, explained to me that large-scale operators are the company's "bread and butter." Edna, an engineer who was also working for one of the world's largest agribusinesses, said that the corporation just could not cater to the smaller, diverse farmers, because "you would have to look at how many small farmers have to work full time to pay for farming … How could the corporation produce these for smaller farmers who have no money to pay for the technology?" But, she continued, her corporation was supporting the "modernization of conventional agriculture," explaining, "We want to showcase modern conventional agriculture, and this includes the reasonable usage of pesticides and GMOs and technology to make better decisions, to be more efficient … It's about not putting more fertilizers in a certain area without needing to. In some cases, the software can help you calculate which areas of your field are not profitable at all ... It's more efficient."

Additional biases related to crop type and the farmers who grow them emerge by looking at the patent applications for specific machine learning used in the decision support tools. N-Manager is an analytics tool within FarmCommand, described in the patent application as a machine learning innovation that is able to "analyze" different environmental conditions and management practices in order to provide nitrogen application recommendations to farmers. The basic premise is that data-driven machine learning can optimize fertilizer use to increase yield and reduce chemical waste and by-products. An obvious bias in this application is that it only works for those farms using chemical inputs (i.e., not organics), though the stated intent behind the development of N-Manager is to help these farmers reduce such inputs. Another obvious bias is that farmers can only follow the advice of the analytics tool if they use variable rates of nitrogen within a field, and this requires extremely expensive "variable rate" equipment, which only a minority of farmers can afford. This lack of affordability affects farmers and researchers working outside of industry. But there are other biases that appear in looking at the specifics of the modelling used for N-Manager. Machine learning in every instance encompasses a number of models that are implemented in the code in different ways, including neural networks, decision trees, and logistic regression. The choice of model depends upon the domain, computational resources and other technical and values-based concerns. As outlined in the US patent application, N-Manager relies on public crop models, such as DSSAT. DSSAT is a public crop modelling platform that allows growers to input information relating to weather, soil, genetics, management practices, pests, and so on. The public sector agricultural research community performed the extensive field trials and other experimentation that enabled the development of every crop model within DSSAT. This kind of agronomic science is incredibly costly because it requires, as one scientist put it in an interview, "boots on the ground." Government granting agencies provide the funding to individual research labs to undertake this research. DSSAT handles genotype (genetic makeup) information, and it either explicitly contains experimentally obtained parameters describing a plant species, ecotype, or cultivar or it has methods for performing statistical approximations of a unique cultivar by borrowing analogously from parameters of similar plant models. This is where biases become apparent.

While the DSSAT system has a variety of models for many types of plant species, the available genotype information for each plant species skews towards broadacre commodity crops. Among those crops, the models focus on varietals that serve as feedstock. Corn is by far the most modelled with 170 cultivars, but the list also includes fifty-five cultivars of rice, fifty-four of millet, and fifty-one of soybean. Compare these numbers against crops such as alfalfa (one), bahia (one), bermudagrass (one), greenbean (one), sugarbeet (two), cabbage (two), faba (two), tomato (four), and pepper (five). Completely absent are models for cultivars of fruiting trees (pears, apples, or avocados), leafy greens (kale, arugula), as well as most types of squash. The Farmers Edge N-Manager thus relies on a system with a partial supply of models; moreover, the patent application (and much of the Farmers Edge promotional material) refers specifically to corn or "maize." Said differently, Farmers Edge has chosen to focus their algorithmic design efforts related to the building of N-Manager on one crop, a tiny fraction of which feeds people (and much of that in the form of high-fructose corn syrup). N-Manager is designed for farms growing commodity corn, which are necessarily large acreage and input-intensive operations.

The bias in agricultural big data and analytics toward large commodity crop farms supports a long-standing and ongoing shift in the relationship between capital and labour. Where once agricultural labourers had a degree of control over the means of production, creativity, skill, and the use of tools and the production of agricultural knowledge, their control has eroded as scientists have actively aimed to displace agricultural labourers with putatively "autonomous" decision-making, like that conducted by N-Manager. Others have written about this problem of increased "alienation" via technological change and privatization of farm technologies, from the seed drill to GMOs (see Kloppenburg 1988). But the current digital bias compounds the social issues raised vis-à-vis Marxist alienation, where the development of smart farming technologies do not, for example, account for the agricultural workers' tremendous, experientially derived knowledge of diverse farm environments and horticultural varieties. Indeed, proponents of smart farming boast that automated decision systems no longer require the brains or presence of labourers. But the farm labourer now not only becomes a "machine minder," they also help to grow datasets without commensurate gain as information gets transferred away from labour and into capital (Harvey 2020). Data bias is thus wrapped up in a larger shift where knowledge, capacity, and skill move from labour to fixed capital external to labour, and this is the entry for science and technology into the production process. Of course, this strategy works better for some food system players – notably historically powerful agribusinesses and relatively powerful farmers – than others (Fine 1994; Goodman and Redclift 1994).

We see through the above examples that while we might borrow from the insights developed by critical data studies analyses of big data and AI in other sectors like social media, there are likely interesting and unique aspects specific to agriculture. Farmers Edge has designed its N-Manager tool to improve upon the task of making fertilizer predictions by drawing on big datasets, but agricultural data are not like other kinds of data. Unlike the "digital breadcrumbs" (Zuboff 2019) easily collected from people's online behaviour, agricultural data are sparse and difficult to collect. Also, research and experimentation related to genotype, environment, and management (GEM) has historically guided agricultural decision-making. Even a superficial reflection on the GEM relationship makes it obvious why agriculture may pose a unique set of circumstances to the machine learning and big data science communities: there are hundreds, if not thousands, of agriculturally relevant crops, and potentially hundreds of cultivars and varieties of each crop. Moreover, there is an enormous range of environmental conditions and management practices within which these crops can be contextualized. The amount of high-quality data necessary for machine learning algorithms to learn and produce high quality (e.g., accurate) decision support models for each and every specific crop is enormous. Given this complicated reality, it becomes obvious that any progress in these methods will come from prioritizing very specific crops under very specific management practices in very specific conditions. Unlike the story of the immaculate conception of data, these are human decisions. I met scientists aiming to diversify and make plant modelling more robust, like Megan, a public sector computer scientist working at a land grant institution in the US. She wanted to design digital tools for organic farms and told me about her work using digital sensors and imaging software in order to develop a greater variety of plant models and more in-depth information on field performance in diverse environments. This work, however, was limited by a lack of access to sophisticated computing:

> The whole system of, like, the varietal descriptions right now are based off of like a not very deep understanding … right now the only standard for what you're told about the variety is the germination percentage which doesn't really tell you very much about how that seed will perform in the field. So, that's why I'm using that imaging software. There is much more well-developed imaging software that's available but I don't have that available to me. So, I'm trying to use that with [the] kind of limited amount of technology I have.

Another recent patent application by Farmers Edge underscores the influence of the human designer's perspective on the production of machine learning tools. The application outlines a strategy that involves using near-infrared spectroscopy and machine learning algorithms to quickly and inexpensively make soil texture predictions. Quantification of soil texture, which classifies the types of particles and their relative material composition (clay, sand, silt) in a given sample, is an incredibly useful way to characterize the suitability of soil for growing certain types of crops. In fact, soil-related measurements are an important input to crop modelling. All farmers test soil, though private enterprises, accredited by provincial ministries, have historically conducted the tests in Canada (e.g., OMAFRA 2016). Farmers interested in testing their soil for moisture, organic, and non-organic compounds must send samples by mail to accredited facilities. Even the university laboratories (at University of Guelph and Dalhousie University) are public only in the sense that they are housed within publicly owned and managed infrastructure, and these labs prioritize tests for public bodies such as the Canadian Food Inspection Agency over the commercial testing. Viewing this existing system as inexpedient, Farmers Edge executives decided to build their own soil testing infrastructure, which includes this machine learning. Key here is that the machine learning algorithm requires data to learn from, and while data collection is always a selection process, this is arguably even more so with soil data. Soil texture differs not just globally but also within the same local environment, and collecting enough variety in soil data to generate a complete or comprehensive "training" dataset for machine learning is infeasible. The patent application does not explicitly state how the company collected the data. However, it does specifically mention a dataset collected using samples from "the Canadian prairies."

Therefore, looking at the types of data the commercial decision platforms collect and the models that these data "feed" into reveals that, like pre-digital agricultural technologies – from Jethro Tull's seed drill to GMOs – these tools actually reproduce the bifurcation of food production practices between large-scale commodity (or "conventional") production and other "unconventional" strategies. Antle, Jones, and Rosenzweig (2017) write that this bias actually inhibits innovation in data science and non-industrial agricultural innovation at once, where "many advances in data, information and communication technology of the past decade have not been fully exploited … [because of the] underinvestment in agricultural research, particularly in non-proprietary public good research, and in research aiming to improve the well-being of poor, smallholder farm households in the developing world." At the same time as commercial databases and decision support systems reproduce historic patterns of variation in food production by favouring some farmers over others, their developers use ICD to pitch these tools as universally liberating; Wade Barnes, for example, has described the value of his company's platform as using "the power of big data analytics and machine learning to implement these strategies to make huge changes to anyone's farm. These tools can be used anywhere wherever you are."

Similar to soil texture machine learning, where both the dataset and the machine programmed to use it skew toward farms operating within a narrow range of soil conditions, Bayer/Monsanto's application Weed ID operates within a narrow environmental range. Bayer/Monsanto's Climate FieldView platform offers this tool for collecting and making sense of weed data. It uses machine learning from crowdsourced (or farmer-sourced) data to identify weeds and map weed pressures. The user interface is a digital mapping tool via a smartphone application. I had a conversation about farming apps with a group of fruit growers from the Canadian Atlantic provinces of New Brunswick and Nova Scotia. All of these farmers were in their thirties and forties, were on the edge of generational farm transition, and were gaining legal title over their farms before feeling a real sense of ownership over it or confidence in their decision-making. They said they found digital apps very helpful because in the digital terrain (reddit versus a local coffee shop) these young farmers could engage with one another outside of the judgment of established producers with years of experiential knowledge but less facility and comfort with digital tools. I asked these growers about common weed identification apps and they pointed out something I had not considered: most are designed in the US and with "training databases" originally over-selected for weed varieties common to the American Midwest. While apps theoretically hold the potential to change over time and use, the machine "learns" from data crowdsourced by users logging novel weed varieties, and given the current dominant user base, the system receives relatively minimal feedback data from growers in Atlantic Canada. The systems are skewed, but developers appear to remain unaware of or unable to seek redress for their work's omissions. Like DSSAT and N-Manager many apps seem to point toward a digital future where power is further concentrated in the hands of those large and capital-intensive farms who are already relatively powerful.

The Reproduction of Corporate Power

While the values and economic interests informing the production of agricultural big data and decision support platforms have implications for equity among farmers, they represent a further and arguably more egregious ethical breach; like genetically modified organisms (see Bronson 2015), the commercial digital agricultural offerings from industry are designed to benefit corporations and their goal of private gain incommensurately compared to the technology user. The soil texture device designed by Farmers Edge continues to draw on soil samples collected via "crowdsourcing" farmers, even as those same farmers pay for and use the machine learning. Because machine learning is as good as the data that ostensibly "teach" it, Farmers Edge continuously improves the algorithm over which it has intellectual property as it grows its soil database. Undeniably, benefits from this improvement accrue to the farmers because the predictive analytics that farmers use get better the more data are collected. A historically common way of sampling soil was for farmers to conduct a "spot sample,"[3] taking soil from sections of the farm, shipping them to soil testing facilities, and then using the resulting data the next year with models that help make predictions. This sampling is labour intensive and necessarily retroactive, whereas Farmers Edge promises that its soil detection AI will be nearer "real time" and predictive. Despite this advantage for the individual farmer, there is, as the saying goes, power in numbers. There are arguably large commercial gains for the corporation that might use the aggregated dataset for a variety of purposes or more likely sell it to other companies. Sandvig et al. (2014) suggest that corporations who develop intelligent machines always have an eye toward their gain and call criticisms of this corporate practice Crandall's complaint, as Robert Crandall once (allegedly) asked, "Why anyone would bother to build and operate an expensive algorithm if they couldn't bias it in their favour?"

The pattern of corporate exploitation of crowdsourced data is also apparent in the example of Weed ID. As we saw in chapter 2, Weed ID may help individual farmers identify weeds but there are likely considerable benefits to Farmers Edge, namely the identification of new chemical needs and therefore new areas of possible investment in research and development. Other benefits to the corporation are related to the fundamental link between big data and machine learning. If the method for quantifying soil texture is sound and the data collected by its use are of reasonable quality, then as data is accumulated the value of the corporate offering increases and the ability of Farmers Edge to dominate sections of the market improves. As we already know, those who start collecting quality data early have an advantage over other offerings in the market. Companies like Google and Amazon, who have been in the business of collecting personal data for more than a decade, are at the forefront of AI development. We know from experience and analysis of other sectors that societal institutions – both public and private – rely increasingly on personal data as means to achieving competitive advantage (Zuboff 2019). We also know that private firms hold huge amounts of personal data, then aggregate them, anonymize them, and sell them for enormous amounts of money (Ghosh and Scott 2018). These firms also use datasets to create spin-off analytics devices: new products and services that were not visible to the farmer who consented to data collection. Over time, these products and services generate even more data, which, in turn, further perpetuates any given firm's market power. We know from other technology companies that this cycle can lead to an incredible amount of market concentration and power in single corporations, which, according to most analysts, is inherently problematic. So, while the immaculate conception of data allows actors to propose their "data-driven" practices as value-free and superior, corporate design decisions – about which data to collect, how to manage them, what information is gleaned from them and for whom – channel technical activities into lucrative economic opportunities for corporations.

Political economists of the agri-food sector have written about the effects of corporate concentration and unequal market power (between corporations and other food system players) for years (Clapp 2012), though to date there has been little exploration of the role that big data and other emergent digital tools play in this concentration (c.f. Duncan et al. 2022; Clapp and Ruder 2021; Fairbairn 2020; Ouma 2020). We know from experience that the market concentration of chemicals and seed companies (see Howard 2016) has given these companies enough clout to operate as near-monopoly corporations who are able to wield tremendous power along the food chain. For instance, input supply companies like Bayer/Monsanto, who supply farmers with seeds and chemicals, have for years used price discrimination, selectively marketing some goods at higher prices for those demographics or particular geographic locations which are seen to depend on them (Valentino-Devries, Singer-Vine, and Soltani 2012). We can infer that corporations who sell chemicals could use data to predict chemical need – for example, about weed or pest pressures on a particular farming region – following in the same pattern of price discrimination. And corporations are likely to use data and proprietary data systems as a currency with farmers, as a means to further solidify a farmer's commitment to their particular platform. Bayer/Monsanto, for example, administers "data-driven" advice putatively derived from its proprietary and "field-tested" algorithms through an "exclusive" corporate-certified dealer network. Initially, farmers who were interested in using Bayer/Monsanto's platform were required to buy in with a minimum of three years of raw corn/soybean yield data (with an average yield of 120 bushels per acre or greater). This was an eligibility requirement for meeting with their nearest dealer, who would guide the farmer through the use of the digital tools and ultimately deliver a "prescription." The prescription consists of recommendations that purportedly match the conditions of a farmer's field to one of Bayer/Monsanto's seeds and proprietary chemicals – products bought as part and parcel of this "prescription," also through the seed dealer. This advice is of course helpful for individual farmers, but what is the line between helpful offerings and consumer manipulation? Use of this digital system tethers farmers to this particular corporation and the tools it sells, a situation very similar to the technological politics of GMO seed systems, which were by design only functional with certain chemicals supplied by agri-chemical corporations growing enormously powerful through their use (Bronson 2015). At a trade show, I bumped shoulders with a group of farm consultants and advisers, and when I asked them if they had any reservations about the collection and use of farmer data by agribusiness, one said to the group,

> I am not sure whether you saw the Canadian Standing Committee report on privacy issues around big data? I gotta tell you … whether it's gonna play out or not, farmers ought to have reservations about their data being collected … companies like the John Deeres are leveraging the data back to farmers by saying the machinery is better … and yes, it probably is, but that's a service a farmer pays for … and so why would I accept that you're selling that to someone else to make money without a portion coming back to me as a farmer?

To assess the likely role of digital technologies in reproducing corporate gain, we can look at our history with agricultural tools, but we can also learn from our more recent history of big data collection and use in other sectors like social media, despite some difference between farm data and other personal data, for example the vast number of environmental variables that a model must incorporate for the agricultural context. We now know that Facebook does not merely (or even primarily) connect us, but they capitalize upon big data as an asset, harvesting our personal experiences or our "behavioural surplus." This surplus exists in the totality of information about our every online action, which is traded for profit in new markets that predict and then shape and direct our needs and desires. Shoshanna Zuboff (2019) splits this use of personal data for predictive marketing from industrial capitalism, giving it the name of surveillance capitalism. The social scientist Isabell Carbonell (2016) has written about the potential that agribusinesses such as Bayer/Monsanto or John Deere will make similar interventions using the farm-level data they now routinely harvest via precision agricultural equipment, for example. Those companies who gain access to these data are "able to construct an unprecedented predictive business model over each aspect of farming" (1). "Big data," she writes, "are very big business" (2).

In response to potential resistance among farmers/consumers, some peripheral industries have developed around the novel social issues raised by digital agriculture, turning ethical snags into market opportunities. In 2014, the American Farm Bureau Federation (AFBF), observing some hesitance among farmer members about technology providers using data for their own gain, convened a number of agricultural organizations (e.g., National Farmers Union) and industry members in roundtable conversations on the topic of data privacy. These conversations resulted in a set of principles for farm data use and a non-profit organization that certifies companies based upon their adherence to these principles. The organization, Ag Data Transparent (ADT), accredits companies using an "audit" of data contracts (see Ag Data Transparent 2020). I spoke with a few farmers who considered this non-profit certification trustworthy, including Bill, a middle-aged grain farmer from the Canadian Prairies who was using ADT certification. Bill's understanding was that the company was rigorously "investigating" data use practices of corporations. Though a lifetime farmer, Bill considered himself a bit of an information technology expert, and he told me,

> If it's true that you're not monetizing or selling my data, then sign up as a company and get certified. The companies have to go through a rigorous investigation process and John Deere just signed up … this tells me that they're meeting something. When I talk to Farmers Business Network that's moving into Canada with a storm, I ask them, "Are you certified?" They say no, because they don't sell my data. But I don't trust you. I know IT and I'm not going to accept your word. And ADT has a list of the companies to sign up and, you know, John Deere was the first big company.

Similarly, in Canada, the province of Ontario is supporting the development of AgBox – an online tool developed through a partnership among Ontario Agri-Food Technologies, Farm Credit Canada, and several corporate entities – which purports to allow farmers to decide how much data to share and for what purposes.

Arguably one of the biggest businesses that stands to gain from the use of big agricultural data and predictive analytics is the insurance industry, which could likely use the visibility on farm environments as an informatic advantage to allocate punishments and rewards and to literally bank on farmer misfortune. We know from other sectors that powerful institutions use big data and analytics to perform a kind of "social ranking" in ways that reproduce disadvantage. For example, the methods internet service providers use to filter spam and consumer credit scoring reproduce discrimination in the allocation of loans (Eubanks 2018; Lyon 2003). In the context of agriculture, no such discrimination has yet come to light but it is possible. We know that re-insurance companies benefit when farmers experience losses and putatively "data-driven" predictions could give these companies the ability to more accurately invest in loss. Farmers Edge executives boasted to me about their "strategic alliances" with insurance companies throughout North and South America. Jim, who works for an international information technology corporation, told me "one of the biggest values to ag data, if you look at the industry as a whole, is re-insurance." Speaking quickly, Jim told me that "if you look at the Farmers Edge of the world – they're the world's largest satellite shot purchaser and continue to gather data, and they spin off companies left, right and centre, and they work with re-insurance companies like Lloyds of London and Ag Swiss." Jim said that he used to work for an insurance crown corporation, and he had contact with re-insurance brokers in that job. He described the process of re-insurance for me, explaining, "They buy blocks of loss coverage to protect themselves from losses … this is significant. In Canada ag insurance is a big deal partly because it's subsidized to the tune of sixty to seventy per cent depending on the province … so these big re-insurance companies are significant because if they are buying a block of loss to the tune of one hundred million dollars, then big data is significant to them."

In the era of big agricultural data, these insurance firms can look not only to historical weather data and a farmer's history – say, the average bushel growth for wheat in the region where they live – they can also use machine learning to predict the likelihood of losses in near real time, using the information not only to validate investments but to drive them into the future. "And," Jim added for emphasis, "these companies are powerful and not public and they are connected to other powerful companies. You look at Global Ag Risk and they're all backed by re-insurance companies." IBM, for example, advertises its intelligence machine, Watson, as participating in this predictive re-insurance. One online advertisement for the Swiss Re Group (IBM n.d.) reads, "Reinsurance and insurance companies will price their products better. Watson reads millions of pages of data, including unstructured data like discussion notes, contracts or tickets to help Swiss Re assess risk factors and make more informed decisions regarding price-risk accuracy. This helps Swiss Re reduce costs while increasing quality."

Some governments are trying to crack down on the escalation of concentration via digitization and the power of "big tech," using claims of unlawful monopoly and anti-trust action as leverage to gain a modicum of governance control over powerful corporations. In other words, as corporations use privacy legislation to close their hands around personal data, some governance actors are using anti-trust legislation to force them back open. Two can play at this game of using legal tools. Take as example the General Data Protection Regulation (GDPR), advanced largely due to the leadership of Margrethe Vestager, the commissioner of competition with the European Commission. The GDPR is a data strategy that sets clear rules on access and re-use of data, protects personal data, accommodates the mixing of public, personal, and proprietary data, and facilitates innovation by academic, business, and governmental sectors. Vestager said in an interview that anti-trust law was the "right tool" she had at her disposal to induce responsible behaviour among corporations (Recode Staff 2017). Corporate lawyers have pointed out that US financial regulators already have legal tools to reform data markets. For instance, the Securities and Exchange Commission (US SEC 2021) already requires that firms report on what they are doing with data in terms of preventing cyber-threats, noting that "cybersecurity is the responsibility of every market participant." Lawyers have also argued that the SEC could mandate transparency for all publicly traded companies, requiring them to disclose how they acquire and use personal data and divulge which firms they sell these data to. Thus far, however, legislators have paid no specific attention to agribusinesses trading in big data, perhaps in part because they continue to perceive these companies as input suppliers rather than data businesses. And yet agribusinesses are some of the longest-standing oligopoly corporations in North America, and they are increasingly centring their business strategies on the collection and processing of data.

Indeed, the centralization of corporate data collection and management can be thought of as a manifestation of historic patterns of consolidation among agribusinesses. Agricultural tools are no stranger to this socio-technical feedback; standardizing the environment by turning to mono-cropping – or intensively cropping one crop exclusively – was historically necessary for the operation of large agricultural machinery. Standardization was thus as much as precondition as a product or outcome of industrial farming. In today's case, pre-existing consolidation and collusion among agribusinesses enables a level of collusion among the companies (e.g., data transfer between machinery and seeds and chemicals companies), engendering streamlined and standardized data systems that are unique to specific firms (i.e., not interoperable), and which justify demands for tight data control. Said differently: the companies who appear to compete against one another with specific data collection and decision systems that farmers license are in fact sharing data behind the scenes.

What is at Stake for Food Justice?

We can look beyond legal compliance to the broader social justice implications of the dominance of powerful agribusinesses in the collection and use of agricultural big data. While legislators have proposed but not yet realized antitrust legislation for the agri-food sector, algorithmic manipulation may be societally problematic far beyond the ways in which corporate practices fail to comply with the law. This is a significant observation for critical data studies exceeding the agricultural sector: we can push beyond scholarship and public attention that has considered algorithmic discrimination from the perspective of law and regulation to take an ecumenical moral justice perspective. As media scholar danah boyd asks in an interview with *Protocol*, "How does a company have values beyond profit for shareholders? Many of the folks on the outside aren't even talking about trade-offs and values. They want justice. Ethics tends to encompass all of this … from the world of legal risk, all the way to justice. As a result, the people on the outside are not at all satisfied by the ideas we're going to get from compliance … We're going to have such contested challenges around this because we don't know how to articulate values within this form of capitalism" (Kinstler 2020).

Considering the broader politics of digital agricultural technologies, or the way they are currently configured, highlights environmental justice concerns; with corporations now controlling the bulk of agricultural big datasets and leading the realization of the dominant vision of farm 4.0 (represented in chapter 2), historic patterns of injustice are likely to be reproduced with implications for society, the non-human environment and everyday lives. For one, a corporate-led food system transition – the so-called digitization of agriculture – is likely to go the same way that historic corporate-led agricultural transitions have gone, from early industrialization to the green revolution to the so-called biotechnology revolution. Since agriculture became an economic sector and "industrialized," it has incorporated automation of labour in search of consistency – a necessity when the goal is mass production – and control over natural (including human) factors in order to reduce cost (Friedmann and McMichael 1989). While the application of technology to food production has led to certain efficiencies and contributed to yield increases, it has also led to soil compaction and reduced soil function (Shah et al. 2017), soil and ground water contamination (from pesticides and herbicides) and biodiversity loss in large part due to targeted breeding (Benton et al. 2021; UNFAO 2019).[4] Industrialized farms currently contribute up to 30 per cent of all anthropogenic greenhouse emissions (counting on-farm and off-farm emissions, like for the transport of commodities) (De Schutter 2015; Friedmann 2005; Lang and Heasman 2015). Moreover, the high cost of large machinery requires large investments, creating debt and path dependency on intensive production methods, technologies, and the corporations who supply agricultural technologies. This process has led to an erosion of the socioeconomic systems in agricultural and rural areas across North America. With consolidated corporations like Bayer/Monsanto colluding with machinery companies like John Deere in the transfer and use of agricultural big data, the digital agricultural landscape is arguably even more concentrated; the division of power between agribusinesses, on whom most farmers depend, and farmers is even more uneven than in the past, and the environmental and social consequences of this inequity are thus likely also reproduced. Amidst the promise that digitization leads inexorably to sustainability, applications of digital tools may raise their own sustainability challenges (see Galaz et al. 2021).

Another example of a broader social justice concern arising from the current politics of agricultural big data is an asymmetry in who is gaining knowledge about which types of farm and broader ecosystems. Agricultural big data are being used to "drive" insights relevant to individual farms, but farm-level and other environmental data collected for the narrow purpose of farm management will also influence our ability to monitor into and intervene into environmental changes like human-induced climate change. The United Nations

Environment Programme (UNEP), aware of this ongoing transformation, is calling for the creation of a "digital ecosystem for our planet" which they define as "a complex distributed network or interconnected socio-technological system" of environmental data collection and sharing, modelling, and mapping (2019). The UN's proposition is that humanity should be able to "leverage this technology effectively" and consequently "be able to assess and predict risks, increase transparency and accountability in the management of natural resources and inform markets as well as consumer choice" However, currently the UNEP reports that more than 90 per cent of world's data have been generated in the last two years, but these datasets have been created with "no common vision, directed strategy or governance framework." In other words, we are "lacking a planetary dashboard" (Campbell and Jensen 2019, 1). This is related to the fact that these data have been gathered by corporations who, despite cooperating in the sharing of data gathered from farm equipment – are competing intensely with their respective proprietary datasets and decision platforms. Said differently, the lack of coordination and cooperation among those corporate players currently collecting the vast majority of environmental data presents issues at the individual level – lack of interoperability among the platforms – but also at the societal level – lack of coordinated effort to collect broadly-relevant data and a lack of open and transparent datasets. Furthermore, of all the new datasets made in the last two years, UNEP reports that 68 per cent of the ninety-three sustainable development goal indicators cannot yet be measured by these data, as the data collected are not relevant to broad ecosystem concerns or services but rather to a narrow set of profit-motivated interests. We might therefore consider the corporate practices and infrastructures around agricultural big data as a kind of digital colonialism that raises issues for individuals – lack of relevant data access for small-scale agroecological or regenerative farmers, for example – but also issues at the global environmental level (UNEP 2019).

Alternative Politics

Quite unlike the story offered by the immaculate conception of data, we can see how human decisions about agricultural environmental data reflect two distinct ethos, which are then concretized into divergent versions of digital agriculture and the food system. The resulting technologies thus intervene into longstanding contestations over the future of food. One ethos aims for control over farm-level environmental data, offering a reductionist approach to environmental monitoring (e.g., capturing one environmental variable such as chemical leaching) and hierarchization of knowledge (e.g., offering graphic interfaces or application programming interfaces to customers). The other aims for a decentralization of data collection and management (more data from as many farms as possible), offering a holistic approach to environmental monitoring and a flattened knowledge hierarchy.

Scientists working in both public and private contexts on digital agricultural tools may leverage a shared vision of data as immaculate and all powerful (the ICD), but they hold markedly different conceptions of good farming. Corporate and activist scientists differ in their perceptions of the environmental, social, and technical challenges they are addressing in their work. For instance, scientists working at the Famers Edge private soil laboratory are proud of their ability to use a predictive tool to measure discrete variables in a timely way that serves large farms, while activist coders working at Wolfe's Neck farm are instead slowly developing soil sensors to locate a complex set of ill-defined variables that they feel will help them, in the words of Anja, "Trace the trajectory of a community of soil organisms as they move through a web of life."

Data scientists and farmers associated with GOAT and its analogue group, called Farm Hack, have developed a prominent hack, the DIY soil sensor, which measures a host of variables, not unlike the tool that Farmers Edge has patented. Dorn Cox has led its comprehensive implementation at Wolfe's Neck Farm. Michael Stenta described this initiative as a "big collaborative effort indicative of open and collaborative science … We have folks from USDA, EPA and commercial farming and software and hardware developers." Like Wade Barnes at Farmers Edge, Stenta, Cox, and the government soil scientists have scientific concerns about the quality of farm-level environmental data; yet in this case the concern is with the "validity" (in Cox's words) of the data. The remedy for potentially unreliable data is to deploy numerous sensors, pairing the less accessible "expensive commercial" soil sensors alongside their "cheapo soil sensors." Cox told me how this strategy allows for cross-comparing the data in order to arrive at a hopefully faithful measure of the variables. While many of these variables (e.g., pH and moisture) are similar to those variables tested at the Farmers Edge soil laboratory (and most soil laboratories),

Cox described how his team wished to move beyond the "extractive" scientific approach of agribusinesses (he mentioned Monsanto), towards a "systems" and "regenerative" perspective on environmental data, including data on soil systems:

> So, we have millions of years of genetic material that's adapted to create life on Earth pretty much everywhere [laughs]. There's something that grows everywhere, so there's value in that … but where that intersects with the current digital world is that we can now exchange knowledge of complexity and how all those genetic materials express themselves … And that's bacterial as well as plants and animals, too. I mean, we're really looking at that whole range – bacterial/fungal relationship. The whole fungal world is still blowing my mind [laughs] how important it is!

Cox put it succinctly later in the interview: "Agriculture isn't rocket science; it's actually far more complex."

While data scientists working in large agribusinesses are as preoccupied with standardized or "clean" data as they are with "clean" farmers' fields (neat rows free of weeds), data and computer scientists working on the farmOS open-source platform do not place a particularly high value on standardization. Instead, they believe that wide participation in data collection and platform design is morally and epistemically beneficial, leading not only to democratically legitimate(d) but also useful tools, defined as ones that will meet a variety of farm management needs. Thus far, under this approach, a variety of contributors have made the farmOS platform distinct from, for example, Farm Command, even though the general aim is precisely the same for both tools: to use farm-level environmental data collection to make more informed agricultural decisions. Farmers use farmOS to collect data on agricultural behaviour and the platform allows for organization and field mapping (using open satellite and public data, such as US Department of Agriculture soil data). Unlike the commercial platforms, however, farmOS allows for the collection of any type of farm data by any means. For instance, some farmers may weigh their grain yield (bag by bag) on a scale, pencil the results on paper/clipboard, and wait until winter to digitize and upload the data to farmOS (as a KML file). There are almost as many data collection methods currently surrounding farmOS as there are participants. One farmer used a fitness self-tracker to collect

GPS data for recording the locations in the field where they had sprayed. Farmos allows for logging any such "event" within the platform, and it is up to the individual farmer to decide what might be a meaningful event, given their farming practice(s) and management goals. Events can be weather, the application of inputs like chemicals or water, or even the process of weeding by tractor or by hand. Farmers can also log their "assets," and again, it is up to them to decide what constitutes an asset. For those farmers using farmos, assets appear to be animals, plantings (crops), equipment, labourers, compost piles, mushroom or soil substrate, maple stands or groves within a farm field, among others.

The ethos held by corporate scientists enables data practices and digital technologies that leave intact the current dominant, industrial agricultural system, amended slightly for more precise and judicious use of the harmful or scarce inputs that this food production strategy and organization demands (Bronson 2020). Therefore, this ethos preserves the current industrial food "regime" (Friedmann and McMichael 1989) because it serves not only particular food production practices but also the global industry players who are central to these practices (e.g., input suppliers like Bayer/Monsanto). In fact, rather than situating the environmental problems raised by industrial agriculture as part of a wider socio-ecological crisis, instead they are framed by most corporate actors principally as a problem of agro-economics, with farmers and technologies inscribed not as vital nodes in ecosystems so much as instruments of economic production, fungible and less capable than intelligent machines. Precision agriculture as an approach to agriculture does not fundamentally seek to avert or mitigate wider ecological food-system crises but rather to foreground the economic opportunities these crises present for industrial agribusinesses and investors offering commercial technological fixes.

Alternately, the activist data and computer scientists hold an ethos that enables scientific decisions which themselves result in tools for producers who work outside of (or against) this agricultural strategy, such as the cooperative permaculture farmers who convene at GOAT. The alternate ethos also leverages a "development methodology" to create new forms of technological, food, and wider social systems. The activist scientist Anja, who works on farmos, said, "By being able to measure biological *systems* better we can make better decisions about agriculture and society." Similarly, a corporate decision-maker summarized their work, saying, "Precision agriculture can help increase yields, it can help decrease costs, and there's ancillary environmental benefits from that." Jon, a farmer who uses Bayer/Monsanto's Climate FieldView platform, explained, "I could just go out there and slap it [herbicide] on and be happy with it, but I wanted to do the best job I could and not waste a bunch of spray. Now, when you waste spray you overlap and whatnot, it's also potentially a pollution, so you know you don't want to do that ... Just enough to do the job." The clear politics of digital agricultural technologies therefore not only call into question ICD but also confirm the science studies perspective that the context of scientific decision-making affects the decisions made (Kloppenburg 1988; Mirowski 2011; Sismondo 2008).

As it stands now, the value-laden decisions made by humans about agricultural big data and computer programing intervene in the long-standing competition between food regimes, but just like other agricultural technologies, the competition between these two visions for the future of farming is asymmetrical. Commercial scientists are currently better organized and better funded, while the activist groups aiming to leverage big data for sustainable agricultural practices float by on surprisingly little money and almost entirely on volunteer labour. Michael Stenta of farmOS is open about the funding he receives and the collaborations which fuel the platform, largely advanced by Michael – who appears to have done about 98 per cent of the coding – and small research projects with US academics.[5] On the other hand, there is a significant promotion engine behind the realization of a productivist farm 4.0: glossy advertising, enormous trade shows, and academic and accrediting associations like the ASABE (American Society of Agricultural and Biological Engineers). Of those trade shows I attended, and in almost all of my conversations with farmers, it was clear that agricultural engineers' associations are powerful sites for the acceptance of novel technologies. Bayer associate Edna told me that it was only because of a paper critiquing the copyright structure around precision tractors, which got a lot of attention at the 2018 American Society of Agricultural and Biological Engineers conference, that John Deere relaxed its "digital lock" the subsequent year. In fact, the trade shows and professional associations complicate the neat picture describing two models of digital agriculture divided by private versus public contexts, where instead the boundary between public and private is porous. For example, if farmOS is explicitly built on open source code, the commercial platforms like Climate FieldView are similarly built on generations of computer science labour and software, much of it coming from the public sector. As one farmOS activist put it to me, "There is not much that the big platforms are doing that doesn't already exist in the public realm … they [Bayer/Monsanto] just stitch it together in a way that makes it useful to farmers and they have the resources to do that. And they have more data from farmers."

Take as a more fulsome illustration of this interplay between public and private a prominent artificial intelligence conference, CVPR 2020, attended by industry and public sector AI scientists alike. According to the conference website, it is "the premier annual computer vision event." Problems related to agriculture have gradually come to the attention of the broader artificial intelligence community, for whom data is a critical component for making any scientific progress; as such, control over these datasets is very important and any biases in public research datasets will shape the direction of research. Often, datasets that are otherwise closed are made public at AI conferences for the purpose of generating competition among scientists, seeding ideas upon which industry can capitalize, and highlighting "human talent" for companies to hire. Partnership between public and private sector research in digital agricultural innovation is much like it is in the tech sector at large, with fundamental research happening in the public sector from which private sector then draws talent and patented ideas (sometimes via the production, first, of a "start-up," which large corporations acquire). Edna, the Bayer employee mentioned above, stated, "What [a large corporation] does is identify a technology that's very good and instead of spending money trying to do it in house, they buy it, and in some cases they leave the branding as it is and in others they do their own branding … in the case of John Deere it gets painted green!" Governments are actively fostering this kind of private–public collaboration. Rob, who at the time of his interview was working to realize a smart test farm in Canada, described the consortia of industry and government interests that came together on his test farm proposal:

> Yes, so the original proposal that we put forward was to work as part of a supercluster. We were looking for solutions for agriculture in the technology sector. The announcement came out for superclusters and we decided to take a shot at it and work with a group in Alberta. It's sort of

> become an open innovation area where companies are coming together and maximizing their expertise in different fields that intersect with agriculture – so, remote sensing, autonomous vehicles, data analytics, agronomy ... the government funding helps bring those together ... Hopefully we can get some momentum going.

At CVPR 2020, a public research dataset focused on plant phenotyping, called the Agriculture-Vision dataset, was made publicly available for the "Vision for Agriculture Workshop." A collaboration between academics and Intelinair (a company involved in smart agriculture using aerial imaging) created the dataset. The "Vision for Agriculture Workshop" was a competition new to the CVPR as of 2020 and awarded US$5,000 to the team who developed a model that performed best on the shared dataset. However, exploring the details of this dataset reveals several significant biases. The Agriculture-Vision dataset (see Chiu et al. 2020) contains 94,986 aerial images of farmlands (presently the largest annotated public research dataset available for aerial agriculture imaging problems). Each image within the dataset is paired with expert annotated labels for a semantic segmentation problem, which is the task of classifying each pixel in an image within some semantic category. There are three important features to consider with this dataset: crop identity, method of collection, and semantic categories. The crops within the fields imaged to create this dataset were predominantly soybean and corn, and a drone collected the images. The challenge put forward at the conference required that a model segment an image into the following seven categories: background, cloud shadow, double plant, planter skip, standing water, waterway, and weed cluster. Important among these semantic categories were the double plant and planter skip categories. A double plant is an error caused by an operator of a planting machine double planting a crop, a redundancy that creates waste in both inputs and time. A planter skip is a planting error where a patch of agricultural land is missing crops. Given this information, it becomes obvious that biases exist within this dataset that mirror those biases within the commercial decision platforms and the data that feed them; the Agriculture-Vision dataset prioritizes corn and soybean farming and in particular, farming operations that can afford expensive planting machinery and UAVs for analyzing their fields. Like FarmCommand, this dataset has the potential to escalate power disparities within the industry, favouring particular food system actors over others by teaching AI and also teams of scientists building these tools on partial data. In this way, agricultural data and computer science happening at Farmers Edge or among PhD students competing at CVPR 2020 are no different from all scientific sorting. As Geoffrey Bowker and Susan Star (1999) put it vividly in their detailed treatment of scientific classification and its consequences, "Each category valorizes some point of view and silences another," and lives are subsequently "torqued by their encounters with classification systems" (5; see also Martin and Lynch 2009).

An analysis of the politics of digital agricultural platforms that looks beyond public–private dichotomies thus reveals something of value for the scholarship on the role of political economy in food and the privatization of science (Mirowski 2011). Despite the obvious role of corporate interest in the digital farming and wider food system trajectory, there exists a complexity that monolithic theories of privatization cannot account for on their own. The movement toward a productivist version of farm 4.0 is not simply a result of the dominance of private interest and power but rather a particular logic about innovation and farming that weaves together private and public R&D in a more complex Gordian knot of shared assumptions and opportunities. We can think again about the patent application for N-Manager, which reveals that biases toward productivist farming exist within the public sector plant modelling used by all computer scientists designing analytics tools for predicting fertilizer needs. And my interviews show close associations between public and private sector research in the smart farming innovation pipeline, such as the CVPR 2020 competition. David Harvey (2020) describes how technological innovation is both dependent upon and feeds back into capitalist interest, with governments subsidizing industry research and development. To stay competitive, capitalist enterprises, from agribusinesses to farms, must use technological innovation and capture technical advancements prior to their competitors (and limit competitor access to such advantages). Because internal R&D is not the only way to achieve this competitiveness, companies have privatized data collection and restricted data access, as well as "rushing" to collect data on crops of economic importance. Increasingly, companies deploy the strategy of technological capture through merger and acquisition, as well as making partnerships that allow them to capitalize on the fruits of public education. The impetus to "capture" and win the technological race is not solely confined to corporate activity; this technological dynamism is built into wider society. Across public and private contexts, I heard about the need to win the technological race and get ahead of the pack. At the meeting for the proposed smart "supercluster" I attended, for example, it became clear that this significant government funding was not so much subsidizing private corporations but rather funding a "business of technology" that spreads across political economic contexts. As a sketch animation video on the Innovation, Science and Economic Development Canada website describes, "Superclusters are dense areas of business activity. Where people with diverse skills work together. Where companies large and small work with universities, colleges and technical schools … We want to speed things up. So we're investing nearly a billion dollars to turn more ideas into solutions. More skills into jobs. And more companies into global successes" (ISED Canada 2018).

Again, as we know from Facebook, Google, and Amazon, those early to collect data and build intelligent systems around them see a significant advantage in the big data and AI marketplace. If farmOS and companies like Bayer/Monsanto all pull from similar public environmental data (e.g., US Department of Agriculture soil survey data) and rely on historic public computer science and agronomic science, the large companies are enabled to "stitch" these data together using human talent, which they can afford. As well, the companies can use their big data gathered from customers (via their precision equipment) to train and perfect their AI systems. The Climate FieldView "data fix-it" tool provides an illustration. To ensure accuracy in the farm field data received into the platform, Bayer/Monsanto has developed an additional "tool" for editing different sets of data in batches. This data includes field-level crop types, hybrid seed name, chemical or other crop treatments made to crops. The platform's planting "prescription" map may indicate where crops were planted in a field, which crops appeared to "take," and roughly what nitrogen levels a farmer will need to maintain application in order to keep up productivity, but the machine does not indicate which seed types or varietals were planted; the farmer must do this work. The corporation's offering then is less AI than combined computer–machine intelligence, relying on farmers verifying their own farm data, which is then said to be "coupled" to satellite imagery of fields. By expediting the process of inputting and verifying the accuracy of data – services that could have been done by corporate scientists

– Climate FieldView has offset a significant amount of data entry labour onto the farmer.

Historically powerful corporations like Bayer/Monsanto and John Deere – those who have been collecting data from farmers and securing data relations with them since the early aughts – are set to entrench their power in the food system and beyond. Just to give a sense of the asymmetry: John Deere has held the dominant position in the tractor market for North America for decades, where retail sales of all wheeled tractors in 2017, their one hundredth year of tractor manufacturing, were approximately 245,000 units. The only Canadian tractor manufacturer is Versatile, a division of Buhler Industries, who claim to have built and sold 100,000 tractor units over their forty years of business. While user data is theoretically hosted on Farmier and could be "fed" "into farmOS, at present farmOS volunteers do not organize or analyze such user data. At least partly as a result of this data gap, the level of specification under Climate Fieldview is overwhelmingly higher than with farmOS, which is furthermore organized on a relatively simple interface.

While a complex private–public ecosystem exists around agricultural big data, agribusinesses like Bayer/Monsanto, and thus private interests, are nonetheless positioned to see enormous gains from digitization given the imbalance in the epistemic resources driving digitization in agri-food. By looking at other sectors, we can project the enormous gains that come from data gathering as a commodifiable service in and of itself, or as an aspect of industrial competitive strategy; in the health sector there is now established research showing that corporations like IMS Health charge hundreds of thousands of dollars for access to research data and thus construct a divide between those scientists who can access crucial information about pharmaceutical prescription patterns and those who cannot (Sismondo 2018). Pharmaceutical companies can also use their data advantage to create invisibility as much as visibility, using pricing to keep exclusive access to information about their (sometimes nefarious) behaviour. One popular *Mother Jones* article from 2014 looked into the data dominance of agribusiness, and the journalist described how Monsanto was "set to take over the world at a resolution level of 10 meter square maps and historic data on all of the 30 million agricultural fields in the United States" (McDonnell 2014). The way one evaluates the consequences of this asymmetry are likely different, depending on one's ideological position on both capitalism and industrial agriculture. For those of who may prioritize equity and environmental sustainability, the current systems around digital agriculture in North America do not augur well.

Radical Politics of the Non-Future, or Staying with the Trouble

The immaculate conception of data coheres with the power of dominant food system actors such that it is tempting to think of ICD as resulting from the evil genius of chief public relations officers working for large industries. Undoubtedly, corporate decision-makers are on some level aware of the benefits of depicting big data algorithms as operating without human intervention, not least because controversy and liability have followed those moments of rupture when the public has understood that algorithms are designed by biased humans. Most ordinary people have been able to pull examples directly from their back pocket since Twitter's trending topics misrepresented the scale of public protest during Occupy, for example (Introna and Nissenbaum 2000). Indeed, "filter bubble" (Pariser 2012) is part of the common lexicon for describing Google Search and Amazon's recommendations. Perhaps ICD is sometimes leveraged tactically for this purpose, just as the framework is put to work for industry spokespeople contending with critique of industrial agriculture's environmental impacts. ICD stabilizes public and consumer trust, providing symbolic reassurances that technologies are fair and accurate, free from subjectivity, error or influence, and thus superior (Edelman 2018; Gillespie 2014, 179). ICD also stabilizes social license in farming by reassuring concerned citizens and consumers that the future of agriculture, even the industrial kind, hinges on immaterial interventions and food production qua abstraction. As we saw in chapter 2, agribusinesses like John Deere use ICD in glossy media texts that depict their "automated decision systems" as efficient, objective, valuable, and powerful. These corporations not only systematically manage the public's image of digital tools, they also manage the information we receive about them via murky relationships with government regulators and intellectual property lawyers (Robin 2008), whose collective work often shields incredibly politicized transactions and materials – such as the datasets themselves and the third party uses of data – from public scrutiny (Drum 2009). Take, for instance, the fact that farmers are prevented by intellectual property law from looking back at their data to assess how they are handled and for whom they are put to use (Zuboff 2019). Legal protections cloak the data that farmers collect (via their precision tractors) as well as the algorithms that use these data to generate advice, while the corporation benefits from these data, commodifying and selling them via a system of transactions that are almost entirely invisible outside of the corporation (Zuboff 2019). During the fieldwork for this book, I witnessed many instances of data science and computation happening under a lack of transparency – including to me as a critical social scientist – and shaped by the narrow goal of economic expansion, both for agribusiness and farmers. Computer science pedagogy even builds obfuscation into its fundamentals, where the term "cloud computing" comes from the symbology of computer network diagrams for engineers (Introna and Nissenbaum 2000). The cloud symbol is used to indicate a part of the diagram whose internal details are irrelevant because they are presumed fluffy and benign.

Yet remember that it is not just corporate actors who circulate ICD; activists and critical social scientists like me – those of us highly critical of industrial agriculture and large agribusinesses – also use the ICD framework. The idea that data-driven readings of the world are the primary (if not the only) means of solving food system problems has captured numerous talented and dedicated people – who work (largely on a volunteer basis) on community-building projects in their spare time. Tarleton Gillespie (2014) has written about a "knowledge logic," which is not specific to agriculture. Gillespie states, "That we are now turning to algorithms to identify what we need to know is as momentous as having relied on credentialed experts, the scientific method, common sense, or the word of God" (168). This is at last a part of ICD, especially as it is used among activists.

While useful, ICD is arguably problematic, functioning to mitigate contestation and negotiation around digital agriculture, where activists who leverage the framework might not consequently readily make visible and contest the current dominant practices in data and computer science – those deeply entangled with hegemonic interests. While the activists I spoke with challenged industrial agriculture and the historic monopolization of scientific knowledge by agribusinesses, they seemed hesitant to see the role of digital agriculture in furthering these processes. These activists therefore displayed what Dawn Nafus and Jamie Sherman of Intel Labs call "soft resistance": challenging some aspects of the hegemonic framework (e.g., productivism) but leaving intact a fundamental logic that serves this system. The widespread circulation of ICD thus works at cross-purposes to activist challenges to the food system status quo by leaving intact assumptions about technology and society that prevent radical change.

And as we saw in chapter 2, academics also subscribe to ICD. The scholarship on digital agriculture has largely been focused on technical debates that get framed under ICD (Klerkx, Jakku, and Labarthe 2019). Notably, there is a now-robust academic conversation about the feasibility of opening public datasets or legal mechanisms for controlling potential data privacy breaches. The majority of the social science and even critical social science on big agricultural data is technical and limited to the legal compliance, rather than the broader social and political legitimacy, of technology companies. Accessibility, however, is not a condition for usability or broader social justice. Beyond data access and infrastructure, digital democracy efforts might call for a redistribution of decision-making power from a small number of corporate stakeholders (or shareholders) to a wider group of stakeholders, including a diversity of producers and food citizens (Dreze 2004; Knupfer 2013). In the case of open data, as Gray (2014) has noted, "While … open data advocacy and policy often places an emphasis on a mix of transparency, accountability, civic participation, democracy and innovation, [it has] historically had a much stronger and more explicit focus on economic opportunity and making it easier for larger established businesses to effectively leverage public sector resources" (8; see also Kitchin 2014). There is still little scholarship interrogating the ways in which values – from explicit corporate business models to the ideas which designers hold – might be influencing which data get collected in the first place, how they are used, and how these values and practices might not conform to what citizens need and demand.

In this way, there is an argument to be made that even critical data studies is also engaging in ICD[6] to the extent that it has not yet adequately considered the actual practices and site-specificity in which data are made and made useful. Critical data studies scholars themselves have flagged this limitation in the scholarship; Aradau and Blanke (2015) claim that "while critical scholars have drawn attention to the social, political and legal challenges to [data] practices," these scholars have failed to "take seriously the critical knowledge developed in information and computer science." The presence of ICD, even among scholars, may explain the focus on "big tech" as a monolithic analytic category, as well as the enormous public attention to the major social media and search platform companies (c.f. Bronson and Sengers 2022).

So if one accepts that ICD is hazardous for data and food justice, what can be done about it?

First of all, we can acknowledge ICD in our own linguistic and ideological practices. Spotting it, calling it out, and avoiding its use are a good first step. In doing so, critical data studies scholars and data activists might be enabled to broaden and deepen understandings of "big tech" by analyzing and comparing how "big techs" in different domains are shaped by contingent constraints and opportunities. If we can take seriously the idea that data collection and processing are far from immaculate but instead are shaped by powerful forces arrayed in particular domains of practice, then those domains cannot be irrelevant to critical understanding of which data-driven technologies are produced in the world. We have seen in this chapter that, in some ways, agriculture reproduces political economies of data familiar from other domains in which big data are used, like social media. Like most internet-derived data, data shared between farmers and corporations are largely shared only in one direction, from farmer *to* corporation. As with other sectors, agribusinesses are using privacy agreements to secure trust with farmers about the usage and potential misusage of their personal data (Newman 2017, see the so-called Monsanto Privacy Model), deploying language in the agreements connoting that their primary purpose is protecting farmer privacy through tight corporate control over data.

But agriculture also produces data practices that build on long histories of corporate consolidation in, and domination tactics specific to, the agricultural sector. Understanding why the current licensing strategy has been successful with farmers requires understanding the specific political economy of agriculture. In conversations with farmers using corporate decision support platforms, I found that most reported being only moderately interested in or concerned about what agribusinesses are doing with their personal data. In part this is cultural: for years being a successful farmer has meant to behave like corporations yourself (see Kneen 1995). In interviews, farmers appear to share in the ethos that sees farmers as businesspeople eager to cut down on the presentational overhead and presumed cognitive work (not to mention digital skill set) that would be required to engage with data directly. While these factors may sound similar to the ease of use preferences of, for example, social media users, there is another factor at play here that is particular to the relationship between farmers and agribusinesses: a history of socio-technical relations defined by what Goodman, Sorj, and Wilkinson (1987) call appropriationism, or the commodification of on-farm labour and biological processes that has left farmers in relationships of dependence with technology supply companies. Thus, when the Goldman Sachs financial report summarized in chapter 2 asks the question, "Who can collect [agricultural] data?" this is not just a question about technical capability; it is not the case that any company can start collecting data from farmers, who research shows depend on historically cultivated relationships with particular input suppliers in their decision-making about which technologies to adopt and from whom (see Busse et al. 2014). Farmers interviewed in this book suggest that they have invested in decision support platforms because of the cost of *not* investing – the possibility of "falling behind" their competition, a message they are getting from their trusted input suppliers. The head of a small agricultural robotics company in the UK and a fourth-generation farmer exemplifies the efficacy of ICD and corporate promotion of digital innovations when he writes, in a forecasting exercise titled "A Vision for 2030" (Jones 2021) that "over the next decade, there will be two types of farms. There will be those that have embraced AI and gradually increased its usage to the point at which some sort of AI is involved in every operational decision they make, and there will be those that have ignored it and are on the way to going out of business."

There are additional unique issues arising specifically in the agricultural context. Unlike the data which are collected from people's online behaviour and aggregated into big datasets used for commercial gain, agricultural data are sparser, geographically dispersed, and difficult to collect. In addition, agricultural environments are complex and open systems that present unique challenges to computer and data scientists intent on making predictions using machine learning and big data. As such, those companies with access not just to the data via historic relationships of control with farmers but also those with the resources to enable expensive computing power are at a further advantage. The already powerful agribusinesses are thus corporations worth watching and because agriculture as an economic sector is unique due to its strategic importance around the world and food is of obvious central importance to us all, it is crucial for both citizens and consumers to think carefully about big data uses (and misuses) in this particular context.

A second strategy following from the first is to examine emergent technologies of food production and trace the ways in which the materialities of their design come together with the discourses which frame their rationale. Engaging in this work would present a challenge to the fundamental bedrock of our large political economic systems, like food production practices as they intersect with global capitalism in the industrial food regime. Being able to see big agricultural data as necessarily touched by humans allows us to see, for example, the articulation of design logics held by scientists working within agribusinesses and within patterns of snowballing private interest. The epistemic focus of dominant big data practices is driven by this interest and it appears to be narrowing our knowledge of farms and wider environments and limiting our options for living well together as humans and non-humans (Global Alliance 2022; UNFAO 2019). And yet as we saw in chapter 2, digital agricultural innovations are introduced, framed, and discussed as "sustainable" technologies with such consistency across media reports, websites, and academic articles that this appears as a recurring discourse. Typically, an initial brief sketch of food system problems – notably the need to feed a growing human global population – sets the stage for the positioning of big data and sophisticated computing as the solution. Any of us can trouble this farming and insist that the conversation about food system ills be situated not narrowly within a technosolutionist frame but rather in a broader conversation about the capitalist and colonialist structures that allow for continuing environmental and other injustices (please read Liboiron 2021). As Robert Soden urges us in relation to environmental (like meteorological) data: "When we attend to the choices we make when deciding how to gather, analyze, and use environmental data, we create the opportunity for things to be otherwise" (46).

A third strategy, following from the insights of this book and for those of us with the technical training and skill, is to intervene by forwarding a feminist or intersectional approach to data science practice, one insistent upon diversity as well as one that is able to acknowledge and prize embodiment (see D'Ignazio and Klein 2020). Data feminism teaches us to value and to build rather than attempt to hide human–machine collaborations into data science and computer science work; in the context of digital agriculture, one might imagine this could inform a soil sensor, for example, that actually senses – which feels and engages in non-digital ways. Computer scientist Stacey Kuznetsov (2011) at the Human Computer Interaction Institute at Carnegie Mellon University has argued for "expanding sensing to include living organisms such as plants and animals, along with traditional tools and digital devices" (228). Kuznetsov and team have studied, in diverse environmental contexts as opposed to just the laboratory, scientists who work with living organisms like fish, reptiles, and bees to find ways of producing meaning from human–computer–organismic interaction through instruments that are both analog and digital. Such sensors could arguably infer a wider range but also depth of environmental conditions and lead to altogether different findings than digital sensors. Similar technical work could be conducted in response to a diversity of food system issues and needs. Take for example the data that are currently generated from remote sensing. Because of who produces these data – private constellations of satellites resulting in proprietary datasets – environmental datasets are used to visualize an increasingly homogenous view of ecosystems. A feminist-inspired or anti-ICD approach to environmental monitoring would value rather than problematize the inherently local, regional, or indeed geospatial nature of remote sensing data. So far, industry has treated as a challenge and something to overcome the fact that data generated from satellites on cropping systems are inherently geospatial because crop types and crop responses obviously vary regionally by latitude or ecological features like watershed and micro-climate (Berry et al. 2003, 2005; Delgado and Berry 2008; Gebbers and Adamchuk 2010; Pierce and Nowak 1999). A feminist, intersectional crop or environmental monitoring could play up and attend to variation, which may in fact mean adapting current monitoring to rely not only on earth observation but also on data generated *in situ*. Geospatial solutions based on imagery from earth observation could be integrated with sensor networks that are regionally situated within a variety of farm types and sizes. Farmers could even be enlisted in developing these networks within and partly by farm communities in a scientific network that integrates the scientific and farming communities. Campbell et al. (1994) and Short et al. (1995) recognized two decades ago that regional databases needed to be developed as a mechanism for providing training data to machine-learning algorithms, which capture local or contextual knowledge.

Last, each of us can counteract not just the pull of ICD but of future-making more broadly (Adam and Groves 2007; Urry 2016). Futurisms abound and come at us from industry and government hype but also from critical academia. Futurisms prevent us from staying with the troubles of today, they prevent us from seeing how current problems and dominant solutions follow from the past, and they also prevent us from seeing that we have at our disposal a suite of "innovations" to help solve our grand challenges, if we could only recognize them as innovative. Sure, a new sensor might help us concentrate soil carbon and mitigate climate change, but caring for the land through intercropping, locally adapted cropping strategies, as just two examples, are known strategies for sustainability. Futurisms related to big data prevent us from asking difficult questions about how human and institutional choices inform data and computational devices as they are brought into being, enlisted, and negotiated in particular settings. Not only is the seemingly static and inhuman datum or the algorithm in actual fact a messy, fragile, and inherently political accomplishment, it is also the case that life is so dazzingly complex it has quiet corners of resistance that allude any form of knowledge creation. No science can claim to be a universal and complete way of knowing – however technically superior it is promised to be, in the future.

Notes

CHAPTER ONE

1 I choose not to capitalize the internet even though it's convention to do so because, to me, Internet connotes a kind of technological agency which I am trying to problematize with this book. In making this decision I enter into a live debate, see: https://www.wired.com/story/hello-world-it-is-i-the-internet/.

2 And the profit is key. At the time of writing, the combined market value of Apple, Amazon, Facebook, Microsoft, and Google (parent company Alphabet) was 10 TRILLION US dollars, a number that is almost five times higher than the combined GDP of all fifty-four African countries. Interestingly, "intangible" assets like data make up a significant percentage of this market value.

3 Since the CA exposé there have been several others, including the whistle-blowing of Frances Haugen, a female data engineer who leaked tens of thousands of pages of internal Facebook documents showing that company executives knew of, hid, and did not act upon evidence that their platform raises harms ranging from its impact on teens' mental health to human traffickers' open use of its services.

4 There are a number of very large projects, particularly across Europe, that are advancing open agricultural data models and systems. See the FATIMA (n.d.) project funded by European Union Horizon 2020 or the FOODIE project funded by the European Commission (EIP-Agri n.d.).

5 The intellectual property business model on precision equipment is such that a farmer who purchases a post-2015 John Deere farm implement, for example, is in a situation where they do not own the technology that operates their equipment. Digital "locks" on machinery manufacturers' proprietary technologies restrict a farmer from making a quick, on-farm fix when equipment breaks down or from "tinkering" with their machinery in order to adapt it to

their specific farm situation (Higgins et al. 2017). Farmers are required by the purchase agreements to use authorized dealership repair, and not doing so is a violation of the legal agreement (see IFIXIT n.d.). In October 2015, the Librarian of Congress ruled in favour of an exception to the Digital Millenium Copyright Act that would allow anyone who owned a tractor to interact with its code, but there remain significant limitations which render this ruling "hollow" (see Carolan 2017).

6 Participant names are pseudonyms, except for cases where people agreed to be identified, or where the person is a public figure speaking in the public sphere.

7 There was a recent very important report that adds to this conversation: https://story.futureoffood.org/the-politics-of-knowledge/.

8 The interviews and observational analysis that inform this book took place between December 2016 and May 2018 across several Canadian provinces (Saskatchewan, Ontario, Quebec, New Brunswick, and Nova Scotia). In total, sixty-five people were interviewed, some of them by telephone but others in their laboratories, farm fields, or experimental research sites. A student research assistant named Matthew Zucca was instrumental in gathering the participants from farm activist groups. Matthew and I asked people open-ended questions about their practice, motivations, and goals in relation to agriculture and technology and we recorded these conversations. I also recorded talks given at big data and AI conventions, and all of this was transcribed and qualitatively coded inductively using the software program NVivo.

9 I do not take a normative position on digital agriculture *per se*, though at times I critique the current social structures configuring agricultural big data and placing its tools and their benefits in the hands of the already powerful. *The Immaculate Conception of Data* touches on but does not treat explicitly the divergence of sustainability intentions circulating around big agricultural data (see Bronson 2019), and it does not explicitly treat the legislative environment around data, including the important issues of data access, privacy, and technological unemployment (Bronson and Knezevic 2019). It does not deal with the abdication of responsibility that occurs when public institutions enlist "data-driven" social policies, a position served by the immaculate conception of data. Others have done a thorough job of questioning "data-driven" governance by interrogating the limits of reliance on algorithms (e.g., O'Neil 2016; Umoja Noble 2018), among other topics.

CHAPTER TWO

1 There have been a few adoption studies of dealerships in the US and Canada as well which show similar patterns as to what tools are being adopted but slightly different geographic patterns of adoption. For more than twenty years, *CropLife* magazine and the Departments of Agricultural Economics and Agronomy at Purdue University have undertaken the Precision Agriculture Dealership Survey. It is the longest-running continuous survey of precision farming adoption in the United States. In 2017, a similar survey in Ontario was conducted by the University of Guelph and the Ontario Ministry of Agriculture, Food and Rural Affairs (OMAFRA) through the membership of the Ontario Agri Business Association (OABA). This survey was repeated in 2019 in Ontario. Shortly after, a similar survey was also sent to members of the Canadian Association of Agri Retailers (CAAR) from across Canada.

2 There are several similar apps available to farmers and gardeners some of which are free but others based on subscription. Top ones based upon use are: Weeds ID, iNaturalist, Leafsnap, PlantSnap, Turf Doctor and Xarvio.

3 To systematically assess the ways in which companies speak to farmers about digital agricultural technologies, I enlisted the help of a research assistant, Megan Beaulieu, to search prominent farm newspapers and trade journals in North America: *Western Producer*; *Farm Forum Magazine*; and *Agri-info Newsletter*. We used the search terms "digital agriculture," "smart farming," and "precision agriculture" and searched between 1 May and 1 December 2017. This yielded sixty-two articles and fifteen advertisements, the vast majority of which appeared in *Western Producer*. I undertook a detailed analysis of the resulting articles and ads.

4 These representations occur across the ideological spectrum, from statues of Vladimir Lenin (Bonnell 1997) to Shepard Fairey's "Hope" portrait of Barack Obama.

5 A Web of Science Core Collection analysis of publications categorized by research areas under a search for "smart farming" from 1990 to 2019 revealed that the vast majority of academic publications are written mainly from those within computer science and engineering, whereas only 10 per cent of publications are from agricultural and biological researchers and only 4 per cent are from environmental sciences and social sciences disciplines. The main publication source, accounting for 27 per cent of this smart farming literature, is conference proceedings, notably the IEEE (Institute of Electrical and Electronics Engineers). The IEEE is a professional network that includes computer scientists, software developers, information technology professionals, physicists, and medical doctors in addition to IEEE's electrical and electronics

engineering core group. In comparison to the 145 conferences within the IEEE, only nine agriculture and two agriculture engineering conferences feature smart farming in their proceedings.

6 Interestingly, all of the focus on targeted and data-based fertilizer applications as a route to sustainability misses a large portion of the pollution picture because it is now known that a significant portion of the greenhouse gas emissions coming from agriculture are related to fertilizer production, not use (see Institute for Agriculture and Trade Policy 2021).

7 This assumption also attended the introduction and promotion of genetically modified organisms, which now dominate the North American food system, despite a lack of evidence that the technology has fulfilled the promises the industry made regarding the yield gains.

8 In fact, these are not only old promises as they relate to historic technologies but they are old promises related to digital ones because the same promises have circulated now for several decades. For instance, an article published in 1998 in the *Canadian Journal of Remote Sensing* (which I had to access in hard copy due to its age) touts the merits of digital agriculture using the very same language as is used today by proponents: "Site specific management allows inputs to be reduced, while optimizing outputs, both of which are attractive to the farm producer. At the same time, by reducing inputs, the run-off of fertilizers and pesticides is reduced, thus improving the environmental condition of the agro-ecosystem" (Brisco et al. 1998, 315).

9 There are indeed variants of "the" agrarian question but generally there are three types: one concerns the contributions of agriculture to capitalist or socialist industrialization which assumes that rising agricultural productivity is the basis of industrialization within a national development framework. A second concerns how the operations of capital work through agriculture, and the third is more explicitly political and is a more populist argument that giant agribusinesses are the villains of contemporary capitalism and its ills (see any work by Henry Bernstein).

10 Arguably, the global food trade made colonialism possible (e.g., the Atlantic triangle).

11 The Netherlands and the US have positioned themselves as the world's leaders in export-oriented agriculture (see AgFunder 2018).

CHAPTER THREE

1 Even supra-national agencies like the Food and Agriculture Organization of the United Nations (UNFAO) put forward this framing. For instance, the UNFAO states that international agricultural policies should aim at raising

levels of nutrition, increasing agricultural productivity, improving the lives of rural people, and contributing to the growth of the world economy (UNFAO 2008).

2 Beyond the (virtual) networked public, "meet-ups" (common among DIYers and "maker movement" participants) also create and strengthen Farm Hack ties. These meet-ups are dispersed around the globe (though concentrated on the east coast of the US). Once a year, Farm Hack community members come together for the Gathering for Open Agricultural Technology (GOAT).

3 The current dominant use for these pis appears to be among horticulturalists tracking the development of delicate fruits like greenhouse peppers or tomatoes, which need to be maintained at precise temperature and moisture levels. Some farmers are using the pis alongside farmOS to alert them (say, on their smartphones) when the pis read anything outside of the desirable range (which they themselves set).

4 For a Harvard University scholar's timeline of the open source movement, see Suber (2009).

5 FarmOS is hosted via GitHub, a web-based version control and source code management tool.

6 In my interviews with public sector data scientists, they showed they were making a clear effort to open datasets at the federal and provincial levels. One female data scientist, working to make public data on precision agricultural use among grain farmers in Ontario, said, "When we started the project, we told the guys we won't publish their names if they don't want it. We try to keep ownership, information, off to one side … But this data is a public data set, it's funded by public dollars as well as the grain farmers of Ontario and … we'd like to share the case studies as best as we can in the future. And this openness just helps them troubleshoot if it's crapping out or if it's not doing something right on various operating systems and various internet browsers."

CHAPTER FOUR

1 Bruno Lamy at Agriculture and Agri-food Canada kindly helped me compile a list of government investments into broadband infrastructure and access projects: The Universal Broadband Fund (ISED Canada 2021b); a CA$600 million agreement with Telesat to secure capacity on its new Low Earth Orbit (LEO) satellites; ISED's CA$500 million Connect to Innovate Program, which received an CA$85 million top-up in the 2019 federal budget (ISED Canada 2021a); the CRTC's CA$750 million broadband fund, which launched in 2019 (CRTC 2021); CA$2 billion in investments from the Canada Infrastructure Bank (CIB-BIC 2020); CA$2 billion through the Investing in Canada Plan

funding stream for rural and northern communities (Infrastructure Canada 2020); a CA$1 billion broadband and cellular investment in Ontario (Government of Ontario 2020); the Internet for Nova Scotia Initiative (Develop Nova Scotia 2021); and Connecting British Columbia (Northern Development Initiative Trust 2021).

2 David Turnbull (2003) furthermore points out the reliance on the science of empire and traditional and Indigenous knowledge, arguing that "the British could only make their general maps of South Asia by combining multiple surveys based on local knowledge and techniques" (122).

CHAPTER FIVE

1 Scholars in Australia have found the same sets of concerns among farmers there (see Jakku et al. 2019). In the United States, farmers appear concerned that information specific to their farming practices could be used for regulatory enforcement purposes or that farm level data might be used in civil or regulatory litigation (Janzen 2017).

2 Ian Kay illustrates procedural rhetoric in analyzing the simulation computer game SimCity's assumptions about criminality. The game responds to increased crime by getting players to install more police stations, as opposed to giving them the choice to increase money for education, build affordable housing, and so on. SimCity thus implicitly makes an argument about crime and prevention, staking out a theoretical position on urban planning from which players cannot deviate by nature of the interface and, of course, the code behind this interface (in Sample 2013).

3 In fact, interns and students often perform this spot sampling and it is known among budding agronomists as a way to "cut one's teeth."

4 Technological advances have also had implications for food security and food-related health worldwide, with the number of under-nourished people at roughly 800 million to one billion, while around two and a half billion adults are overweight or obese (UNFAO 2018).

5 According to their budget statement, they received only US$2,387.34 over the last twelve months. The Farmos Github indicates that over one month when I scanned in the year 2020, only two developers had committed changes.

6 I want to thank and credit a reviewer of the book manuscript for this idea.

Bibliography

Adam, Barbara, and Chris Groves. 2007. *Future Matters: Action, Knowledge, Ethics*. Leiden, Netherlands: Brill.

Advisory Council on Economic Growth. 2017. "Unlocking Innovation to Drive Scale and Growth." Government of Canada. https://www.budget.gc.ca/aceg-ccce/pdf/innovation-2-eng.pdf.

Ag Data Transparent. 2020. "About." https://www.agdatatransparent.com/about.

AgFunder. 2018. "AgriFood Tech Investment Report." https://agfunder.com/research/agrifood-tech-investing-report-2018/.

Agriculture and Agri-Food Canada. 2020. "Managing Agroclimate Risk." Government of Canada. https://www.agr.gc.ca/eng/agriculture-and-climate/drought-watch/managing-agroclimate-risk/?id=1463575241811.

Akhtman, Y., E. Golubeva, O. Tutubalina, and M. Zimin. 2017. "Application of Hyperspectural Images and Ground Data for Precision Farming." *Geography, Environment, Sustainability* 10, no. 4: 117–28. https://doi.org/10.24057/2071-9388-2017-10-4-117-128.

Albritton, Robert. 2009. *Let Them Eat Junk: How Capitalism Creates Hunger and Obesity*. London: Pluto.

Alperovitz, Gar. 2017. "The Possibility of a Pluralist Commonwealth Evolutionary Reconstruction Toward a Caring and Just Political Economy." *Interdisciplinary Journal of Partnership Studies* 4, no. 1. https://doi.org/10.24926/ijps.v4i1.154.

Altieri, Miguel A. 2009. "Agroecology, Small Farms, and Food Sovereignty." *Monthly Review* 61, no. 3 (July–August): 102–13. https://doi.org/10.14452/mr-061-03-2009-07_8.

Anderson, Chris. 2008. "The End of Theory: The Data Deluge Makes the Scientific Method Obsolete." *Wired*. 23 June. https://www.wired.com/2008/06/pb-theory/.

Anderson, Gina. 2018. "How NASA and John Deere Helped Tractors Drive Themselves." NASA. 18 April. http://www.nasa.gov/feature/directorates/spacetech/spinoff/john_deere.

Antle, John M., James W. Jones, and Cynthia E. Rosenzweig. 2017. "Next Generation Agricultural System Data, Models, and Knowledge Products: Introduction." *Agricultural Systems* 155 (July): 186–90. https://doi.org/10.1016/j.agsy.2016.09.003.

Aradau, Claudia, and Tobias Blanke. 2015. "The (Big) Data-Security Assemblage: Knowledge and Critique." *Big Data and Society* 2, no. 2 (October). https://doi.org/10.1177/2053951715609066.

Aubert, Benoit A., Andreas Schroeder, and Jonathan Grimaudo. 2012. "IT as Enabler of Sustainable Farming: An Empirical Analysis of Farmers' Adoption Decision of Precision Agriculture Technology." *Decision Support Systems* 54, no. 1 (December): 510–20. https://doi.org/10.1016/j.dss.2012.07.002.

Bajaj, Jatinder K. 1990. "Francis Bacon, the First Philosopher of Modern Science: A Non-Western View." In *Science, Hegemony and Violence*, edited by Ashis Nandy. Tokyo: United Nations University Press.

Basok, Tanya. 2002. *Tortillas and Tomatoes: Transmigrant Mexican Harvesters in Canada*. Montreal and Kingston: McGill-Queen's University Press.

Bates, Jo. 2012. "'This Is What Modern Deregulation Looks Like: Co-optation and Contestation in the Shaping of the UK's Open Government Data Initiative." *The Journal of Community Informatics* 8, no. 2 (April). http://cijournal.net/index.php/ciej/article/view/845.

Batte, Marvin T., and Michael W. Arnholt. 2003. "Precision Farming Adoption and Use in Ohio: Case Studies of Six Leading-Edge Adopters." *Computers and Electronics in Agriculture* 38, no. 2: 125–39. https://doi.org/10.1016/S0168-1699(02)00143-6.

Baum Hedlund Law. 2021. "Baum Hedlund Law Homepage." https://www.baumhedlundlaw.com/.

Bauwens, Michel, and Alekos Pantazis. 2018. "The Ecosystem of Commons-Based Peer Production and Its Transformative Effects." *The Sociological Review* 66, no. 2 (March): 302–19. https://doi.org/10.1177/0038026118758532.

Bayer-Monsanto. 2020. "Smart Fields." https://www.cropscience.bayer.com/innovations/data-science/a/smart-fields.

Benton, T.G., C. Bieg, H. Harwatt, R. Pudasaini, and L. Wellesley. 2021. "Food System Impacts on Biodiversity Loss: Three Levers for Food System Transformation in Support of Nature." London: Chatham House, Royal Institute of International Affairs.

Berlan, Jean-Pierre, and Richard C. Lewontin. 1986. "Technology, Research, and the Penetration of Capital: The Case of US Agriculture." *Monthly Review* 38, no. 3 (July–August): 21–35. https://doi.org/10.14452/mr-038-03-1986-07_4.

Berry, J.K., J.A. Delgado, R. Khosla, and F.J. Pierce. 2003. "Precision Conservation for Environmental Sustainability." *Journal of Soil and Water Conservation* 58, no. 6: 332–9.

Berry, J.K., J.A. Delgado, F.J. Pierce, and R. Khosla. 2005. "Applying Spatial Analysis for Precision Conservation Across the Landscape." *Journal of Soil and Water Conservation* 60, no. 6: 363–70.

Beyer, Susanne, and Lothar Gorris. 2009. "Spiegel Interview with Umberto Eco: 'We Like Lists Because We Don't Want to Die.'" *Der Spiegel*. 11 November. https://www.spiegel.de/international/zeitgeist/spiegel-interview-with-umberto-eco-we-like-lists-because-we-don-t-want-to-die-a-659577.html.

Biddle, Justin B. 2014. "Can Patents Prohibit Research? On the Social Epistemology of Patenting and Licensing in Science." *Studies in History and Philosophy of Science* 45 (March): 14–23. https://doi.org/10.1016/j.shpsa.2013.12.001.

Bijker, Wiebe E., Thomas Parke Hughes, and Trevor Pinch, eds. 2012. *The Social Construction of Technological Systems: New Directions in the Sociology and History of Technology*. Cambridge, MA: MIT Press. First published 1987.

Birch, Kean and Kelly Bronson. 2022. "Big Tech, introduction to special issue on Big Tech." *Science as Culture?*: 1–14.

Bishop, Kevin D., and Adrian A.C. Phillips. 1993. "Seven Steps to Market – The Development of the Market-Led Approach to Countryside Conservation and Recreation." *Journal of Rural Studies* 9, no. 4 (October): 315–38. https://doi.org/10.1016/0743-0167(93)90045-L.

Blanke, Tobias. 2014. *Digital Asset Ecosystems: Rethinking Crowds and Clouds*. Elsevier.

Blumenfeld, J. 2019. *Meeting Data User Needs: A Look Behind the Curtain*. https://earthdata.nasa.gov/meeting-data-user-needs.

Bogost, Ian. 2015. "The Cathedral of Computation." *The Atlantic*. 15 January. https://www.theatlantic.com/technology/archive/2015/01/the-cathedral-of-computation/384300/.

Bolaria, P. Singh, and Peter S. Li. 1988. *Racial Oppression in Canada*. Toronto: Garamond.

Bongiovanni, R., and J. Lowenberg-Deboer. 2004. "Precision Agriculture and Sustainability." *Precision Agriculture* 5, no. 4 (August): 359–87. https://doi.org/10.1023/B:PRAG.0000040806.39604.aa.

Bonnell, Victoria E. 1997. *Iconography of Power: Soviet Political Posters Under Lenin and Stalin*. Berkeley: University of California Press.

Bowker, Geoffrey C. 2005. *Memory Practices in the Sciences*. Cambridge, MA: MIT Press.

Bowker, Geoffrey C., and Susan Leigh Star. 1999. *Sorting Things Out: Classification and its Consequences*. Cambridge, MA: MIT Press.

boyd, danah, and Kate Crawford. 2012. "Critical Questions for Big Data: Provocations for a Cultural, Technological, and Scholarly Phenomenon." *Information, Communication & Society* 15, no. 5: 662–79. https://doi.org/10.1080/1369118X.2012.678878.

Bramley, R.G.V. 2009. "Lessons from Nearly 20 Years of Precision Agriculture Research, Development, and Adoption as a Guide to Its Appropriate Application." *Crop and Pasture Science* 60, no. 3: 197–217. https://doi.org/10.1071/CP08304.

Brisco, B., R. Brown, T. Hirose, R. McNairn, and K. Staenz. 1998. "Precision Agriculture and the Role of Remote Sensing: A Review." *Canadian Journal of Remote Sensing*: 315–27.

Brockway, Lucile H. 2011. "Science and Colonial Expansion: The Role of the British Royal Botanic Gardens." In *The Postcolonial Science and Technology Studies Reader*, edited by Sandra Harding, 127–39. Durham, NC: Duke University Press.

Bronson, Kelly. 2014. "Reflecting on the Science in Science Communication." *Canadian Journal of Communication* 39, no. 4: 523–37. https://doi.org/10.22230/cjc.2014v39n4a2751.

– 2015. "Responsible to Whom? Seed Innovations and the Corporatization of Agriculture." *Journal of Responsible Innovation* 2, no. 1: 62–77. https://doi.org/10.1080/23299460.2015.1010769.

– 2018. "Smart Farming: Including Rights Holders for Responsible Agricultural Innovation." *Technology Innovation Management Review* 8, no. 2 (February): 7–14. https://doi.org/10.22215/timreview/1135.

– 2019. "Digitization and Big Data in Food Security and Sustainability." In *Encyclopedia of Food Security and Sustainability* 2, 582–7. https://doi.org/10.1016/B978-0-08-100596-5.22462-1.

– 2020. "A digital 'revolution' in agriculture? Critically viewing digital innovations through a regenerative food systems lens." In *Routledge Handbook of Sustainable and Regenerative Food Systems*, edited by Jessica Duncan, Michael Carolan, Michael and Johannes Wiskere, 336–50. New York: Routledge.

Bronson, Kelly, and Irena Knezevic. 2016. "Big Data in Food and Agriculture." *Big Data & Society* 3, no. 1 (June). https://doi.org/10.1177/2053951716648174.

– 2019. "The Digital Divide and How It Matters for Canadian Food System Equity." *Canadian Journal of Communication* 44, no. 2: 63–8. https://doi.org/10.22230/cjc.2019v44n2a3489.

Bronson, Kelly and Phoebe Sengers. 2022. "Big Tech Meets Big Ag: Diversifying Epistemologies of Data and Power," *Science as Culture*: 10.1080/09505431.2021.1986692.

Brown, Meghan. 2018. "Smart Farming: Automated and Connected Agriculture."

Engineering.com. 14 March. https://www.engineering.com/story/smart-farming-automated-and-connected-agriculture.

Brynjolfsson, Erik, and Andrew McAfee. 2011. *Race Against the Machine: How the Digital Revolution Is Accelerating Innovation, Driving Productivity, and Irreversibly Transforming Employment and the Economy*. Lexington, MA: Digital Frontier.

Burch, David, and Geoffrey Lawrence. 2013. "Financialization in Agri-Food Supply Chains: Private Equity and the Transformation of the Retail Sector." *Agriculture and Human Values* 30, no. 2 (June): 247–58. https://doi.org/10.1007/s10460-012-9413-7.

Burrell, Jenna. 2016. "How the Machine 'Thinks': Understanding Opacity in Machine Learning Algorithms." *Big Data & Society* 3, no. 1 (January). https://doi.org/10.1177/2053951715622512.

– 2020. "On Half-Built Assemblages: Waiting for a Data Center in Prineville, Oregon," *Engaging Science and Technology Studies* 6 (283): https://estsjournal.org/index.php/ests/article/view/447.

Burwood-Taylor, Louisa. 2016. "Why Monsanto Invested in Ag Image Analytics Company Resson." *AgFunder News*. 24 June. https://agfundernews.com/why-monsanto-invested-in-ag-image-analytics-company-resson6053.html.

– 2017. "What Is AgriFoodTech?" *AgFunder News*. 15 August. https://agfundernews.com/what-is-agrifood-tech.html.

Busse, M., A. Doernberg, R. Siebert, A. Kuntosch, B. König, and W. Bokelmann. 2014. *Precision Agriculture* 15, no. 4 (August): 403–26. https://doi.org/10.1007/s11119-013-9337-2.

Buttel, Frederick H. 1993. "Ideology and Agricultural Technology in the Late Twentieth Century: Biotechnology as Symbol and Substance." *Agriculture and Human Values* 10, no. 2 (March): 5–15. https://doi.org/10.1007/BF02217599.

– 2003. "Environmental Sociology and the Explanation of Environmental Reform." *Organization & Environment* 16, no. 3 (September): 306–44. https://doi.org/10.1177/1086026603256279.

Cadwalladr, Carole, and Emma Graham-Harrison. 2018. "Revealed: 50 Million Facebook Profiles Harvested for Cambridge Analytica in Major Data Breach." *The Guardian*. 17 March. https://www.theguardian.com/news/2018/mar/17/cambridge-analytica-facebook-influence-us-election.

Campbell, Jillian, and David Jensen 2019. "UN Environment Foresight Brief: Building a Digital Ecosystem for the Planet." https://wedocs.unep.org/bitstream/handle/20.500.11822/30612/Foresight014.pdf?sequence=1&isAllowed=y.

Campbell, T., J. Magnay, S. Ibrahim, and B. Rabatsky. 2014. "Jumping into the Future: How Leapfrog Technologies Will Change Agriculture." Presented at the Rural Sociological Society Webinar.

Campbell, W., N. Short, P. Coronado, and R. Cromp. 1994. "Distributed Earth Science Validation Centers for Mission to Planet Earth." In *Methodologies for Intelligent Systems*, edited by Z.W. Raś and M. Zemankova, 1–12. Vol. 869 of *Lecture Notes in Computer Science.* Berlin: Springer.

CAPÉ (Coopérative Pour l'Agriculture de Proximité Écologique). n.d. "Autoconstruction." https://www.cape.coop/autoconstruction/.

Carbonell, Isabelle M. 2016. "The Ethics of Big Data in Big Agriculture." *Internet Policy Review* 5, no. 1. https://doi.org/10.14763/2016.1.405.

Carolan, Michael. 2017. "Publicising Food: Big Data, Precision Agriculture, and Co-Experimental Techniques of Addition." *Sociologia Ruralis* 57, no. 2 (April): 135–54. https://doi.org/10.1111/soru.12120.

CBC. "'Eat Less Steak and Ice Cream': What Climate Change Means for the Food You Love." 2018. *CBC Radio*. 11 October. https://www.cbc.ca/radio/thecurrent/the-current-for-october-11-2018-1.4857639/eat-less-steak-and-ice-cream-what-climate-change-means-for-the-food-you-love-1.4858288.

Cheney-Lippold, John. 2011. "A New Algorithmic Identity: Soft Biopolitics and the Modulation of Control." *Theory, Culture & Society* 28, no. 6 (November): 164–81. https://doi.org/10.1177/0263276411424420.

Chiles, Robert Magneson. 2013. "If They Come, We Will Build It: In Vitro Meat and the Discursive Struggle Over Future Agrofood Expectations." *Agriculture and Human Values* 30, no. 4 (December): 511–23. https://doi.org/10.1007/s10460-013-9427-9.

Chiu, Mang Tik, Xingqian Xu, Yunchao Wei, Zilong Huang, Alexander G. Schwing, Robert Brunner, Hrant Khachatrian, Ivan Dozier, Greg Rose, David Wilson, Adrian Tudor, Naira Hovakimyan, Thomas S. Huang, and Honghui Shi. 2020. "Agriculture-Vision: A Large Aerial Image Database for Agricultural Pattern Analysis." In *Proceedings of the IEEE/CVF Conference on Computer Vision and Pattern Recognition*, 2828–38. https://openaccess.thecvf.com/content_CVPR_2020/html/Chiu_AgricultureVision_A_Large_Aerial_Image_Database_for_Agricultural_Pattern_Analysis_CVPR_2020_paper.html.

Chun, Wendy Hui Kyong. 2011. *Programmed Visions: Software and Memory*. Cambridge, MA: MIT Press.

CIB-BIC (Canada Infrastructure Bank). 2020. "Prime Minister Announces Infrastructure Plan to Create Jobs and Grow the Economy." 1 October. https://cib-bic.ca/en/the-canada-infrastructure-bank-announces-a-plan-to-create-jobs-and-grow-the-economy/.

Clapp, Jennifer. 2012. *Food*. Cambridge, UK: Polity.

– 2015. "Food Security and International Trade: Unpacking Disputed Narratives:

Background Paper for *The State of Agricultural Commodity Markets 2015–2016*." Rome: Food and Agriculture Organization of the United Nations. http://www.fao.org/3/a-i5160e.pdf.
– 2016. "Too Much at Stake for Canada to Ignore Agribusiness Mega-Mergers." *The Hill Times*. 13 July. https://www.hilltimes.com/2016/07/13/too-much-at-stake-for-canada-to-ignore-agribusiness-mega-mergers/73554.
– 2021. "The problem with growing corporate concentration and power in the global food system," *Nature Food* 2: 404–8
Clapp, Jennifer, and Eric Helleiner. 2012. "Troubled Futures? The Global Food Crisis and the Politics of Agricultural Derivatives Regulation." *Review of International Political Economy* 19, no. 2: 181–207. https://doi.org/10.1080/09692290.2010.514528.
Clapp, Jennifer and Sarah-Louise Ruder. 2021. "Precision Technologies for Agriculture: Digital Farming, Gene-Edited Crops, and the Politics of Sustainability," *Global Environmental Politics* 20, no. 3: 49–69.
Cleveland, David A., Nora M. Müller, Alexander C. Tranovich, D. Niki Mazaroli, and Kai Hinson. 2014. "Local Food Hubs for Alternative Food Systems: A Case Study from Santa Barbara County, California." *Journal of Rural Studies* 35 (July): 26–36. https://doi.org/10.1016/j.jrurstud.2014.03.008.
Clifford Chance. 2018. "Facebook, Data Misuse and Why It Matters." https://www.cliffordchance.com/content/dam/cliffordchance/briefings/2018/03/facebook-data-misuse-and-why-it-matters.pdf.
Climate Corporation. 2020. "Digital Farming's Leading Software Platform: Climate Fieldview." https://climatefieldview.ca/.
Clinton, Hillary Rodham. 2011. "Secretary of State Hillary Rodham Clinton Remarks on Internet Freedom." *Electronic Frontier Foundation*. 15 February. https://www.eff.org/files/filenode/clinton_internet_rights_wrongs_20110215.pdf.
Cloke, Paul, and Mark Goodwin. 1992. "Conceptualizing Countryside Change: From Post-Fordism to Rural Structured Coherence." *Transactions of the Institute of British Geographers* 17, no. 3: 321–36. https://doi.org/10.2307/622883.
Cochrane, Willard. 1958. *Farm Prices, Myth and Reality*. Minneapolis: University of Minnesota Press.
Cochrane, Willard Wesley. 1979. *The Development of American Agriculture: A Historical Analysis*. Minneapolis: University of Minnesota Press.
Cohen, Noam. 2017. *The Know-It-Alls: The Rise of Silicon Valley as a Political Powerhouse and Social Wrecking Ball*. New York: The New Press.
Conway, Gordon. 1998. *The Doubly Green Revolution: Food for All in the Twenty-First Century*. Ithaca, NY: Cornell University Press.

Conway, Gordon R., and Edward B. Barbier. 1988. "After the Green Revolution: Sustainable and Equitable Agricultural Development." *Futures* 20, no. 6 (December): 651–70. https://doi.org/10.1016/0016-3287(88)90006-7.

Cosgrove, Emma. 2018. "Why Syngenta Acquired FarmShots: 'It's Definitely a Race.'" *AgFunder News*. 16 March. https://agfundernews.com/syngenta-acquired-farmshots.html.

Couldry, Nick, and Joseph Turow. 2014. "Advertising, Big Data and the Clearance of the Public Realm: Marketers' New Approaches to the Content Subsidy." *International Journal of Communication* 8: 1710–26.

Cox, Dorn. 2014. "Open Source for Agricultural Resilience." Presented at the Vermont Organic Farmers, Vermont, USA.

Cox, Sidney. 2002. "Information Technology: The Global Key to Precision Agriculture and Sustainability." *Computers and Electronics in Agriculture* 36, no. 2–3 (November): 93–111. https://doi.org/10.1016/S0168-1699(02)00095-9.

Crawford, Kate. 2013. "The Hidden Biases in Big Data." *Harvard Business Review* 1, no. 4 (April). https://static1.squarespace.com/static/5b5df2f5fcf7fd7290ff04a4/t/5b8d8261562fa736b2002818/1536000609606/05+The+Hidden+Biases+in+Big+Data+%28Crawford%29.pdf.

– 2015. "The Partial Witness: Data, Bodies and the Trouble with Truth." Presented at the Annual Attallah Lecture, Carleton University, Ottawa, 10 March.

Crawford, Kate, Kate Miltner, and Mary L. Gray. 2014. "Critiquing Big Data: Politics, Ethics, Epistemology." *International Journal of Communication* 8: 1663–72.

Cribb, Julian. 2010. "The Coming Famine: Risks and Solutions for Global Food Security." *Agricultural Science* 22, no. 1 (March): 24–30.

Cronon, William. 1991. *Nature's Metropolis: Chicago and the Great West*. New York: Norton.

Crossley, Nick, Elisa Bellotti, Gemma Edwards, Martin G. Everett, Johan Koskinen, and Mark Tranmer. 2015. *Social Network Analysis for Ego-Nets*. London: SAGE.

CRTC (Canadian Radio-Television and Telecommunications Commission). 2021. "Broadband Fund: Closing the Digital Divide in Canada." Last modified 19 March 2021. https://crtc.gc.ca/eng/internet/internet.htm.

CSIRO (Commonwealth Scientific and Industrial Research Organisation). n.d. "Digiscape Future Science Platform." https://research.csiro.au/digiscape/.

CVPR (Computer Vision and Pattern Recognition). n.d. "CVPR Virtual." http://cvpr2020.thecvf.com/.

Daberkow, Stan G., and William D. McBride. 2003. "Farm and Operator Characteristics Affecting the Awareness and Adoption of Precision Agriculture Technologies in the US." *Precision Agriculture* 4, no. 2 (June): 163–77. https://doi.org/10.1023/A:1024557205871.

Daston, Lorraine, and Peter Galison. 2007. *Objectivity*. Cambridge, MA: Zone Books.

"Data Is Power." 2011. *Popular Science Magazine*. 13 October. https://www.popsci.com/technology/article/2011-10/data-power/.

Davis, Gary. 2007. "History of the NOAA Satellite Program," *Journal of Applied Remote Sensing* 1, no. 1 (January): 2–18. https://www.spiedigitallibrary.org/journals/Journal-of-Applied-Remote-Sensing/volume-1/issue-1/012504/History-of-the-NOAA-satellite-program/10.1117/1.2642347.short?SSO=1.

de Beer, Jeremy. 2005. "Reconciling Property Rights in Plants." *The Journal of World Intellectual Property* 8, no. 1 (January): 5–31. https://doi.org/10.1111/j.1747-1796.2005.tb00235.x.

De Schutter, Olivier. 2015. "Don't Let Food Be the Problem." *Foreign Policy*. https://foreignpolicy.com/2015/07/20/starving-for-answers-food-water-united-nations/.

Debinski, D.M., K. Kindscher, and M.E. Jakubauskas. 1999. "A Remote Sensing and GIS-Based Model of Habitats and Biodiversity in the Greater Yellowstone Ecosystem." *International Journal of Remote Sensing* 20, no. 17: 3281–91. https://doi.org/10.1080/014311699211336.

Delgado, Jorge A. 2016. "4 Rs Are Not Enough: We Need 7 Rs for Nutrient Management and Conservation to Increase Nutrient Use Efficiency and Reduce Off-Site Transport of Nutrients." In *Social-Specific Farming: Precision Agriculture*, edited by R. Lal and B.A. Stewart, 89–126. Boca Raton: CRC Press.

Delgado, Jorge A., and Joseph K. Berry. 2008. "Advances in Precision Conservation." *Advances in Agronomy* 98: 1–44. https://doi.org/10.1016/s0065-2113(08)00201-0.

Delgado, Jorge A., Nicholas M. Short Jr., Daniel P. Roberts, and Bruce Vandenburg. 2019. "Big Data Analysis for Sustainable Architecture on a Geospatial Cloud Framework." *Frontiers in Sustainable Food Systems* 3 (July). https://www.frontiersin.org/articles/10.3389/fsufs.2019.00054/full#B18.

Develop Nova Scotia. 2021. "Internet for Nova Scotia Initiative." https://internet.developns.ca/.

D'Ignazio, Catherine, and Lauren F. Klein. 2020. *Data Feminism*. Cambridge, MA: MIT.

Driessen, Clemens, and Leonie F.M. Heutinck. 2015. "Cows Desiring to Be Milked? Milking Robots and the Co-Evolution of Ethics and Technology on Dutch Dairy Farms." *Agriculture and Human Values* 32, no. 1: 3–20. https://doi.org/10.1007/s10460-014-9515-5.

Drum, Kevin. 2009. "Betting the Farm." *Mother Jones*. https://www.motherjones.com/environment/2009/10/betting-farm/.

Durkheim, Emile. 1912. *The Elementary Forms of the Religious Life*. Alcan.

Eastwood, C., L. Klerkx, and R. Nettle. 2017. "Dynamics and Distribution of Public and Private Research and Extension Roles for Technological Innovation and Diffusion: Case Studies of the Implementation and Adaptation of Precision Farming Technologies." *Journal of Rural Studies* 49 (January): 1–12. https://doi.org/10.1016/j.jrurstud.2016.11.008.

Edelman, Richard. 2018. "Silicon Valley: The New Focus on Trust." *Edelman*. 15 February. https://www.edelman.com/post/silicon-valley-new-focus-on-trust.

Edney, Matthew H. 1993. "The Patronage of Science and the Creation of Imperial Space: The British Mapping of India, 1799–1843." *Cartographica: The International Journal for Geographic Information and Geovisualization* 30, no. 1: 61–7. https://doi.org/10.3138/4622-L321-1214-1XR7.

Edwards, Paul N. 2010. *A Vast Machine: Computer Models, Climate Data, and the Politics of Global Warming*. Cambridge, MA: MIT Press.

EIP-Agri (European Union Agriculture & Innovation). n.d. "FOODIE – Farm-Oriented Open Data in Europe." https://ec.europa.eu/eip/agriculture/en/find-connect/projects/foodie-farm-oriented-open-data-europe.

Elliott, Kevin C. 2017. *A Tapestry of Values: An Introduction to Values in Science. A Tapestry of Values*. Oxford: Oxford University Press.

Escobar, Arturo. 1995. *Encountering Development: The Making and Unmaking of the Third World*. Princeton, NJ: Princeton University Press.

Estes, Vonnie. 2016. "How Big Data Is Disrupting Agriculture from Biological Discovery to Farming Practices." *AgFunder News*. 9 June. https://agfundernews.com/how-big-data-is-disrupting-agriculture-from-biological-discovery-to-farming-practices5973.html.

ETC Group. 2016. "Software vs. Hardware vs. Nowhere: Deere & Co. Is Becoming 'Monsanto in a Box.'" Val David, QC: ETC Group.

Eubanks, Virginia. 2018. *Automating Inequality: How High-Tech Tools Profile, Police, and Punish the Poor*. New York: St Martin's.

Ezrahi, Yaron. 1990. *The Descent of Icarus: Science and the Transformation of Contemporary Democracy*. Cambridge, MA: Harvard University Press.

– 2004. "Science and the Political Imagination in Contemporary Democracies." In *States of Knowledge: The Co-Production of Science and Social Order*, edited by Sheila Jasanoff, 254–73. London: Routledge.

Fairbairn, Madeleine. 2020. *Fields of Gold: Financing the Global Land Rush*. Ithaca, NY: Cornell University Press.

Farm Forum. n.d. "Farm Forum." https://farmforum.ca/.

Farmers Edge. 2015. "Farmers Edge Story." YouTube video, 6 April. https://www.youtube.com/watch?v=RHhe8QS3bPo.

– 2016. "Empowering Farmers, Improving Sustainability – CEO, Wade Barnes, Explains the Farmers Edge Impact." YouTube video, 16 June. https://www.youtube.com/watch?v=-opKKojEuME.

– n.d. "FarmCommand" https://www.farmersedge.ca/farmcommand/.

FarmHack. n.d. "Farm Hack Tools." https://farmhack.org/tools.

farmOS. n.d. "Homepage." https://farmos.org/.

FATIMA (Farming Tools for External Nutrient Inputs and Water Management). n.d. "Home Page." http://fatima-h2020.eu.

Federici, Silvia. 2004. "Women, Land-Struggles and Globalization: An International Perspective." *Journal of Asian and African Studies* 39, no. 1–2 (April): 47–62. https://doi.org/10.1177/0021909604048250.

Felt, Mylynn. 2016. "Social Media and the Social Sciences: How Researchers Employ Big Data Analytics." *Big Data & Society* 3, no. 1 (April). https://doi.org/10.1177/2053951716645828.

Fine, Ben. 1994. "A Response to My Critics." *Review of International Political Economy* 1, no. 3: 579–86. https://doi.org/10.1080/09692299408434302.

Finn, Ed. 2018. *What Algorithms Want: Imagination in the Age of Computing.* Cambridge, MA: MIT Press.

Fischhoff, David. 2016. "Digitization: The Next Revolution in Agriculture." Presented at the Monsanto Climate Corporation, 6 January. https://www.ofc.org.uk/sites/ofc/files/papers/david-fischhoff-digitization-next-revolution-agriculture-presentation-notes-final.pdf.

Fitzgerald, Chris. 1993. *Environmental Management Information Systems.* New York: McGraw-Hill.

Fitzgerald, Deborah. 1993. "Farmers Deskilled: Hybrid Corn and Farmers' Work." *Technology and Culture* 34, no. 2 (April): 324–43. https://doi.org/10.2307/3106539.

Foroohar, R. 2019. *Don't Be Evil.* New York: Currency.

Foucault, Michel. 1977. "What Is an Author?" In *Language, Counter-Memory, Practice: Selected Essays and Interviews*, edited by Donald F. Bouchard, translated by Donald F. Bouchard and Sherry Simon, 113–38. Ithaca, NY: Cornell University Press.

Fountas, S., S. Blackmore, D. Ess, S. Hawkins, G. Blumhoff, J. Lowenberg-Deboer, and C.G. Sorensen. 2005. "Farmer Experience with Precision Agriculture in Denmark and the US Eastern Corn Belt." *Precision Agriculture* 6, no. 2 (April): 121–41. https://doi.org/10.1007/s11119-004-1030-z.

Fox Keller, Evelyn. 1992. *Secrets of Life, Secrets of Death: Essays on Language, Gender, and Science.* New York: Routledge.

Franklin, Ursula. 1999. *The Real World of Technology*. Toronto: House of Anansi.

Fraser, Alistair. 2019. "Land Grab/Data Grab: Precision Agriculture and Its New Horizons." *The Journal of Peasant Studies* 46, no. 5: 893–912. https://doi.org/10.1080/03066150.2017.1415887.

Fraser, Evan. 2018. "Canada's Agriculture System on the Cusp of a Circular Revolution." *The Hill Times*. 5 December. https://www.hilltimes.com/2018/12/05/canadas-agriculture-system-cusp-circular-revolution/179064.

Frickel, Scott, Sahra Gibbon, Jeff Howard, Joanna Kempner, Gwen Ottinger, and David J. Hess. 2010. "Undoing Science: Charting Social Movement and Civil Society Challenges to Research Agenda Setting." *Science, Technology, & Human Values* 35, no. 4: 444–73. https://doi.org/10.1177/0162243909345836.

Friedmann, Harriet. 1980. "Household Production and the National Economy: Concepts for the Analysis of Agrarian Formations." *The Journal of Peasant Studies* 7, no. 2: 158–84. —https://doi.org/10.1080/03066158008438099.

– 1987. "International Regimes of Food and Agriculture since 1870." In *Peasants and Peasant Societies*, edited by Teodor Shanin, 258–76. Oxford: Basil Blackwell.

– 2005. "Feeding the Empire: The Pathologies of Globalized Agriculture." *Socialist Register* 41 (January): 124–43.

Friedmann, Harriet, and Philip McMichael. 1989. "Agriculture and the State System: The Rise and Decline of National Agricultures, 1870 to the Present." *Sociologia Ruralis* 29, no. 2 (August): 93–117. https://doi.org/10.1111/j.1467-9523.1989.tb00360.x.

Fromer, Jeanne C. 2009. "Patent Disclosure." *Iowa Law Review* 94: 539–606.

Fuller, Steve. 2018. *Post-Truth: Knowledge as a Power Game*. New York: Anthem.

Galaz, Victor, Miguel Centeno, Peter Callahan, Amar Causevic, Thayer Patterson, Irina Brass, Seth Baum Darryl Farber, Joern Ficher, David Garcia, Timon McPhearson, Daniel Jimenez, Brian King, Paul Larcey, and Karen Levy. 2021. "Artificial Intelligence, Systemic Risks, and Sustainability," *Technology in Society* 67: https://doi.org/10.1016/j.techsoc.2021.101741.

Garvey, Scott. 2018. "Self-Driving Versus the Lawyers: Fully Autonomous Farm Vehicles Are Already Here, but Setting the Rules for Their Use Won't Be Simple." *Country Guide*. 24 October. https://www.country-guide.ca/machinery/fully-autonomous-farm-vehicles-are-here-but-what-are-their-rules-for-use/.

Gates, Bill. 2018. "Can the Wi-Fi Chip in Your Phone Help Feed the World?" *GatesNotes: The Blog of Bill Gates*. 9 October. https://www.gatesnotes.com/Development/FarmBeats.

Gebbers, Robin, and Viacheslav I. Adamchuk. 2010. "Precision Agriculture and Food Security." *Science* 327, no. 5967 (February): 828–31. https://doi.org/10.1126/science.1183899.

Ghaffarzadeh, K., J. Harrop, and H. Zervos. 2017. "Agricultural Robots and Drones 2017–2027: Technologies, Markets, Players, the Future of Farming; Ultra Precision Farming; Autonomous Farming." *Cision* PR *Newswire.* 16 August. https://www.prnewswire.com/news-releases/agricultural-robots-and-drones-2017-2027-technologies-markets-players-300505653.html.

Ghosh, Dipayan, and Ben Scott. 2018. "Digital Deceit: The Technologies Behind Precision Propaganda on the Internet." *New America.* 23 January. http://newamerica.org/public-interest-technology/policy-papers/digitaldeceit/.

Ghosh, Rishab Aiyer. 1998. "FM Interview with Linus Torvalds: What Motivates Free Software Developers?" *First Monday.* https://firstmonday.org/ojs/index.php/fm/article/download/583/504/2539.

Gillam, Carey. 2019. "Former Monsanto CEO Ordered to Testify at Roundup Cancer Trial." *US Right to Know.* 7 December. https://usrtk.org/monsanto-roundup-trial-tacker/former-monsanto-ceo-ordered-to-testify-at-roundup-trial-in-person/.

Gillespie, Tarleton. 2014. "The Relevance of Algorithms." In *Media Technologies: Essays on Communication, Materiality, and Society*, edited by Tarleton Gillespie, Pablo J. Boczkowski, and Kirsten A. Foot, 167–94. Cambridge, MA: MIT Press. https://doi.org/10.7551/mitpress/9780262525374.003.0009.

Girardi, Giulio. 1987. *Sandinismo, Marxismo, Cristianismo: La Confluencia.* Managua, Nicaragua: Centro Ecuménico Antonio Valdivieso.

Gitelman, Lisa, ed. 2013. *"Raw Data" Is an Oxymoron.* Infrastructures Series. Cambridge, MA: MIT Press.

Gitelman, Lisa, and Virginia Jackson. 2013. "Introduction." In *"Raw Data" Is an Oxymoron*, edited by Lisa Gitelman, 1–14. Infrastructures Series. Cambridge, MA: MIT Press.

Glaros, Alesandros, Sarah Marquis, Chelsea Major, Philip Quarshie, Lisa Ashton, Arthur Green, B. Krishna, Lenore Newman, Robert Newell, Yada Rickey, and Evan Fraser. 2022. "Horizon Scanning and Review of the Impact of Five Food and Food Production Models for the Global Food System in 2050," *Trends in Food Science and Technology*, 119: 560–4.

Gliessman, Steve. 2015. "A Global Vision for Food System Transformation." *Agroecology and Sustainable Food Systems* 39, no. 7: 725–6. https://doi.org/10.1080/21683565.2015.1039159.

Global Alliance for the Future of Food. 2021. "The Politics of Knowledge" report online at https://futureoffood.org/insights/global-alliance-launches-new-compendium-the-politics-of-knowledge/.

GODAN (Global Open Data for Agriculture & Nutrition). n.d. "Government Open-Up Guide for Agriculture." https://www.godan.info/pages/government-open-guide-agriculture.

GODAN, and Jeremy de Beer. 2016. "Ownership of Open Data: Governance Options for Agriculture and Nutrition." Wallingford, UK: GODAN. https://www.godan.info/sites/default/files/documents/Godan_Ownership_of_Open_Data_Publication_lowres.pdf.

Goldman Sachs. 2016. "Precision Farming: Cheating Malthus with Digital Agriculture." Equity Research.

Goodman, David, and Michael Redclift. 1994. "Constructing a Political Economy of Food." *Review of International Political Economy* 1, no. 3: 547–52. https://doi.org/10.1080/09692299408434298.

– 2002. *Refashioning Nature: Food, Ecology and Culture.* London: Routledge.

Goodman, David, Bernardo Sorj, and John Wilkinson. 1987. *From Farming to Biotechnology: A Theory of Agro-Industrial Development.* Oxford: Basil Blackwell.

Goodman, David, and Michael Watts. 1994. "Reconfiguring the Rural or Fording the Divide?: Capitalist Restructuring and the Global Agro-Food System." *The Journal of Peasant Studies* 22, no. 1: 1–49. https://doi.org/10.1080/03066159408438565.

Gorski, Paul. 2003. "Privilege and Repression in the Digital Era: Rethinking the Sociopolitics of the Digital Divide." *Race, Gender & Class* 10, no. 4: 145–76. https://www.jstor.org/stable/41675106.

Government of Ontario. 2020. "Ontario Investing Nearly $1 Billion to Expand and Improve Broadband and Cellular Access." *Newsroom.* 4 November. https://news.ontario.ca/en/release/59057/ontario-investing-nearly-1-billion-to-expand-and-improve-broadband-and-cellular-access.

Gray, Jonathan. "Towards a Genealogy of Open Data." 2014. *General Conference of the European Consortium for Political Research,* 3 September. Glasgow. https://doi.org/10.2139/ssrn.2605828.

Hacking, Ian. 1992. "Statistical Language, Statistical Truth and Statistical Reason: The Self-Authentication of a Style of Reasoning." In *The Social Dimensions of Science,* edited by Ernan McMullin, 130–57. Notre Dame, IN: University of Notre Dame Press.

Haight, Michael, Anabel Quan-Haase, and Bradley A. Corbett. 2014. "Revisiting the Digital Divide in Canada: The Impact of Demographic Factors on Access to the Internet, Level of Online Activity, and Social Networking Site Usage." *Information, Communication & Society* 17, no. 4: 503–19. https://doi.org/10.1080/1369118X.2014.891633.

Halfacree, Keith. 1999. "A New Space Or Spatial Effacement?: Alternative Futures for the Post-Productivist Countryside." In *Reshaping the Countryside: Perceptions and Processes of Rural Change*, edited by N. Walford, J.C. Everitt, and D.E. Napton. Wallingford, UK: CABI.

Hall, Mark A., and Kevin A. Schulman. 2009. "Ownership of Medical Information." *Journal of the American Medical Association* 301, no. 12 (March): 1282–4. https://doi.org/10.1001/jama.2009.389.

Haraway, Donna. 1988. "Situated Knowledges: The Science Question in Feminism and the Privilege of Partial Perspective." *Feminist Studies* 14, no. 3: 575–99. https://doi.org/10.2307/3178066.

– 2016. *Staying with the Trouble: Making Kin in the Chthulucene*. Durham, NC: Duke University Press.

Harding, Sandra G. 2008. *Sciences from Below: Feminisms, Postcolonialities, and Modernities*. Next Wave. Durham, NC: Duke University Press.

Harvey, David. 2020. "We Need a Collective Response to the Collective Dilemma of Coronavirus." *Jacobin*. 4 April. https://jacobinmag.com/2020/4/david-harvey-coronavirus-pandemic-capital-economy.

Harvey, David, and Mark Riley. 2005. "Country Stories: The Use of Oral Histories of the Countryside to Challenge the Sciences of the Past and Future." *Interdisciplinary Science Reviews* 30, no. 1: 19–32. https://doi.org/10.1179/030801805X19681.

Heaton, Tim, and David Brown. 1982. "Farm Structure and Energy Intensity: Another Look." *Rural Sociology* 47, no. 1: 17–31.

Hecht, Gabrielle, ed. 2011. *Entangled Geographies: Empire and Technopolitics in the Global Cold War*. Cambridge, MA: MIT Press.

Higgins, Vaughan, Melanie Bryant, Andrea Howell, and Jane Battersby. 2017. "Ordering Adoption: Materiality, Knowledge and Farmer Engagement with Precision Agriculture Technologies." *Journal of Rural Studies* 55 (October): 193–202. https://doi.org/10.1016/j.jrurstud.2017.08.011.

Holmgren, David. 2002. *Permaculture: Principles & Pathways Beyond Sustainability*. Holmgren Design.

Howard, Philip H. 2016. *Concentration and Power in the Food System: Who Controls What We Eat?* London: Bloomsbury Academic.

Hughes, Thomas. 1987. "The Evolution of Large Socio-Technical Systems." In *The Social Construction of Technological Systems*, edited by Wiebe E. Bijker, Thomas P. Hughes, and Trevor Pinch, 45–77. Cambridge, MA: MIT Press.

IAASTD (International Assessment of Agricultural Knowledge, Science and Technology for Development). 2009. "Agriculture at a Crossroads: The Global Report," edited by Beverly Mcintyre, Hans Herren, Judi Wakhungu, and Robert Watson.

– 2015. "Agriculture at a Crossroads: IAASTD Findings and Recommendations for

Future Farming," edited by Angelika Beck, Benedikt Haerlin, and Lea Richter. https://www.globalagriculture.org/fileadmin/files/weltagrarbericht/English Brochure/BrochureIAASTD_en_web_small.pdf.

IBM. n.d. "What Does a World with IBM Watson Look Like?" Accessed 8 September 2016. http://www.ibm.com/watson/aworldwithwatson/.

IEEE (Institute of Electrical and Electronics Engineers). 2016. "2016 IEEE International Conference on Big Data." http://cci.drexel.edu/bigdata/bigdata2016/index.html.

IFIXIT. n.d. https://www.ifixit.com/Right-to-Repair.

Infrastructure Canada. 2020. "Investing in Canada Plan Funding Stream: Rural and Northern Communities Infrastructure." Last modified 2 November 2020. https://www.infrastructure.gc.ca/plan/rnc-crn-eng.html.

Institute for Agriculture Trade and Policy, "New research shows 50 year binge on chemical fertilisers must end to address the climate crisis," 1 November 2020, online at https://www.iatp.org/new-research-chemical-fertilisers.

Introna, Lucas D., and Helen Nissenbaum. 2000. "Shaping the Web: Why the Politics of Search Engines Matters." *The Information Society* 16, no. 3: 169–85. https://doi.org/10.1080/01972240050133634.

IoF2020 (Internet of Food & Farm 2020). 2020. "Introducing Internet of Food and Farm 2020." https://www.iof2020.eu/about.

IPES Food (International Panel of Experts on Sustainable Food Systems). 2015. "The New Science of Sustainable Food Systems." http://www.ipes-food.org/_img/upload/files/NewScienceofSusFood.pdf.

– 2016. "From Uniformity to Diversity: A Paradigm Shift from Industrial Agriculture to Diversified Agroecological Systems." http://www.ipesfood.org/_img/upload/files/UniformityToDiversity_FULL.pdf.

Isakson, S. Ryan. 2015. "Derivatives for Development? Small-Farmer Vulnerability and the Financialization of Climate Risk Management." *Journal of Agrarian Change* 15, no. 4 (October): 569–80. https://doi.org/10.1111/joac.12124.

ISED Canada (Innovation, Science, and Economic Development Canada). 2018. "What Is A Supercluster?" https://www.ic.gc.ca/eic/site/093.nsf/eng/home.

– 2021a. "Connect to Innovate." Last modified 10 June 2021. https://www.ic.gc.ca/eic/site/119.nsf/eng/home.

– 2021b. "Universal Broadband Fund." Last modified 23 April 2021. https://www.ic.gc.ca/eic/site/119.nsf/eng/home.

ISRIC (International Soil Reference and Information Centre). n.d. "ISRIC-World Soil Information." https://www.isric.org/.

Jakku, Emma, Bruce Taylor, Aysha Fleming, Claire Mason, Simon Fielke, Chris Sounness, and Peter Thorburn. 2019. "'If They Don't Tell Us What They Do with

It, Why Would We Trust Them?' Trust, Transparency and Benefit-Sharing in Smart Farming." NJAS-*Wageningen Journal of Life Sciences* 90–1 (December). https://doi.org/10.1016/j.njas.2018.11.002.

Janzen, Todd. 2017 "LinkedIn Case Shows the Limits of Data Ownership." *Janzen Ag Tech Blog*. 17 October. https://www.aglaw.us/janzenaglaw/2017/10/16/linkedin-case-shows-the-limits-of-data-ownership.

Jasanoff, Sheila, and Sang-Hyun Kim. 2009. "Containing the Atom: Sociotechnical Imaginaries and Nuclear Power in the United States and South Korea." *Minerva* 47, no. 2. https://doi.org/10.1007/s11024-009-9124-4.

– 2015. *Dreamscapes of Modernity: Sociotechnical Imaginaries and the Fabrication of Power*. Chicago: University of Chicago Press.

Jasanoff, Sheila, and Hilton R. Simmet. 2017. "No Funeral Bells: Public Reason in a 'Post-Truth' Age." *Social Studies of Science* 47, no. 5 (October): 751–70. https://doi.org/10.1177/0306312717731936.

Jensen, Hans Grinsted, Lars-Bo Jacobsen, Søren Marcus Pedersen, and Elena Tavella. 2012. "Socioeconomic Impact of Widespread Adoption of Precision Farming and Controlled Traffic Systems in Denmark." *Precision Agriculture* 13, no. 6 (December): 661–77. https://doi.org/10.1007/s11119-012-9276-3.

John Deere. 2012. "Farm Forward." YouTube video, 23 August. https://www.youtube.com/watch?v=jEh5-zZ9jUg.

– 2015. "Feet on the Ground, Eyes on the Horizon: Deere and Company Annual Report 2015." http://www.annualreports.com/HostedData/AnnualReportArchive/d/NYSE_DE_2015.pdf.

Jones, Sam Watson. 2021. "A Vision for 2030." *Sam Watson Jones*. 17 March. https://sam-51837.medium.com/three-ways-that-farmers-can-own-the-future-of-food-production-6cd030721020.

Kamilaris, Andreas, Andreas Kartakoullis, and Francesc X. Prenafeta-Boldú. 2017. "A Review on the Practice of Big Data Analysis in Agriculture." *Computers and Electronics in Agriculture* 143 (December): 23–37. https://doi.org/10.1016/j.compag.2017.09.037.

Kaminski-Killiany, Kara, and Tom Walker. 2016. "Responsibly Opening Agriculture Data." *The Engine Room*. 8 June. https://www.theengineroom.org/responsibly-opening-agriculture-data/.

Kanaracus, Chris. 2013. "Monsanto Bets Nearly $1 Billion on Big Data Analytics." IDG *News Service*. 2 October. https://www.cmo.com.au/article/print/528098/monsanto_bets_nearly_1_billion_big_data_analytics/.

Keen, Andrew. 2018. *How to Fix the Future*. New York: Grove Atlantic.

Kelly, Kevin. 2002. "God Is the Machine." *Wired*. 1 December. https://www.wired.com/2002/12/holytech/.

Kinchy, Abby J. 2012. *Seeds, Science, and Struggle: The Global Politics of Transgenic Crops.* Cambridge, MA: MIT Press.

Kinstler, Linda. 2020. "Researcher danah boyd on How to Protect the Census and Fix Tech." *Protocol.* 8 March. https://www.protocol.com/danah-boyd-q-a.

Kitchin, Rob. 2014. *The Data Revolution: Big Data, Open Data, Data Infrastructures & Their Consequences.* Los Angeles: SAGE.

Kitzinger, Jenny, and Clare Williams. 2005. "Forecasting Science Futures: Legitimising Hope and Calming Fears in the Embryo Stem Cell Debate." *Social Science & Medicine* 61, no. 3 (August): 731–40. https://doi.org/10.1016/j.socscimed.2005.03.018.

Klerkx, Laurens, Emma Jakku, and Pierre Labarthe. 2019. "A Review of Social Science on Digital Agriculture, Smart Farming, and Agriculture 4.0: New Contributions and a Future Research Agenda." *NJAS – Wageningen Journal of Life Sciences* 90–1 (December). https://doi.org/10.1016/j.njas.2019.100315.

Kline, Ronald R. 2000. *Consumers in the Country: Technology and Social Change in Rural America.* Baltimore: Johns Hopkins University Press.

Kloppenburg, Jack Ralph, ed. 1988. *Seeds and Sovereignty: The Use and Control of Plant Genetic Resources.* Durham, NC: Duke University Press.

– 2005. *First the Seed: The Political Economy of Plant Biotechnology.* Madison: University of Wisconsin Press.

Kneen, Brewster. 1995. *From Land to Mouth: Understanding the Food System.* Toronto: NC Press. First published 1989.

Koç, Mustafa, Jennifer Sumner, and Anthony Winson, eds. 2012. *Critical Perspectives in Food Studies.* Toronto: Oxford University Press.

Konrad, Kornelia, Harro van Lente, Christopher Groves, and Cynthia Sellin. 2017. "Performing and Governing the Future in Science and Technology." In *The Handbook of Science and Technology Studies*, edited by Ulrike Felt, Rayvon Fouché, Clark A. Miller, and Laurel Smith-Doerr, 465–94. Cambridge, MA: MIT Press.

Krimsky, Sheldon, and Carey Gillam. 2018. "Roundup Litigation Discovery Documents: Implications for Public Health and Journal Ethics." *Journal of Public Health Policy* 39, no. 3 (August): 318–26. https://doi.org/10.1057/s41271-018-0134-z.

Kuhn, Thomas. 1962. *The Structure of Scientific Revolutions.* Chicago: University of Chicago Press.

Kuznetsov, Stacey, William Odom, James Pierce, and Eric Paulos. 2011. "Nurturing Natural Sensors." *Proceedings of the 13th International Conference on Ubiquitous Computing: UbiComp*: 227–36. https://doi.org/10.1145/2030112.2030144.

Kurzweil, Ray. 2010. *The Singularity Is Near: When Humans Transcend Biology.* London: Penguin.

Lakoff, George. 2015. "Linguistics and Politics." In *The Routledge Handbook of Linguistics*, edited by Keith Allan, 562–76. London: Routledge.

Lambert, Dayton, Burton English, David Harper, Sherry Larkin, James Larson, Daniel Mooney, Roland Roberts, Margarita Velandia, and Jeanne Reeves. 2014. "Adoption and Frequency of Precision Soil Testing in Cotton Production." *Journal of Agricultural and Resource Economics* 39, no 1 (April): 106–23. https://doi.org/10.22004/ag.econ.168262.

Lang, Tim, and Michael Heasman. 2015. *Food Wars: The Global Battle for Mouths, Minds and Markets*. London: Routledge. First published 2004.

Langlois, Ganaele, Joanna Redden, and Greg Elmer, eds. 2015. *Compromised Data: From Social Media to Big Data*. New York: Bloomsbury.

Latour, Bruno. 1987. *Science in Action: How to Follow Scientists and Engineers through Society*. Cambridge, MA: Harvard University Press.

– 1988. *The Pasteurization of France*. Translated by Alan Sheridan and John Law. Cambridge, MA: Harvard University Press.

Levidow, Les, and Susan Carr. 2007. "GM Crops on Trial: Technological Development as a Real-World Experiment." *Futures* 39, no. 4 (May): 408–31. https://doi.org/10.1016/j.futures.2006.08.002.

Levidow, Les, and Joyce Tait. 1991. "The Greening of Biotechnology: GMOs as Environment-Friendly Products." *Science and Public Policy* 18, no. 5 (October): 271–80. https://doi.org/10.1093/spp/18.5.271.

Lévi-Strauss, Claude. 1964. *The Raw and the Cooked*. Vol. 1 of *Mythologiques*. Chicago: University of Chicago Press, 1964–71.

Liboiron, Max. 2021. *Pollution is Colonialism*. Durham, NC: Duke University Press.

Limer, Eric. 2018. "Elon Musk Quit Facebook and So Can You." *Popular Mechanics*. 23 March. https://www.popularmechanics.com/technology/apps/a19576169/elon-musk-quit-facebook-and-so-should-you/.

Linkogle, Stephanie. 1998. "The Revolution and the Virgin Mary: Popular Religion and Social Change in Nicaragua." *Sociological Research Online* 3, no. 2 (June): 1–11. https://doi.org/10.5153/sro.164.

Lohr, Steven. 2001. *Go To*. New York: Basic Books.

– 2016. "IBM Is Counting on Its Bet on Watson, and Paying Big Money for It." *The New York Times*. 17 October. https://www.nytimes.com/2016/10/17/technology/ibm-is-counting-on-its-bet-on-watson-and-paying-big-money-for-it.html.

Lyon, David. 2003. *Surveillance as Social Sorting: Privacy, Risk, and Digital Discrimination*. London: Routledge.

– 2014. "Surveillance, Snowden, and Big Data: Capacities, Consequences, Critique." *Big Data & Society* 1, no. 2 (July). https://doi.org/10.1177/2053951714541861.

MacIntyre, Alasdair and Dorothy Emmet, eds. 1970. *Sociological Theory and Philosophical Analysis*. London: Macmillan.

Magnan, Andre. 2004. "Social and Political Implications of Genetically Modified Crops in Saskatchewan." *Prairie Forum* 29, no. 2: 301–16.

Mann, Susan A., and James M. Dickinson. 1980. "Obstacles to the Development of a Capitalist Agriculture." *The Journal of Peasant Studies* 5, no. 4: 466–81. https://doi.org/10.1080/03066157808438058.

Manovich, Lev. 2001. *The Language of New Media*. Cambridge, MA: MIT Press.

Markham, Annette N. 2003. "Metaphors Reflecting and Shaping the Reality of the Internet: Tool, Place, Way of Being." Presented at *International Association of Internet Researchers Conference*, Toronto, Canada. https://annettemarkham.com/writing/MarkhamTPW.pdf.

Marsden, Terry, Richard Munton, Sarah Whatmore, and Jo Little. 1986. "Towards a Political Economy of Capitalist Agriculture: A British Perspective." *International Journal of Urban and Regional Research* 10, no. 4 (December): 498–521. https://doi.org/10.1111/j.1468-2427.1986.tb00026.x.

Martin, Aryn, and Michael Lynch. 2009. "Counting Things and People: The Practices and Politics of Counting." *Social Problems* 56, no. 2 (May): 243–66. https://doi.org/10.1525/sp.2009.56.2.243.

Marvin, Carolyn. 1988. *When Old Technologies Were New: Thinking About Electric Communication in the Late Nineteenth Century*. New York: Oxford University Press.

Marx, Karl. 1889. *Capital: A Critical Analysis of Capitalist Production*. London: Sonnenschein.

Marx, Leo. 2010. "*Technology*: The Emergence of a Hazardous Concept." *Technology and Culture* 51, no. 3 (July): 561–77. https://doi.org/10.1353/tech.2010.0009.

Marx, Leo, and Merritt Roe Smith, eds. 1994. *Does Technology Drive History? The Dilemma of Technological Determinism*. Cambridge, MA: MIT Press.

Mayer-Schonberger, Viktor, and Kenneth Cukier. 2014. *Big Data: A Revolution That Will transform How We Live, Work, and Think*. London: John Murray.

McBratney, Alex, Brett Whelan, Tihomir Ancev, and Johan Bouma. 2005. "Future Directions of Precision Agriculture." *Precision Agriculture* 6, no. 1 (February): 7–23. https://doi.org/10.1007/s11119-005-0681-8.

McDonnell, Tim. 2014. "Monsanto Is Using Big Data to Take over the World." *Mother Jones*. 19 November. https://www.motherjones.com/environment/2014/11/monsanto-big-data-gmo-climate-change/.

McMichael, Philip. 2001. *Development and Social Change: A Global Perspective*. Thousand Oaks, CA: SAGE.

– 2009. "A Food Regime Genealogy." *The Journal of Peasant Studies* 36, no. 1: 139–69. https://doi.org/10.1080/03066150902820354.

– 2012. "Food Regime Crisis and Revaluing the Agrarian Question." In *Rethinking Agricultural Policy Regimes: Food Security, Climate Change and the Future*, edited by Reider Almas and Hugh Campbell, 99–122. Bingley: Emerald Group.

Menne, Tobias. 2017. "Digital Farming Set to Revolutionize Agriculture." *Politico*. 6 July. https://www.politico.eu/sponsored-content/digital-farming-set-to-revolutionize-agriculture/.

Merchant, Carolyn. 1990. *The Death of Nature: Women, Ecology, and the Scientific Revolution*. New York: Harper & Row.

Merton, Robert. 1942. *The Sociology of Science: Theoretical and Empirical Investigations*. Edited by Norman Storer. Chicago: University of Chicago Press.

Michalopoulos, Sarantis. 2015. "Europe Entering the Era of 'Precision Agriculture.'" *EurActiv*. 23 October. https://www.euractiv.com/section/science-policymaking/news/europe-entering-the-era-of-precision-agriculture/.

Micheels, Eric T., and James F. Nolan. 2016. "Examining the Effects of Absorptive Capacity and Social Capital on the Adoption of Agricultural Innovations: A Canadian Prairie Case Study." *Agricultural Systems* 145 (June): 127–38. https://doi.org/10.1016/j.agsy.2016.03.010.

Miller, Toby. 2010. "Surveillance: The 'Digital Trail of Breadcrumbs,'" *Culture Unbound*, 2: 9–14.

Mirowski, Philip. 2011. *Science-Mart*. Cambridge, MA: Harvard University Press.

– 2018. "The Future(s) of Open Science." *Social Studies of Science* 48, no. 2 (April): 171–203. https://doi.org/10.1177/0306312718772086.

Mitchell, Timothy. 2002. *Rule of Experts: Egypt, Techno-Politics, Modernity*. Berkeley: University of California Press.

Mollison, Bill. 1988. *Permaculture: A Designer's Manual*. Tyalgum, Australia: Tagari.

Mooney, Patrick. 2000. "Specifying the 'Rural' in Social Movement Theory." *Polish Sociological Review* 129: 35–55.

Moore Lappé, Frances. 1991. *Diet for a Small Planet*. New York: Ballantine.

Morning, Ann. 2008. "Reconstructing Race in Science and Society: Biology Textbooks, 1952–2002." *American Journal of Sociology* 114, no. S1: 106–37. https://doi.org/10.1086/592206.

Mosco, Vincent. 2014. *To the Cloud: Big Data in a Turbulent World*. Boulder, CO: Paradigm.

– 2015. "The Political Economy of Communication: A Living Tradition." In *Power, Media, Culture: A Critical View from the Political Economy of Communication*, edited by Luis A. Albornoz, 35–57. London: Palgrave Macmillan.

Mosier, Kathleen L. 2009. "Searching for Coherence in a Correspondence World." *Judgment and Decision Making* 4, no. 2 (March): 154–63. http://www.sjdm.org/~baron/journal/ccm/ccm.pdf.

Muller, Birgit. 2008. "Still Feeding the World? The Political Ecology of Canadian Prairie Farmers." *Anthropologica* 50, no. 2: 389–407.

Nadler, Andrew. 2017. "Weather Monitoring Means Less Guessing and More Knowing." *Farm Forum*. https://farmforum.ca/article/weather-monitoring-means-less-guessing-and-more-knowing/.

Nafus, Dawn and Jamie Sherman. 2014. "This One Does Not Go Up to 11: The Quantified Self Movement as an Alternative Big Data Practice," *International Journal of Communication* 8:1784–94. https://ijoc.org/index.php/ijoc/article/view/2170/1157.

National Research Council. 2010. *Toward Sustainable Agricultural Systems in the 21st Century*. https://doi.org/10.17226/12832.

National Telecommunications and Information Administration. 1991. "The NTIA Infrastructure Report: Telecommunications in the Age of Information." Washington, DC: US Government Printing Office.

Neate, Rupert. 2016. "Bayer's $66bn Takeover Bid of Monsanto Called a 'Marriage Made in Hell.'" *The Guardian*. 14 September. https://www.theguardian.com/business/2016/sep/14/bayer-takeover-monsanto-66-billion-deal.

Nesheim, Malden C., Maria Oria, and Peggy Tsai Yih, eds. 2015. "Nitrogen in Agroecosystems." In *A Framework for Assessing Effects of the Food System*. Washington: National Academies Press.

Newby, Howard. 1979. "Urbanization and the Rural Class Structure: Reflections on a Case Study." *The British Journal of Sociology* 30, no. 4 (December): 475–99. https://doi.org/10.2307/589634.

Newby, Sir Howard. 2008. "Reflections on Colin Bell and the Past and Future of Community Studies." *International Journal of Social Research Methodology* 11, no. 2: 93–6. https://doi.org/10.1080/13645570801940731.

Newman, Nathan. 2017. "The Monsanto Privacy Model? Monsanto and Farmer Organizations May Be Forging New Path to Data Cooperation." *Huffington Post*. 27 March. https://www.huffpost.com/entry/the-monsanto-privacy-mode_b_6955640.

Newman, Nathan, and Jesse Bunge. 2016. "Bayer Deal for Monsanto Caps Reshaping of Seed and Pesticide Sector. *Wall Street Journal*. 14 September. https://www.wsj.com/articles/bayer-deal-for-monsanto-caps-reshaping-of-seed-and-pesticide-sector-1473864494.

Nielson, David, Yuan-Ting Meng, Anna Buyvolova, and Artavazd Hakobyan. 2018. "Unleashing the Power of Digital on Farms in Russia – and Seeking Opportunities for Small Farms." World Bank. https://documents1.worldbank.org/curated/en/174171539109767548/pdf/126745-P164457-RussiaDigitalAgreport.pdf.

Northern Development Initiative Trust. 2021. "Connecting British Columbia." https://www.northerndevelopment.bc.ca/funding-programs/partner-programs/connecting-british-columbia/.

Obar, Jonathan A., and Anne Oeldorf-Hirsch. 2020. "The Biggest Lie on the Internet: Ignoring the Privacy Policies and Terms of Service Policies of Social Networking Services." *Information, Communication & Society* 23, no. 1: 128–47. https://doi.org/10.1080/1369118X.2018.1486870.

Office of the Privacy Commissioner of Canada. 2013. "Drones in Canada. Will the Proliferation of Domestic Drone Use in Canada Raise New Concerns for Privacy?" https://www.priv.gc.ca/en/opc-actions-and-decisions/research/explore-privacy-research/2013/drones_201303/.

OHCHR (United Nations Human Rights Office of the High Commissioner). n.d. "Special Rapporteur on the Right to Food." https://www.ohchr.org/en/issues/food/pages/foodindex.aspx.

OKFN (Open Knowledge Foundation). n.d. "Open Knowledge Canada." https://ca.okfn.org/.

OKFN and Access Info Europe. 2011. "Beyond Access: Open Government Data & the Right to (Re)Use Public Information." https://www.access-info.org/wp-content/uploads/Beyond_Access_7_January_2011_web.pdf.

Olson, Parmy. "Much 'Artificial Intelligence' Is Still People Behind a Screen," *Bloomberg Opinion*, 13 October 2021, online at https://www.bloomberg.com/opinion/articles/2021-10-13/how-good-is-ai-much-artificial-intelligence-is-still-people-behind-a-screen.

OMAFRA (Ontario Ministry of Agriculture, Food and Rural Affairs). 2016. "Accredited Soil Testing Laboratories in Ontario." Last modified 5 May 2021. http://www.omafra.gov.on.ca/english/crops/resource/soillabs.htm.

O'Neil, Cathy. 2016. *Weapons of Math Destruction: How Big Data Increases Inequality and Threatens Democracy*. New York: Crown.

Open Data Charter. n.d. "Executive Summary." Agriculture Open Data Package. https://opendatacharter.net/agriculture-open-data-package/.

Osler, Hoskin & Harcourt. 2018. "Canada." In *The International Comparative Legal Guide to: Data Protection 2018*, edited by Suzie Levy and Caroline Collingwood, 54–65. London: Global Legal Group. https://iapp.org/media/pdf/resource_center/Legal_Guide_To_Data_Protection_2018.pdf.

Ouma, Stefan. 2020. *Farming as Financial Asset, Global Finance and the Making of Institutional Landscapes*. New York: Columbia University Press.

Parthasarathy, Shobita. 2017. *Patent Politics: Life Forms, Markets, and the Public Interest in the United States and Europe*. Chicago: University of Chicago Press.

Pasquale, Frank. 2010. "Data and Power: From Individual Consent to Societal Transparency." Unpublished manuscript.

– 2015. *The Black Box Society*. Cambridge, MA: Harvard University Press.

Pasquale, Frank, and Tara Adams Ragone. 2014. "Protecting Health Privacy in an Era of Big Data Processing and Cloud Computing." *Stanford Technology Law Review* 17: 595–653.

Patel, Raj. 2007. "The World Bank and Agriculture: A Critical Review of the World Bank's World Development Report 2008." *ActionAid International*. http://rajpatel.org/wp-content/uploads/2009/11/actionaid.pdf.

PayScale. n.d. "Average Salary in Silicon Valley, California." https://www.payscale.com/research/US/Location=Silicon-Valley-CA/Salary.

Pentland, Alex. 2015. *Social Physics: How Social Networks Can Make Us Smarter*. New York: Penguin.

Perelman, Michael. 2003. "Myths of the Market: Economics and the Environment." *Organization & Environment* 16, no. 2 (June): 168–226. https://doi.org/10.1177/1086026603016002002.

Perry, J. Adam. 2012. "Barely Legal: Racism and Migrant Farm Labour in the Context of Canadian Multiculturalism." *Citizenship Studies* 16, no. 2: 189–201. https://doi.org/10.1080/13621025.2012.667611.

Phillips, Peter W.B., Jo-Anne Relf-Eckstein, Jobe Graeme, and Brian Wixted. 2019. "Configuring the New Digital Landscape in Western Canadian Agriculture." NJAS — *Wageningen Journal of Life Sciences* 90–1 (December). https://doi.org/10.1016/j.njas.2019.04.001.

Philpott, Tom. 2018. "Along with Monsanto, Chemical Giant Bayer Inherits its Pests." *Mother Jones*. 24 August. https://www.motherjones.com/food/2018/08/along-with-monsanto-chemical-giant-bayer-inherits-its-pests/.

Pierce, J. Francis, and Peter Nowak. 1999. "Aspects of Precision Agriculture." *Advances in Agronomy* 67: 1–85. https://doi.org/10.1016/s0065-2113(08)60513-1.

Polanyi, Michael. 1967. *The Tacit Dimension*. Terry Lectures. Garden City, NY: Anchor.

Poppe, Krijn, Sjaak Wolfert, Cor Verdouw, and Alan Renwick. 2015. "A European Perspective on the Economics of Big Data." *Farm Policy Journal* 12, no. 1: 11–19.

Porter, Theodore M. 1996. *Trust in Numbers: The Pursuit of Objectivity in Science and Public Life*. History and Philosophy of Science. Princeton, NJ: Princeton University Press.

Pozen, David E. 2010. "Deep Secrecy." *Stanford Law Review* 62, no. 2: 257–339.

Pugliese, Patrizia. 2001. "Organic Farming and Sustainable Rural Development: A

Multifaceted and Promising Convergence." *Sociologia Ruralis* 41, no. 1 (January): 112–30. https://doi.org/10.1111/1467-9523.00172.

Purdon, Nick, and Leonardo Palleja. 2020. "'I Thought I Was Going to Die': Canadian Farmers Open Up about Struggles with Mental Health." CBC. 17 February. https://www.cbc.ca/news/health/the-national-farmers-mental-health-1.5431158.

Pursell, Carroll. 1993. "The Rise and Fall of the Appropriate Technology Movement in the United States, 1965-1985." *Technology and Culture* 34, no. 3 (July): 629–37. https://doi.org/10.2307/3106707.

Qualman, Darrin. 2019. "Tackling the Farm Crisis and the Climate Crisis." Saskatoon: National Farmers Union. https://www.nfu.ca/wp-content/uploads/2019/12/Tackling-the-Farm-Crisis-and-the-Climate-Crisis-Final-with-covers.pdf.

Ramsay, Stephen. 2011. *Reading Machines: Toward an Algorithmic Criticism*. Topics in the Digital Humanities. Urbana: University of Illinois Press.

Raymond, Eric S. 2001. *The Cathedral and the Bazaar: Musings on Linux and Open Source by an Accidental Revolutionary*. Cambridge, MA: O'Reilly. Originally published 1999.

Recode Staff. 2017. "European Union Competition Commissioner Margrethe Vestager on Recode Decode." *Vox*. 9 December. https://www.vox.com/2017/12/9/16752750/european-union-eu-competition-commissioner-margrethe-vestager-recode-decode-lisbon-web-summit.

Reichardt, M., and C. Jürgens. 2009. "Adoption and Future Perspective of Precision Farming in Germany: Results of Several Surveys Among Different Agricultural Target Groups." *Precision Agriculture* 10, no. 1 (February): 73–94. https://doi.org/10.1007/s11119-008-9101-1.

Reichardt, M., C. Jürgens, U. Klöble, J. Hüter, and K. Moser. 2009. "Dissemination of Precision Farming in Germany: Acceptance, Adoption, Obstacles, Knowledge Transfer and Training Activities." *Precision Agriculture* 10, no. 6 (December): 525–45. https://doi.org/10.1007/s11119-009-9112-6.

Reif, Linda. 1987. "Farm Structure, Industry Structure, and Socioeconomic Conditions in the United States." *Rural Sociology* 52, no. 4: 462–82.

"The Revolution in North American Agriculture." 1972. *National Geographic Magazine*.

Roberts, Roland K., Burton C. English, James A. Larson, Rebecca L. Cochran, W. Robert Goodman, Sherry L. Larkin, Michele C. Marra, Steven W. Martin, W. Donald Shurley, and Jeanne M. Reeves. 2004. "Adoption of Site-Specific Information and Variable-Rate Technologies in Cotton Precision Farming." *Journal of Agricultural and Applied Economics* 36, no. 1 (April): 143–58. https://doi.org/10.1017/S107407080002191X.

Robin, Marie-Monique. 2008. *The World According to Monsanto*. Image et

Compagnie, ARTE, Office national du film du Canada, Productions Thalie, and Westdeutscher Rundfunk.

Rosenberg, Daniel. 2013. "Data Before the Fact." In *'Raw Data' Is An Oxymorn*, edited by Lisa Gitelman, 15–40.

Rossel, Raphael A., and Johan Bouma. 2016. "Soil Sensing: A New Paradigm for Agriculture." *Agricultural Systems* 148 (October): 71–4. https://doi.org/10.1016/j.agsy.2016.07.001.

Rotz, Sarah, and Evan D.G. Fraser. 2015. "Resilience and the Industrial Food System: Analyzing the Impacts of Agricultural Industrialization on Food System Vulnerability." *Journal of Environmental Studies and Sciences* 5, no. 3 (September): 459–73. https://doi.org/10.1007/s13412-015-0277-1.

Rotz, Sarah, Evan D.G. Fraser, and Ralph C. Martin. 2017. "Situating Tenure, Capital and Finance in Farmland Relations: Implications for Stewardship and Agroecological Health in Ontario, Canada." *The Journal of Peasant Studies* 46, no. 1: 142–64. https://doi.org/10.1080/03066150.2017.1351953.

Russell, Matthew A., and Mikhail Klassen. 2019. *Mining the Social Web: Data Mining Facebook, Twitter, LinkedIn, Instagram, GitHub, and More*. Sebastopol, CA: O'Reilly.

Sample, Mark. 2013. "Criminal Code: Procedural Logic and Rhetorical Excess in Videogames," *Digital Humanities Quarterly* 7, no. (1). http://www.digitalhumanities.org/dhq/vol/7/1/000153/000153.html.

Sandvig, Christian, Kevin Hamilton, Karrie Karahalios, and Cedric Langbort. 2014. "Auditing Algorithms: Research Methods for Detecting Discrimination on Internet Platforms." *Data and Discrimination: Converting Critical Concerns into Productive Inquiry.* 64th Annual Meeting of the International Communication Association, 22 May. Seattle, WA.

Santos Valle, Santiego, and Josef Kienzle. 2020. *Agriculture 4.0 – Agricultural Robotics and Automated Equipment for Sustainable Crop Production*. Food and Agriculture Organization of the United Nations. Report online at, http://www.fao.org/3/cb2186en/CB2186EN.pdf.

Sarewitz, Daniel. 1996. *Frontiers of Illusion: Science, Technology and the Politics of Progress*. Philadelphia, PA: Temple University Press.

Sawhney, Harmeet. 1996. "Information Superhighway: Metaphors as Midwives." *Media, Culture & Society* 18, no. 2 (April): 291–314. https://doi.org/10.1177/016344396018002007.

Schnaiberg, Allan. 1980. *The Environment: From Surplus to Scarcity*. New York: Oxford University Press.

Schumacher, Ernst Friedrich. 2010. *Small Is Beautiful: Economics as if People Mattered.* New York: Harper Perennial. First published 1973.

Sciadas, George. 2002. *The Digital Divide in Canada*. Science, Innovation and Electronic Information Division, Statistics Canada. https://www.deslibris.ca/ID/201029.

Scott, James C. 1998. *Seeing Like a State: How Certain Schemes to Improve the Human Condition Have Failed*. Yale University Press.

– 2014. *Two Cheers for Anarchism: Six Easy Pieces on Autonomy, Dignity, and Meaningful Work and Play*. Princeton, NJ: Princeton University Press.

Selin, Cynthia. "Expectations and the Emergence of Nanotechnology." *Science, Technology, & Human Values* 32, no. 2 (March): 196–220. https://doi.org/10.1177/0162243906296918.

Shah, Adnan Noor, Mohsin Tanveer, Babar Shahzad, Guozheng Yang, Shah Fahad, Saif Ali, Muhammad Adnan Bukhari, Shahbaz Atta Tung, Abdul Hafeez, and Biangkham Souliyanonh. 2017. "Soil Compaction Effects on Soil Health and Crop Productivity: An Overview." *Environmental Science and Pollution Research* 24 (January): 10056–67. https://doi.org/10.1007/s11356-017-8421-y.

Shapin, Steven. 2010. *Never Pure: Historical Studies of Science as if It Was Produced by People with Bodies, Situated in Time, Space, Culture, and Society, and Struggling for Credibility and Authority*. Baltimore: Johns Hopkins University Press.

Shapin, Steven, and Simon Schaffer. 1985. *Leviathan and the Air-Pump: Hobbes, Boyle, and the Experimental Life*. Princeton, NJ: Princeton University Press.

Shildrick, Margrit. 2005. "The Disabled Body, Genealogy and Undecidability." *Cultural Studies* 19, no. 6: 755–70. https://doi.org/10.1080/09502380500365754.

Shirky, Clay. 2009. "A Speculative Post on the Idea of Algorithmic Authority."

Short, N., R. Cromp, W.J. Campbell, J.C. Tilton, J.J. LeMoigne, G. Fekete, N.S. Netanyahu, K. Wichmann, and W.B. Ligon. 1995. "Mission to Planet Earth: AI Views the World." *IEEE Expert* 10, no. 6 (December): 24–34. https://doi.org/10.1109/64.483009.

Silva, Claudia, Marcia Moraes, and Jose Molin. 2011. "Adoption and Use of Precision Agriculture Technologies in the Sugarcane Industry of São Paulo State, Brazil." *Precision Agriculture* 12, no. 1 (February): 67–81. https://doi.org/10.1007/s11119-009-9155-8.

Sismondo, Sergio. 2008. "How Pharmaceutical Industry Funding Affects Trial Outcomes: Causal Structures and Responses." *Social Science & Medicine* 66, no. 9 (May): 1909–14. https://doi.org/10.1016/j.socscimed.2008.01.010.

– 2018. *Ghost-Managed Medicine: Big Pharma's Invisible Hands*. Mattering Press.

Smith, Benjamin, and Jared W. Magnani. 2019. "New Technologies, New Disparities: The Intersection of Electronic Health and Digital Health Literacy." *International Journal of Cardiology* 292 (October): 280–2. https://doi.org/10.1016/j.ijcard.2019.05.066.

Soden, Robert. 2021. "Reimagining Environmental Data," *Interactions* (January–February 2022): 45–7, DOI: 10.1145/3501302.

Solon, Olivia. 2017. "A Right to Repair: Why Nebraska Farmers Are Taking on John Deere and Apple." *The Guardian*. 6 March. https://www.theguardian.com/environment/2017/mar/06/nebraska-farmers-right-to-repair-john-deere-apple.

Sonka, Steven. 2015. "Big Data: From Hype to Agricultural Tool." *Farm Policy Journal* 12 (January): 1–9.

Stafford, John V. 2000. "Implementing Precision Agriculture in the 21st Century." *Journal of Agricultural Engineering Research* 76, no. 3 (July): 267–75. https://doi.org/10.1006/jaer.2000.0577.

Stanford Graduate School of Business. 2017. Chamath Palihapitiya, Founder and CEO Social Capital, on Money as an Instrument of Change." YouTube video, 13 November. https://www.youtube.com/watch?v=PMotykwoSIk.

Statistics Canada. 2016. "2016 Census of Agriculture." Last modified 8 April 2021. https://www.statcan.gc.ca/eng/ca2016.

Steele, Dale. 2017. "Analysis of Precision Agriculture Adoption & Barriers in Western Canada." Agriculture and Agri-Food Canada. http://static.albertafarmexpress.ca/wp-content/uploads/2017/05/Final-Report-Analysis-of-Precision-Agriculture-Adoption-and-Barriers-in-western-Canada-April-2017.pdf#_ga=2.133338444.371781874.1623806639-1802075309.1623806639.

Stenta, Michael. 2018. "Mapping in Farmos." YouTube video, 4 December. https://www.youtube.com/watch?v=LOtHcWVc4T8.

Stokstad, Erik. 2008. "Dueling Visions for a Hungry World." *Science* 319, no. 5869 (March): 1474–6. https://doi.org/10.1126/science.319.5869.1474.

Stoll, Steven. 1998. *The Fruits of Natural Advantage: Making the Industrial Countryside in California*. Oakland: University of California Press.

Streitfeld, David, Natasha Singer, and Steven Erlanger. 2018. "How Calls for Privacy May Upend Business for Facebook and Google." *The New York Times*. 24 March. https://www.nytimes.com/2018/03/24/technology/google-facebook-data-privacy.html.

Strubenhoff, Heinz, and Roy Parizat. 2018. "Can the Digital Revolution Transform Agriculture?" *Brookings Institute*. 28 February. https://www.brookings.edu/blog/future-development/2018/02/28/can-the-digital-revolution-transform-agriculture/.

Suber, Peter. 2009. "Timeline of the Open Access Movement." https://dash.harvard.edu/bitstream/handle/1/4724185/suber_timeline.htm.

Tannahill, Reay. 1973. *Food in History*. New York: Stein and Day.

Tansey, Geoff, and Tasmin Rajotte, eds. 2008. *The Future Control of Food: A Guide to International Negotiations and Rules on Intellectual Property, Biodiversity and*

Food Security. London: Earthscan and the International Development Research Centre.

Taplin, Jonathan. 2017. *Move Fast and Break Things: How Facebook, Google, and Amazon Cornered Culture and Undermined Democracy.* New York: Little, Brown and Company.

Taylor, Charles. 2003. *Modern Social Imaginaries*. Durham, NC: Duke University Press.

TED. 2012. "Clay Shirky: How the Internet Will (One Day) Transform Government." YouTube video, 25 September. https://www.youtube.com/watch?v=CEN4XNth61o&feature=youtube.

te Kulve, Haico, Kornelia Konrad, Carla Alvial Palavicino, and Bart Walhout. 2013. "Context Matters: Promises and Concerns Regarding Nanotechnologies for Water and Food Applications" *NanoEthics* 7, no. 1 (April): 17–27. https://doi.org/10.1007/s11569-013-0168-4.

Tesfom, Goitom, and Nancy Birch. 2010. "Do They Buy for Their Dogs the Way They Buy for Themselves?" *Psychology and Marketing* 27, no. 9 (September): 898–912. https://doi.org/10.1002/mar.20364.

Thompson, John, and Ian Scoones. 2009. "Addressing the Dynamics of Agri-Food Systems: An Emerging Agenda for Social Science Research." *Environmental Science & Policy* 12 (4): 386–97. https://doi.org/10.1016/j.envsci.2009.03.001.

Tidwell, Abraham S.D., and Jessica M. Smith. 2015. "Morals, Materials, and Technoscience: The Energy Security Imaginary in the United States." *Science, Technology, & Human Values* 40, no. 5 (September): 687–711. https://doi.org/10.1177/0162243915577632.

Treinen, Sophie, and Alice van der Elstraeten. 2018. "Gender and ICTs: Mainstreaming Gender in Use of Information and Communication Technologies (ICTs) for Agriculture and Rural Development." United Nations Food and Agriculture Organization. https://www.comminit.com/global/content/gender-and-icts-mainstreaming-gender-use-information-and-communication-technologies-icts.

Trimble Agriculture. n.d. "Agricultural Intelligence in Your Hands." 2020. https://agriculture.trimble.com/.

Tunney, Catherine. 2017 "To Take Advantage of Coming Agriculture 'Revolution' Canada Needs Investment, Says Expert." *CBC News*. 18 February. https://www.cbc.ca/news/politics/evan-fraser-barton-report-agri-food-1.3987948.

Turkle, Sherry. 1985. *The Second Self: Computers and the Human Spirit.* Cambridge, MA: MIT Press.

Turnbull, David. 2003. *Masons, Tricksters and Cartographers: Comparative Studies in the Sociology of Scientific and Indigenous Knowledge.* London: Routledge.

Turner, Billie Lee. 1989. "The Specialist–Synthesis Approach to the Revival of Geography: The Case of Cultural Ecology." *Annals of the Association of American Geographers* 79, no. 1: 88–100. https://doi.org/10.1111/j.1467-8306.1989.tb00252.x.

Umoja Noble, Safiya. 2018. *Algorithms of Oppression: How Search Engines Reinforce Racism*. New York: New York University Press.

UNFAO (The Food and Agriculture Organization of the United Nations). 2008. *The State of Food Insecurity in the World, 2008*. Rome: UNFAO. http://www.fao.org/3/i0291e/i0291e00.htm.

– 2014a. *Agroecology for Food Security and Nutrition: Proceedings of the FAO International Symposium*. Rome: UNFAO. https://foodfirst.org/wp-content/uploads/2015/11/a-i4729e.pdf.

– 2014b. "Putting Family Farmers First to Eradicate Hunger." 16 October. http://www.fao.org/news/story/en/item/260535/icode/.

– 2018. "FAO's Work on Agricultural Innovation: Sowing the Seeds of Transformation to Achieve the SDGs." http://www.fao.org/policy-support/tools-and-publications/resources-details/en/c/1365983/.

Urban, Dean L., Robert V. O'Neill, and Herman H. Shugart. 1987. "Landscape Ecology." *BioScience* 37, no. 2 (February): 119–27. https://doi.org/10.2307/1310366.

Urry, John. 2016. *What is the Future?* Cambridge, UK: Polity.

US SEC (United States Securities and Exchange Commission). 2021. "Cybersecurity." Last modified 26 February 2021. https://www.sec.gov/spotlight/cybersecurity.

US Senate. 2017. "Hearing Before the United States Senate Committee on the Judiciary Subcommittee on Crime and Terrorism: Testimony of Colin Stretch." 31 October. https://www.judiciary.senate.gov/imo/media/doc/10-3117%20Stretch%20Testimony.pdf.

Väliverronen, Esa. 2004. "Stories of the Medicine Cow: Representations of Future Promises in Media Discourses." *Public Understanding of Science* 13, no. 4 (October): 363–77. https://doi.org/10.1177%2F0963662504046635.

Valentino-Devries, Jennifer, Jeremy Singer-Vine, and Ashkan Soltani. 2012. "Websites Vary Prices, Deals Based on Users' Information." *Wall Street Journal*. 24 December. https://www.wsj.com/articles/SB10001424127887323777204578189391813881534.

Vasisht, Deepak, Zerina Kapetanovic, Jongo Won, Xinxin Jin, Ranveer Chandra, Ashish Kapoor, Sudipta N. Sinha, and Manhusudhan Sudarshan. 2017. "FarmBeats: An IoT Platform for Data-Driven Agriculture." Proceedings of the 14th USENIX Symposium on Networked Systems Design and Implementation. Boston. https://www.usenix.org/system/files/conference/nsdi17/nsdi17-vasisht.pdf.

Via Campesina. 1996. "The Right to Produce and Access to Land: Position of the Via Campesina on Food Sovereignty." Rome: World Food Summit.

Vieri, Marco, Riccardo Lisci, Marco Rimediotti, and Daniele Sarri. 2013. "The RHEA-Project Robot for Tree Crops Pesticide Application." *Journal of Agricultural Engineering* 44, no. S2. https://doi.org/10.4081/jae.2013.313.

Viviano, Frank. 2018. "How the Netherlands Feeds the World." *National Geographic Magazine*. https://www.nationalgeographic.com/magazine/2017/09/holland-agriculture-sustainable-farming/.

Vogt, Willie. 2015. "Drilling Down on John Deere, Climate Corp Deal" *Farm Industry News*. 3 November.

von Neumann, John. 1948. "Electronic Methods of Computation." *Bulletin of the American Academy of Arts and Sciences* 1, no. 3 (March): 2–4. https://doi.org/10.2307/3824008.

– 1949. *Theory of Self-Reproducing Automata*. University of Illinois Lectures on the Theory and Organization of Complicated Automata. Urbana: University of Illinois Press.

Weinberger, David. 2010. "The Problem with the Data-Information-Knowledge-Wisdom Hierarchy." *Harvard Business Review*. 2 February. https://hbr.org/2010/02/data-is-to-info-as-info-is-not.

Weingarten, Debbie. 2018. "Why Are America's Farmers Killing Themselves?" *The Guardian*. 11 December. https://www.theguardian.com/us-news/2017/dec/06/why-are-americas-farmers-killing-themselves-in-record-numbers.

Weis, Anthony John. 2007. *The Global Food Economy: The Battle for the Future of Farming*. London: Zed Books.

Weizenbaum, Joseph. 1975. *Computer Power and Human Reason: From Judgment to Calculation*. San Francisco: W.H. Freeman.

Welsh, Rick, and Leland Glenna. 2006. "Considering the Role of the University in Conducting Research on Agri-Biotechnologies." *Social Studies of Science* 36, no. 6 (December): 929–42. https://doi.org/10.1177/0306312706060062.

Wheat Growers. 2019. "Western Canadian Wheat Growers: Advocating for Us." Western Canadian Wheat Growers Association. https://wheatgrowers.ca/.

Wiener, Norbert. 2007. *Cybernetics: Or Control and Communication in the Animal and the Machine*. Cambridge, MA: MIT Press.

Wilson, Geoff A. 2001. "From Productivism to Post-Productivism … and Back Again? Exploring the (Un)Changed Natural and Mental Landscapes of European Agriculture." *Transactions of the Institute of British Geographers* 26, no. 1 (March): 77–102. https://doi.org/10.1111/1475-5661.00007.

Winner, Langdon. 1980. "Do Artifacts Have Politics?" *Daedalus* 109, no. 1: 121–36.
– 1986. *The Whale and the Reactor: A Search for Limits in an Age of High Technology*. Chicago: University of Chicago Press.
Winograd, Terry. 2006. "Shifting Viewpoints: Artificial Intelligence and Human–Computer Interaction." *Artificial Intelligence* 170, no. 18 (December): 1256–8. https://doi.org/10.1016/j.artint.2006.10.011.
Wolf, Steven A., and Frederick H. Buttel. 1996. "The Political Economy of Precision Farming." *American Journal of Agricultural Economics* 78, no. 5 (December): 1269–74. https://doi.org/10.2307/1243505.
Wolf, Steven A., and Spencer D. Wood. 1997. "Precision Farming: Environmental Legitimation, Commodification of Information, and Industrial Coordination." *Rural Sociology* 62, no. 2 (June): 180–206. https://doi.org/10.1111/j.1549-0831.1997.tb00650.x.
Wong, Yu Cheung, John Yat Chu Fung, Chi Kwong Law, Jolie Chi Yee Lam, and Vincent Wan Ping Lee. 2009. "Tackling the Digital Divide." *British Journal of Social Work* 39, no. 4 (June): 754–67. https://doi.org/10.1093/bjsw/bcp026.
Woolley, Samuel C., and Philip N. Howard. 2016. "Political Communication, Computational Propaganda, and Autonomous Agents." *International Journal of Communication* 10 (January): 4882–90.
World Bank. 2013. "World Bank Group Agriculture Action Plan 2013-2015." 25 March. http://documents.worldbank.org/curated/en/639551468163485999/World-Bank-Group-agriculture-action-plan-2013-2015.
– 2016. "World Bank Group Climate Change Action Plan 2016–2020." 17 January. http://documents.worldbank.org/curated/en/755721468011421594/World-Bank-Group-Climate-Change-Action-Plan-2016-2020.
– 2017. "Mobile Technologies and Digitized Data to Promote Access to Finance for Women in Agriculture." Washington: World Bank Group. https://openknowledge.worldbank.org/bitstream/handle/10986/29104/122110-WP-PUBLIC-DFSforwomeninagrireport.pdf?sequence=1&isAllowed=y.
World Bank Group and China Development Bank, 2017. "Leapfrogging: The Key to Africa's Development? From Constraints to Investment Opportunities." https://openknowledge.worldbank.org/bitstream/handle/10986/28440/119849-WP-PUBLIC-Africa-Leapfrogging-text-with-dividers-9-20-17-web.pdf?sequence=1&isAllowed=y.
Wyatt, Sally. 2004. "Danger! Metaphors at Work in Economics, Geophysiology, and the Internet." *Science, Technology, & Human Values* 29, no. 2 (April): 242–61. https://doi.org/10.1177/0162243903261947.
Wynne, Brian. 2011. "Intolerance: Science Informs, Not Defines." *Nature* 471 (March). https://doi.org/10.1038/471305b.

Yearly, Steven. 2005. *Making Sense of Science: Understanding the Social Study of Science*. London: SAGE.
Zuboff, Shoshana. 2019. *The Age of Surveillance Capitalism: The Fight for a Human Future at the New Frontier of Power*. New York: PublicAffairs.

Index

"Addressing the Shortage of Appropriate Farm Technologies Through DIY," (Oslund), 67–8
AFBF (American Farm Bureau Federation), 131
AgBox (data-sharing tool), 131
Ag Data Transparent (ADT), 131
agrarian question, 45, 158n9
agribusinesses: and capitalism, 158n9; criticized by UN, 52; and the future, 18–19; legislation on trade in data, 133; purchase versus development of technology, 143–4; relationship with farmers, 26, 36, 61, 150; view of environmental issues, 139. *See also* Bayer/Monsanto Corporation; Deere & Company; Monsanto Corporation; precision agriculture (PA); productivism; sustainable agriculture (agribusinesses)
Agriculture and Agri-Food Canada, 86
"Agriculture at a Crossroads" (IAASTD), 17, 51
"Agriculture Open Data Package" (Open Data Charter), 72–3
Agriculture-Vision dataset, 142
Agri-Food Technologies, Ontario, 131
Agroclimate Impact Reporter (AIR), 104
agro-ecology, 52, 78, 80
algorithms: about, 31, 82, 90; bias and discrimination, 90–2; gap in predictions, 102; and humans, 19, 106; as if they had agency, 84, 89, 97, 99; need for data, 124, 125–6; patents on, 117; precision agriculture use of, 43; procedural rhetoric, 119, 160n2; as proprietary for agribusinesses, 12; and regional, contextual knowledge, 152; in social media, 7, 89; in software applications, 33. *See also* artificial intelligence (AI); data; immaculate conception of data (ICD)
Algorithms of Oppression (Noble), 92
Alloway, Reid, 67–9, 77
Alperovitz, Gar, 79
Amazon, 7, 34, 128, 144, 146, 155n2
American Farm Bureau Federation (AFBF), 131
American Society of Agricultural and Biological Engineers (ASABE), 140
anti-trust regulations, 133, 134
Antle, John M., 126
Apple, 155n2
appropriate technology movement, 64–5, 67–70, 80–1
Aradau, Claudia, 148
Arell Food Institute (University of Guelph), 59
artificial intelligence (AI): awareness of consequences, 21–3; conventions on, 3,

13, 60; CVPR, 141; data collection, 99, 128, 144; discrimination, 143; gap between AI and reality, 103; historic processes, 90; and human input, 96; investment in, 59; only as good as your data, 34; positioned as the solution, 44–5, 53; pressure to embrace, 150; as proprietary for agribusinesses, 18; and social media, 34; soil detection, 128. *See also* algorithms; data; immaculate conception of data (ICD)
ASABE (American Society of Agricultural and Biological Engineers), 140
Asia Pacific Economic Cooperation, 85, 109
Australia, 59, 160n1
Autoconstruction (agri-tech cooperative), 64, 67–9, 78
automated decision system/technology platform: about, 31–2; as authoritative, 14, 95; conceived of as all-powerful, 12; DSSAT (Decision Support System for Agrotechnology Transfer), 122–3; FarmCommand (decision platform), 20, 22, 120–2, 137–8, 142; and human input, 91, 123; as inputs, 26; used to save money, 57; value of, 110, 146. *See also* Farmers Edge Inc (precision agriculture company); Trimble Agriculture (software)
Automating Inequality (Eubanks), 7, 91
auto-steering guidance equipment, 28–9, 32–3
AutoTrac, 28
"A Vision for 2030" (Jones), 150

Bacon, Francis, 94
Bajaj, Jatinder K., 94
Barnes, Wade, 20, 53–4, 99, 113–15, 126
Bar-Sever, Yoaz, 28
BASF Corporation, 8, 52
Bayer CropScience, 8, 36
Bayer/Monsanto Corporation: and Deere & Company, 135, 145; and digital transformation, 35–6; lawsuits against, 52; price discrimination, 129; and privacy agreements, 118; promotion of sustainability, 42; purchase of Monsanto, 7–8, 11; relationship with farmers, 36; on replacement of human decision making, 33; suite of digital software, 33
Beaulieu, Megan, 157n3
Bhojwani, Yash, 13
bias and discrimination, 90–2, 116, 122–3, 126–7, 134, 142–3
big data: as anti-democratic, 88; created recently, 136; government involvement in, 58, 104–5; human decisions involved, 113, 144, 151; monetary profits from, 37; as social imaginary, 82; as superior, 104. *See also* Amazon; Facebook; Google; Microsoft
big data, agricultural: and automation of machinery, 30–1; farmer reservations, 130; as fix of the future, 23; genotype, environment, and management (gem), 124; harder to collect, 124; and insurance, 132; market for, 39; repoliticization of, 19; research into, 10; shared between large companies, 135. *See also* agribusinesses
Big Data Congress (conference), 9, 37, 83, 109–10
biodiversity, 81, 135
bioremediation, 74
Bishop, Kevin D., 46
BIXS (Business Info Exchange System), 39
black box of data and assumptions, 116–19
Blanke, Tobias, 148
Blaser, Earl, 49
Bogost, Ian, 104, 105, 119
Bongiovanni, R., 43, 109
Borne, Jacob van den, 48
Bowker, Geoffrey, 90, 143
boyd, danah, 134

Brexit, 5
broadband infrastructure, 18, 86–8, 159–60n1
Bronson, Kelly: about research, 11–16, 18–23, 40–1, 82–3, 96, 112–13, 156n8; at conventions, 3, 9–10, 13, 37, 60, 83, 89, 144; on government panel, 110–11; photo of, *30*; plant identification, 33–4
Business Info Exchange System (BIXS), 39
Buttel, Frederick, 47

Cambridge Analytica (CA), 5–6, 88
Campbell, W., 152
Canadian Association of Agri Retailers (CAAR), 157n1
Canadian government: investments into broadband infrastructure, 159–60n1; technological use compared to US, 32, 157n1
Canadian government agencies and departments: Agriculture and Agri-Food Canada, 86; Canada Infrastructure Bank, 159–60n1; Environment Canada, 74; Farm Credit Canada, 131; Food Inspection Agency Canada, 126; Food Secure Canada, 67; Innovation, Science and Economic Development Canada, 85, 87, 144
Canadian Journal of Remote Sensing, 158n8
CAPÉ (Coopérative pour l'Agriculture de Proximité Écologique), 67–9
capitalism, 134, 143, 151, 158n9
Carbonell, Isabelle, 8, 130
Carolan, Michael, 10, 67
"The Cathedral of Computation" (Bogost), 104
Cerf, Vint, 88
chemical fertilizers, 16–17, 43, 50, 55, 121, 124, 158n6
chemical herbicides and pesticides, 16, 49, 77, 121
Cheney-Lippold, John, 119
Christianity, 96
citizen science, 72
climate change, 135–6
Climate Corporation (Monsanto), 8, 35, 37
Climate FieldView (Bayer/Monsanto), 22, 36, 53, 80, 126, 144
colonialism, 15, 158n10
commodity crops: about, 120, 126, 133–4; corn, 32, 38, 123, 142; soybeans, 20, 32, 123, 129, 142
Commonwealth Science and Industrial Research Organisation (CSIRO), Australia, 59
community-supported agriculture programs (CSAS), 79
Conference on Computer Vision and Pattern Recognition (CVPR), 141–3
Connecting British Columbia, 159–60n1
Connect to Innovate program (Canada), 87, 159–60n1
Coopérative pour l'Agriculture de Proximité Écologique (CAPÉ), 67–9
copyright protection, 117
corn, 32, 38, 123, 142
corporate power, 127–34, 143
Cox, Dorn, 13, 63, 67, 70–80, 103, 107, 137–8; "Open Source for Agricultural Resilience," 109
Coxe, Tench, 15
Crandall, Robert, 128
Crawford, Kate, 104
criminality, 160n2
critical data studies, 5, 10, 14, 21, 124, 134, 148–9
crop yields, 38, 48, 59
crowdsourcing, 33–4, 126–8
CSIRO (Commonwealth Science and Industrial Research Organisation, Australia), 59
Cukier, Kenneth, 35

CVPR (Conference on Computer Vision and Pattern Recognition), 141–3
cybersecurity, 133

data: access to, 4, 18, 70, 85–92, 115–16, 117; and articles, conferences, organizations, tools, AgBox (data-sharing tool), 131; Ag Data Transparent (ADT), 131; "Agile Data-Oriented Research Tools to Support Smallholder Farm System Transformation," (*Frontiers*), 45; "Agriculture Open Data Package" (Open Data Charter), 72–3; Agriculture-Vision dataset, 142; Data Congress (conference), 60; "Data Is Power" (*Popular Science*), 109; Data Power (conference), 10; DIK (data to information to knowledge), 99–100; General Data Protection Regulation (GDPR), 133; Global Open Data for Agriculture and Nutrition (GODAN), 9, 13, 73, 74, 117; black box of assumptions, 116–19; critical data studies, 5, 10, 14, 21, 124, 134, 148–9; critiques, 9–11; as having agency, 83, 88; and the human element, 3, 19, 90–1; as objective, trustworthy, 97; open data and sustainable farming systems, 13, 72–3, 107, 140; privacy breaches, 148; from public institutions, 115–16; raw, 12–16, 19, 74, 83, 92; term usage, 84–5; value of, 6, 25. *See also* algorithms; artificial intelligence (AI); immaculate conception of data (ICD); open access; weather
debt, 29, 50, 135
decision platforms. *See* automated decision system/technology platform
decisions: by algorithms, 90, 119; data-driven, 41, 91, 122; DSSAT (Decision Support System for Agrotechnology Transfer), 122–3; FarmCommand (decision platform), 20, 22, 120–2, 142; and humans, 25, 33, 38, 44–5, 59, 99. *See also* automated decision system/technology platform
Decision Support System for Agrotechnology Transfer (DSSAT), 122–3
Deere & Company: and Ag Data Transparent (ADT), 131; and Bayer CropScience, 8; and Bayer/Monsanto, 135, 145; and collection of data, 35; and digital innovation, 27; digital lock, 140; *Farm Forward*, 24–5, 44, 46, 61, 97–8; and GPS, 28; on replacement of human decision making, 25; streaming data from tractors, 5. *See also* John Deere tractors
Delgado, Jorge A., 43
Diet for a Small Planet (Moore Lappé), 79
Digiscape (software), 59
digital agriculture: advertised by Deere & Company, 97; agricultural automation, 25–34; articles and ads about, 40, 157n3; benefit to corporations, 127–34; black boxing of, 116–19; *Canadian Journal of Remote Sensing* (1998), 158n8; democratized access to data, 70; and farmers, 39–40, 56–7; funding of, 87–8; gap between machines and humans, 102, 105–6; human decision making, 62, 66–7, 80–1, 99, 124; moral claims, 54–5; public and private sector partnerships, 141; research papers on, 109; social impacts of, 86; soft resistance to, 147–8; use of UAVS, 38, 48, 87, 102, 108, 142; validation of human knowledge, 103; and workers, 98–9, 123–4. *See also* agribusinesses; automated decision system/technology platform; decisions; future of agriculture; immaculate conception of data (ICD)
digital divide, 86
digital positivism, 97
DIK (data to information to knowledge), 99–100

discrimination and bias, 90–2, 116, 122–3, 126–7, 134, 142–3
DIY workshops, 67–8
Dow/DuPont, 36
drones. *See* uncrewed aerial vehicles (UAV)
Drupal, 62
DSSAT (Decision Support System for Agrotechnology Transfer), 122–3

East India Company, 112
Eco, Umberto, 108
Elabed, Ghada, 85
Elliott, Kevin, 93–4
"Empowering Farmers, Improving Sustainability" (Farmers Edge), 54
environmental mapping, 121
Environment Canada, 74
equity, 127, 129
ETC Group (watchdog organization), 9, 35
ethical issues. *See* morality
Eubanks, Virginia, 91
European Commission, 58–9, 133, 155n4
European Union, 5
European Union Horizon 2020 (FATIMA), 155n4
Ezrahi, Yaron, 94

Facebook, 4–6, 7, 21, 130, 144, 155n2, 155n3
Farallon Institute, California, 64
FarmBeats (Microsoft), 87
FarmCommand (decision platform), 20, 22, 120–2, 137–8, 142
Farm Credit Canada, 131
farmers: as business executives, 49, 149–50; controlled by purchase of inputs, 26; feelings on digital agriculture, 56, 57; income of, 120; networks, 52; pressure to use technologies, 28; promotion of digital agriculture to, 39–40; and raw data, 118–19
Farmers Business Network, 131
Farmers Edge Inc (precision agriculture company): about, 20; beginnings of, 53; biases, 113–16, 143; FarmCommand, 20, 22, 120–2, 137–8, 142; and insurance companies, 132; N-Manager, 122–4, 143; saves time, 99; selling of advice, 31–2; soil-testing lab, 125, 127–8, 137; and "sustainability," 54
Farm Forward (John Deere), 24, 44, 46, 61, 97–8
Farm Hack (community), 67, 137, 159n2
Farmier, 63
farmOS (open-source farm management platform): about, 13, 62–3, 70, 137–9, 159n5, 160n5; as activist platform, 22; compared to Farm Command, 137; data for research, 76; development methodology, 72; funding, 140, 160n5; participants, 63; people programming, 160n5; scale of, 80–1; shared values, 78; sharing of data from smallholdings, 77; visibility for challenges of smallholdings, 66
farms: the future (4.0), 61, 80–1, 86, 134, 140, 143; drones, 26; farm-to-table information, 39; farm workers, 49, 98, 121, 123–4; regulatory oversight, 26–7; size of, 48, 120; tools, 67–9
Fathi, Eli, 3
FATIMA (European Union Horizon 2020), 155n4
feminism, 100, 111–12, 151–2
field map, 32
filter bubble, 146
Fischhoff, David, 38
Flood, Geoff, 9, 83
FOODIE (European Commission), 155n4
Food Inspection Agency Canada, 126
food justice/security, 46, 51, 66, 79, 134–6, 160n4
Food Secure Canada, 67
food studies: and agricultural tech-

nologies, 4, 10, 50, 78; with data studies and science studies, 21; and farmers, 26, 63; and productivism, 22, 45–6, 65–6, 114
food systems, 4, 11–14, 16–18, 22, 78–9, 81
food traceability, 39
Ford, Henry, 47–8
Foroohar, R., 9
FORTRAN, 71
Fox Keller, Evelyn, 112
Fraley, Robert, 38
Fraser, Evan, 59
Frickel, Scott, 70
"From Uniformity to Diversity" (International Panel on Environmental Sustainability), 52
future of agriculture: activist vision of, 81; and agribusinesses, 18–19, 140; agricultural big data as fix, 23, 44–5; and agroecological farmers, 19; broadband infrastructure, 18, 86–8, 159–60n1; compared to today, 22; corporate messaging, 42; data-mediated economy, 60; expectations, 40; farm (4.0), 60–1, 80, 86, 134, 140, 143; Internet of Things (IoT), 13, 38, 59, 87, 108; labourless farming, 98–9; large farms, 127; prevents focus on current challenges, 152; representations of, 82–3; works on: "A Vision for 2030" (Jones), 150; "The Future of Agricultural Intelligence" (Trimble), 41; "Future of Agrifood Industry" (IoTForum), 13; "The Future of Food" (World Bank), 58; *How to Fix the Future* (Keen), 7. *See also* digital agriculture; sustainable farming systems

Gates, Bill, 60
Gate-to-Plate food traceability, 39
Gathering for Open Agricultural Technologies (GOAT). *See* GOAT
gender, binary model of, 119–20
General Data Protection Regulation (GDPR), 133
genetically modified organisms (GMOs), 11, 16–17, 36, 50, 121, 129–30, 158n7
genotype, environment, and management (gem), 124
Ghosh, Dipayan, 6
Gillespie, Tarleton, 92, 147
Girardi, Giulio, 96
GitHub, 62–3, 159n5, 160n5
Global Ag Risk (insurance), 132
globalization, 47
global North, 18, 64, 65
Global Open Data for Agriculture and Nutrition (GODAN), 9, 13, 73, 74, 117
Global Positioning System (GPS), 27
global South, 58, 84, 118
glyphosate herbicide (Roundup), 11, 52
GMOs (genetically modified organisms), 11, 16–17, 36, 50, 121, 129–30, 158n7
GOAT (Gathering for Open Agricultural Technologies): about, 19, 62; and anti-consumerism, 77–8; and community, 79; DIY sensors, 69–70, 137; and Farm Hack meet-ups, 159n2; food sovereignty, 66; mission statement, 76; values of, 79
GODAN (Global Open Data for Agriculture and Nutrition), 9, 13, 73, 74, 117
Goldman Sachs, 38–9, 108, 150
Goodman, David, 150
Google (Alphabet): and AI, 128, 144; Cerf as Internet Evangelist, 88; collection of data, 34; data storehouses of, 99; as ethical miscreant, 4; maps provided by, 105; market value, 155n2; public sentiment, 7; and search returns, 92, 146
Gore, Al, 84
"Government Open-Up!" (GODAN), 75
GPS (Global Positioning System), 27
Gray, Jonathan, 148
greenhouse climate controller, 68–9

greenhouse gas emissions, 135, 158n6
growth hormones, 50

Hambly, Helen, 86
Handbook of Science and Technology Studies (Konrad), 14
Haraway, Donna, 22, 83, 95–6, 112
Harvey, David, 143
Haugen, Frances, 155n3
health, 51, 52
high-fructose corn syrup, 123
Holmgren, David, 78
hormones, growth, 50
How to Fix the Future (Keen), 7
Human Computer Interaction Institute, Carnegie Mellon University, 152
human–machine collaboration, 105, 144, 151–2
hybrid seeds, 48, 50
HYDRA (software), 74, 101–2

IAASTD (International Assessment of Agricultural Knowledge, Science and Technology for Development), 17, 51
IBM, 31–2, 34, 60, 132
IC-ETITE international conference, 13
ICTS (Information and Communications Technologies), 15, 86
IEEE (Institute of Electrical and Electronics Engineers), 157–8n5
imaginaries: and big data, 21, 82–3; and science/science studies, 14, 21, 82, 107; sociotechnical, 85, 107, 113. *See also* immaculate conception of data (ICD)
immaculate conception of data (ICD): about, 4, 12–13, 83; and academics, 108–9; actions against, 149; data having agency, 12–13, 15–16; as framework, 4, 13–14, 18–19, 96; *versus* human mediated, 13–14, 19; multiple users, 147–8; need for and use of, 107–8; neutrality of, 107–8; reassurance of, 146; as vehicle for value of digital agriculture, 110. *See also* algorithms; artificial intelligence (AI); data
Impact AI convention, 3
IMS Health, 145
iNaturalist (plant identification app), 157n2
Indigenous knowledge, 51, 160n2
industrial food systems, 16, 22, 25
information and communications technologies (ICTS), 15, 86
information superhighways, 84
Innis, Harold, 88
Innovation, Science and Economic Development Canada, 85, 87, 144
inputs. *See* chemical fertilizers; chemical herbicides and pesticides; data
Institute of Electrical and Electronics Engineers (IEEE), 157–8n5
insurance companies, 131–2
intellectual property, 117, 146–7, 155–6n5
International Assessment of Agricultural Knowledge, Science and Technology for Development (IAASTD), 17, 51
International Panel of Experts on Sustainable Food Systems, 17
International Panel on Environmental Sustainability, 52
International Peasant's Movement (La Via Campesina), 67
International Soil Reference and Information Centre (ISRIC) World Soil Information, 74
International Telecommunication Union, 109
internet: ability to access as a right, 86–7; Internet for Nova Scotia Initiative, 159–60n1; Internet of Food and Farm 2020 (IoF2020), 59; Internet of Things (IoT), 13, 38, 59, 87, 108
intersectional approaches, 151

Investing in Canada Plan, 159–60n1
IoF2020 (Internet of Food and Farm 2020), 59
IoT (Internet of Things), 13, 38, 59, 87, 108
IoTForum's "Future of Agrifood Industry," 13
ISRIC (International Soil Reference and Information Centre) World Soil Information, 74

Jacobs, Jenna, 68, 77
Jasanoff, Sheila, 82
Jet Propulsion Lab (JPL), 28
John Deere tractors, 5, 29–33, 155–6n5. *See also* Deere & Company
Johnson, Dewayne, 11
Jones, James W., 126
Journal of Precision Agriculture, 42–3

Kay, Ian, 160n2
Kelly, Kevin, 96
Kienzle, Josef, 45
Kim, Sang-Hyun, 82
The Know-It-Alls (Cohen), 7
Konrad, Kornelia, 14, 85
Kuhn, Thomas, 93
Kuznetsov, Stacey, 152

La Ferme Coopérative aux Champs qui Chantent, 68
Lamy, Bruno, 159–60n1
Land O'Lakes, 36–7
La Via Campesina (International Peasant's Movement), 67
Leafsnap (plant identification app), 157n2
Lightbar (equipment), 56–7
Linkogle, Stephanie, 96
Liveris, Andrew, 36
logical positivist movement, 14
Low Earth Orbit (LEO) satellites, 159–60n1
Lowenberg-Deboer, J., 43, 109

Manovich, Lev, 106
Marvin, Carolyn, 22
Marx, Karl, 25, 45, 83
Marx, Leo, 15, 111
Mayer-Schonberger, Viktor, 35
Menne, Tobias, 42–3, 52, 109
Merchant, Carolyn, 94
Merton, Robert, 93–5, 112
Micheels, Eric T., 56
Microsoft Corporation, 34, 36–7, 44–5, 87, 155n2
Microsoft Research Summit (2021), 13
Millennium Ecosystem Assessment, 51
Mining the Social Web (Russell and Klassen), 88
Ministry of Agriculture, Canada, 86
Ministry of Innovation, Science and Economic Development, Canada, 85
Mirowski, Philip, 72
MIT Media Lab, 60
moisture level controls, 159n3
Mollison, Bill, 78
monocrops, 20, 133–4. *See also* commodity crops
Monsanto Corporation: agreements with Deere for data from tractors, 5; and data analytics, 35; divesting from seeds and chemicals to BASF, 52; and Facebook and Google, 3–24; and GMOs, 51; law suits against, 11; purchase by Bayer, 7–8, 11; purchase of agricultural data analytics, 88. *See also* Bayer/Monsanto
Moore Lappé, Frances, 79
morality: and agribusinesses, 11, 53–4; and alternative farming systems, 138; and colonialism, 15, 158n10; and digitization, 41, 45; and justice, 134–6; obfuscated by ICD, 4; and power, 22; and the World Bank, 58
Morning, Ann, 16
Mosco, Vincent, 97
Move Fast and Break Things (Taplin), 7

Musk, Elon, 7

Nafus, Dawn, 147
NASA (National Aeronautics and Space Administration), 27–8, 116
National Geographic, 48
National Rifle Association, US, 93
NavCom, 27–8
navigation systems, 27
near-infrared spectroscopy, 126
neoliberalism, 49
neo-productivism, 46, 53, 55, 56, 60. *See also* productivism
Netherlands, 158n11
New Alchemy Institute, Massachusetts, 64
nitrogen, 122
N-Manager (FarmCommand), 122–4, 143
Noble, Safiya Umoja, 92
Nokia, 36
Nolan, James F., 56
Novum Organum (Bacon), 94

obesity, 160n4
O'Neil, Kathy, 91–2
Ontario Agri Business Association (OABA), 157n1
Ontario Ministry of Agriculture, Food and Rural Affairs (OMAFRA), 157n1
open access: "Agriculture Open Data Package" (Open Data Charter), 72–3; open data and sustainable farming systems, 13, 72–3, 107, 140; Open Knowledge Foundation, 72; Open Pipe Kit, 69–70; "Open Source for Agricultural Resilience" (Cox), 109; open-source movement, 71–6, 80–1, 137. *See also* farmOS; GOAT; GODAN
organic farming: about, 49–50; access to big data, 121; and appropriate technology, 64, 80; CAPÉ (Coopérative pour l'Agriculture de Proximité Écologique), 67–9; innovation in, 77; La Ferme Coopérative aux Champs qui Chantent, 68; and open data, 72; and re-use of machinary, 33; Vermont Organics Growers' Meeting, 103, 109
Oslund, Sam, 67–8

Palihapitiya, Chamath, 6–7
Pasquale, Frank, 117
patents/patent law, 117, 122, 125–6
Pentland, Sandy, 60, 83, 108–9
permaculture, 139
Permaculture: A Designers' Manual (Mollison), 78
Permaculture: Principles and Pathways Beyond Sustainability (Holmgren), 78
pharmaceutical data, 145
Phillips, Adrian A.C., 46
PlantSnap (plant identification app), 157n2
plant/weed identification apps, 126–7, 157n2
politics, alternative, 136–46
post-colonialism, 111–12
postmodernism, 111
precision agriculture (PA): about, 8, 28; adoption of, 32, 108; and data, 34, 35, 43, 115; and Deere & Company products, 25, 27, 30–1; example of, 48; and farmers' income crisis, 46; Goldman Sachs on, 38, 108; growth of market, 35; IoF2020 fostering uptake of, 59; *Journal of Precision Agriculture*, 42–3; and large farms, 20, 120; and openness of datasets, 159n6; and power for agribusinesses, 18; requirements of, 121; research papers on, 109; shift to global sustainability, 44; surveys, 157n1. *See also* automated decision system/technology platform; autosteering guidance equipment
precision analytics, 102

privacy: agreements to, 149; breaches of, 148; third party corporations, 32, 39, 146
productivism: and agricultural research, 65–6; compared to resilience and community, 77; complex path to, 143; critiques of, 50–1; defining success, 114; dominant ethos in ag-tech firms, 53; in family history, 104; marketed for efficiency and sustainability, 45–8, 60; and UNFAO, 158–9n1
Pursell, Carroll, 64

quotidian insubordination, 77–81

racism, 7, 16, 92, 94–5, 111–12
Ramsay, Stephen, 111
raspberry pi sensors, 67, 159n3
Raymond, Eric, 71
Reed, Cory, 36
regenerative agriculture, 63, 66–7, 80–1, 103
religion, 96
Report of the Task Force on Agriculture (Canada), 47
resilience, 63–4
"The Revolution in North American Agriculture" (*National Geographic*), 48
RHEA Research Project (Robot Fleets for Highly Effective Agriculture and Forestry Management), 59
Roe Smith, Merritt, 15
Rosenberg, Daniel, 84
Rosenzweig, Cynthia E., 126
Roundup (glyphosate herbicide), 11, 52

Sandvig, Christian, 128
Santos Valle, Santiego, 45
Schumacher, Ernst, 65
science/science studies: and imaginaries, 14, 21, 82, 107; and knowledge, 21, 94, 95, 112; and objectivity, 92–101; and open science, 72; and power, 15; and rule of experts, 16; and technology, 85, 112; "undone science," 70
Scott, Ben, 6
Scott, James, 77
seed corporations, 5
seed drills, 46, 123
Sherman, Jamie, 147
Shirky, Clay, 88, 97
Short, N., 152
SimCity (computer game), 160n2
smallholdings: and access to data, 70, 118, 121, 136; "Agile Data-Oriented Research Tools to Support Smallholder Farm System Transformation," (*Frontiers*), 45; alternative farming as, 50; and appropriate technology, 65; Autoconstruction for, 64, 67–9, 78; in the developing world, 126; difficulties of scale, 69–70; digitization as necessary, 15, 45; Farm Hack (community) for, 67, 137, 159n2; importance of, 52; innovation on, 77; La Ferme Coopérative aux Champs qui Chantent, 68; and minor crops (not commodity crops), 120; Open Pipe Kit for, 69–70; support through ICTS, 15; visibility for challenges of, 66. *See also* farmOS; organic farming
Small is Beautiful: Economics as if People Mattered (Schumacher), 65
smart farming: farm of the future (4.0), 61, 80–1, 86, 134, 140, 143; field school on, 33; future of, 57–8; research into, 114, 143, 157–8n5, 157n3; smart equipment/tools, 25, 32, 97; worker alienation with, 123
social media. *See* Facebook
social physics, 6, 109
social policies/action, 19
Soden, Robert, 151
soil systems, 74, 126, 135, 137–8
Sorj, Bernardo, 150
soybeans, 20, 32, 123, 129, 142
spot sampling, 127, 160n3

Star, Susan, 143
StarFire receivers, 28
Stenta, Michael, 13, 65–6, 70, 72, 76, 137, 140
Stretch, Colin, 6
superclusters, 85, 87, 141–2, 144
surveillance capitalism, 130
sustainable agriculture (agribusinesses): consequences of digitization, 135; farm (4.0), 61, 80–1, 86, 134, 140, 143; positioning of big data as the solution, 151; profit *versus* global development goals, 136; through AI capabilities, 37–45, 59. *See also* productivism
sustainable farming systems: agro-ecology, 52, 78, 80; appropriate technology movement, 64–5, 67–70, 80–1; Autoconstruction (agri-tech cooperative), 64, 67–9, 78; biodiversity, 81, 135; CAPÉ (Coopérative pour l'Agriculture de Proximité Écologique), 67–9; Farm Hack (community), 67, 137, 159n2; and Indigenous knowledge, 51–2; intersectional approaches, 151; La Via Campesina (International Peasant's Movement), 67; organic farming, 49–50, 77, 121, 125–6; permaculture, 78, 139; recommended by UN reports, 17, 52; regenerative agriculture, 63, 66–7, 80–1, 103; rural need for ICTs, 15; through open data, 13, 72–3, 107, 140. *See also* farmOS; future of agriculture; GOAT (Gathering for Open Agricultural Technologies); GODAN; smallholdings
Swiss Re Group (insurance), 132–3

T4G (data company), 109–10
techlash, 9, 11
technological determinism, 85
technologies: capitalism, 143; criteria for appropriateness, 65; development and marketing of, 25; effects of, 50; inevitability of, 107; participatory development of, 72; pressure to use, 28; repair person for, 106; and social institutions, 91; and worker alienation, 123–4
temperature controls, 159n3
third party corporations, 32, 39, 146
"This Tiny Country Feeds the World" (*National Geographic*), 48
Torvalds, Linus, 71
Tourne Sol (cooperative farm), 68
tractors. *See* John Deere tractors; Versatile, Buhler Industries (tractors)
transhumanist movement, 100
transnational corporations, 18
transparency, 117, 147
Trimble Agriculture (software), 31–2, 41
Tuckaway Farm, 77
Tull, Jethro, 46
Turf Doctor (plant identification app), 157n2
Turnbull, David, 160n2

uncrewed aerial vehicles (UAV): demonstration of, 26–7; use of for farmOS, 67, 77; use of in digital agriculture, 38, 48, 87, 102, 108, 142
United Nations (UN): Broadband Commission for Digital Development, 88; Environment Programme (UNEP), 135–6; Food and Agriculture Organization (UNFAO), 15, 16, 52, 158–9n1; Global Open Data for Agriculture and Nutrition (GODAN), 9; Human Rights Council, 52
United States: and export-oriented agriculture, 158n11; farmers and privacy of data, 160n1; influence of voters by Facebook, 5–6; technological use compared to Canada, 32, 157n1; UAV regulations, 27
United States government and institutions: American Farm Bureau Feder-

ation (AFBF), 131; American Society of Agricultural and Biological Engineers (ASABE), 140; Department of Agriculture, 32, 73, 87; Geological Survey, 116; National Institute of Food and Agriculture, 59; National Rifle Association, 93; Senate Judiciary Subcommittee on Crime and Terrorism, 6
Universal Broadband Fund, 87, 159–60n1
University of Guelph (Arell Food Institute), 59

van den Borne, Jacob, 48
Vermont Organic Farmers meeting, 103, 109
Versatile, Buhler Industries (tractors), 145
Vestager, Margrethe, 133
Vienna Circle, 14–15
"Vision for Agriculture Workshop" (CVPR), 142

Watson, (IBM), 132
Watson, Robert, 51
Weapons of Math Destruction (O'Neil), 91
weather: big data approaches to monitoring, 40; data collection of, 24, 73, 104, 114–15, 122, 139; dependence on, 115; historical data of, 132; risks from, 55, 105
"Weather Monitoring Means Less Guessing and More Knowing" (FarmForum.ca), 40, *41*, 95
Weed ID (Bayer/Monsanto), 33, 126, 128, 157n2
weed identification apps, 126–7, 157n2
Weinberger, David, 99
Western Canadian Wheat Growers Association, 47
When Old Technologies Were New (Marvin), 22
WHO (World Health Organization), 17
Wilkinson, John, 150
Winner, Langdon, 23, 94
Wolfe's Neck Center for Agriculture & the Environment, 63, 77, 137
World Bank, 16, 58, 85
World Health Organization (WHO), 17
Wylie, Christopher, 5
Wynne, Brian, 95

Xarvio Weed Scout (plant identification app), 33, 157n2

Yearly, Steven, 111

Zuboff, Shoshanna, 130
Zucca, Matthew, 156n8
Zuckerberg, Mark, 6